PSYCHOTHERAPY WITH LESBIAN CLIENTS

Theory Into Practice

PSYCHOTHERAPY WITH LESBIAN CLIENTS

Theory Into Practice

KRISTINE L. FALCO, Psy.D.

BRUNNER/MAZEL, *Publishers* • NEW YORK

Library of Congress Cataloging-in-Publication Data

Falco, Kristine L.
Psychotherapy with lesbian clients : theory into practice / by
Kristine L. Falco.
p.   cm.
Includes bibliographical references and indexes.
ISBN 0-87630-622-9
1. Lesbian—Mental health.   2. Psychotherapy.   I. Title.
[DNLM: 1. Homosexuality—psychology.   2. Psychotherapy.   WM 420
F181p]
RC558.F36   1990
616.85'8340651'082—dc20
DNLM/DLC
for Library of Congress   90-15083
                                                              CIP

Published by
BRUNNER/MAZEL, Inc.
19 Union Square
New York, New York 10003

Manufactured in the United States of America

10 9 8 7 6 5 4 3 2 '

For women who love women,
everywhere

CONTENTS

PREFACE

Writing this book is really the product of a lifelong process. Writing doesn't come easily to me, but it has always been a strong draw-of-the-heart—so much so, in fact, that my whole family remembers when, at the age of 10, I informed my parents that I was not getting a good enough education at the school I was attending; the other children were not serious about learning how to read and write well, and I wanted to be sent to a Catholic school instead. I don't have any idea where I got the notion that a Catholic school would provide me with a different educational atmosphere, and I cannot even say whether it really did or whether I simply created that atmosphere for myself—whichever the case, I did learn to write.

A decade later, in college, I found that I actually enjoyed writing all those term papers, and I found solace in the written words of others when I was searching for perspectives outside of my own. At that time, I was also coming to see that the emotional ties and crushes I had had on females over the past years (including those during a stint in the convent) really had a "meaning"—and that meaning was lesbianism. I read everything I could find on the subject, which in 1970 wasn't much. And what did exist usually was not lesbian-affirmative. So three other budding gay psychology undergraduates and I approached the local free medical clinic with a proposal to create a gay drop-in and peer counseling center. That was my introduction to counseling and it fueled a desire to compensate for the gaps in the written literature on a lesbian-positive approach to counseling, and to life. Our subsequent discussions about what a "healthy homosexual" was began a process of commitment to a highly critical approach to the older literature on the subject, and it underscored the importance of listening to gays and lesbians themselves about what was healthy and enhancing and what was not.

Through my 20s I continued doing volunteer peer counseling at lesbian resource centers. I worked during this time as a medical writer and editor, further honing the skills required to interpret scientific literature. I also went back to school to get a masters in counseling. Increasingly, I began to be able to define what was missing in the literature. By this time, a number of books were available in the popular press that were gay- and lesbian-positive, but these tended to go out of print within a few years. In addition, they usually addressed gay men more than lesbian women.

By the time I began work on my doctorate, in the mid 1980s, *The Journal of Homosexuality* was gaining in circulation, and occasional articles began appearing in other mainstream psychology and psychiatry journals. Anthologies also began to appear. However, it was a rare psychotherapist training program that included even one course on a positive approach to therapy with gays and lesbians (which was an elective course if the school had one), and nowhere was this subject incorporated into the overall training program. And one would have to have access to a large academic library and loads of research time to find the scattered articles on the subject. I began to provide in-service training seminars to the staffs of mental health agencies, but it seemed that such training required more depth than a two-hour staff presentation or one session of a graduate class.

When dissertation time arrived in my life, the goal was clear to me: to broaden the knowledge about lesbians. But even after the dissertation was finished, I still felt the pull to do more. This pull took the shape of wanting to gather the majority of the literature on lesbians and therapy in one place—of wanting to discuss the issues in more clinical depth than had previously been done, and of wanting to contribute to a solid theoretical and clinical basis for providing psychotherapy to this clientele. The dissertation had to become a book.

My research method is commonly called the "snowball" method. From each article that was useful, I would search out all the articles among the references that looked helpful too, and then I would search the references from those articles as well. This investigation was rounded out by reading the relevant journals and making frequent trips to bookstores that carry lesbian literature. These materials seemed to fall into place quite naturally, and in this way, the chapters almost named themselves. It was hard to find a stopping point, because even as this book goes to press, new literature is appearing—a welcome change from the state of the literature in the 1970s, when I first started looking into it.

As the book developed, my client-centered focus guided me. Over my years in clinical practice, I was still seeing clients who had been harmed by uninformed or outright biased therapists; clients who still believed they were inferior to heterosexual people; who believed that being in the closet was a requirement for survival; who had not allowed themselves to see the impact of a life of self-censorship and constriction; who believed they had become lesbian out of a trauma or an inability to be with men; who could only make love with their partners when intoxicated. I wanted them to see their strengths as well. It takes a special strength of character for a person to be able to define herself so differently from what her culture tells her she must be— especially when the culture implies that what she is is not good. To live without the support of a male, who still has greater access to higher wages and less responsibility for children; to creatively invent herself and her relationships without the automatic reliance on sex roles or cultural models; to find a dynamic resolution to living with external disapproval in order to be internally syntonic—these things create a strength of character that deserves validation.

In 1989, I was diagnosed with breast cancer. During that time of outrage and fear, feeling that I must be somehow responsible for this, I came to the decision not to finish this book. It was taking up too much of what might turn out to be a pretty short time left on the planet, and maybe the stress of writing it had influenced my cancer. But after several months of psychological recovery, and some of the greatest support a person can experience, I changed my mind. The desire to finish the book continued to call to me. And, I came to see that the book itself was important to my recovery. In the meantime, the dissertation had won the Best Unpublished Manuscript Award in Lesbian Psychologies from the Association for Women in Psychology, which refueled a belief in the usefulness of the material it contains. So here it is. I find that a one-breasted woman can do all the things she used to do, but do them with even more heart.

Ever since I realized I was a lesbian myself, I have been fascinated by the psychological process that people go through to discover this about themselves, and by the diversity of ways they find to live with the realization. My hope is that this book will make it easier for lesbians of the future to have access to appropriate standards of mental health and an affirmative approach when they seek therapy—and easier for therapists to facilitate a healing process that respects individual identities.

ACKNOWLEDGMENTS

I would like to thank many people for their contributions to this project, beginning with those authors who gave me their published works, their unpublished works, and their ideas. My clients have my respect and admiration for showing me the diverse ways in which we can establish our own self-defined health, and for showing me the importance of disseminating information about the value and distinctiveness of lesbian-affirmative psychotherapy.

My doctoral dissertation was the first draft of this work, on which Peggy Hanley-Hackenbruck, Elaine Breshgold, Marci Nemhauser, Rocky Garrison, Joan Dayger Behn, and Deborah Zita provided editing, encouragement, suggestions, perspective, and enthusiasm when my motivation waned.

During the preparation of this book length version, my family has frequently expressed their pride in me: my parents, Arlene and Paul Falco, and my sisters, Karen Sendelback, Paula Falco Wilson, and Lori Bixler. Jane Clausen provided help with research. Rita Maynard and Julie Gudmestad were my cheerleaders. And Peggy Hanley-Hackenbruck read the manuscript a second time (!), offering the most helpful of editorial and clinical suggestions. My editors, Suzi Tucker and Natalie Gilman, were a pleasure to work with, offering both enthusiasm and guidance.

My computer, "The Palomino" I call her, was a requisite for this project. If personal computers had not yet been invented, I never would have undertaken this, and I think wistfully of the hours spent gazing at the computer screen and the tall fir trees that fill the window beyond.

My "farm family"—my horses, cats, ducks, geese, and chickens—adjusted gracefully to my sometimes cramped schedule during the writing of this book, and yet continued to teach me just how a life close to the earth can be lived.

And Catherine Keith fed me, nurtured me, provided financial support, did research, ran errands, brought me trinkets for pleasure, and stayed ever-available for whatever back-up I needed, all while keeping her own life in balance. She has my deepest appreciation for uncountable weekends when writing took precedence over our time together. We finally made it!

I

THE
CONTEXT
OF
THERAPY

1

INTRODUCTION

Until 1973, homosexuality was considered a mental illness by most mental health professionals. In that year, homosexuality was deleted from the mental disorders of the *Diagnostic and Statistical Manual* of the American Psychiatric Association. Over the next 15 years, other professional therapist organizations have made policy statements in recognition of the nonillness status of homosexuality. Such policy statements have come from the National Association of Social Workers, the American Association of Marriage and Family Therapists, and the American Psychological Association, among others. Typical of this new stance is the American Psychological Association's policy, which states:

1. Homosexuality implies no impairment of judgment, stability, reliability, or general social or vocational capabilities;
2. Mental health professionals should take the lead in removing the stigma of mental illness long associated with homosexuality; and
3. All discrimination against gays is to be deplored, and civil rights legislation is urged to meet that end.

Many further efforts have been made by mental health professionals to see lesbians and gay men in a more realistic, nonpathological light. For example:

- The American Psychological Association has an official division called the Society for the Psychological Study of Lesbian and Gay Issues (Division 44) as well as a Committee for Lesbian and Gay Concerns.
- An independent group of psychologists has formed the Association of Lesbian and Gay Psychologists.
- The American Psychiatric Association has developed the Committee on Gay, Lesbian, and Bisexual Issues and the Caucus of Homosexually Identified Psychiatrists.

1

- An independent group of psychiatrists has formed the Association of Gay and Lesbian Psychiatrists.
- The National Association of Social Workers has established the Committee on Lesbian and Gay Issues.
- The Association of Marriage and Family Therapists has established the Caucus of Gay, Lesbian, and Bisexual Concerns.

Other organizations of mental health professionals have undertaken similar approaches. In addition, many professional journals publish theory, research, and clinical articles that represent a nonillness model of homosexuality. Two specialty journals are now in print: *Journal of Homosexuality* and *Journal of Gay and Lesbian Psychotherapy*. (The addresses for these journals and committees can be found in Appendix C, Resources.)

The newer outlook on lesbians and gay men not only attempts to eliminate negative judgment, but it seeks to actively portray the positive value of this lifestyle. As psychologist Don Clark (1987) describes it,

> Gay is a descriptive label we have assigned to ourselves as a way of reminding ourselves and others that awareness of our sexuality facilitates a capability rather than creating a restriction. It means that we are capable of fully loving a person of same gender by involving ourselves emotionally, sexually, spiritually, and intellectually. (pp. 144–145)

Similarly, in their text *Counseling with Gay Men and Women*, Woodman and Lenna (1980) state:

> Being gay is not merely the ability and willingness to engage in homosexual behavior. Indeed, being gay is being different, having a distinct identity, frequently in a way that is felt even before it is conscious or sexually expressed. Gayness is a special affinity and a special feeling toward people of the same gender; it is not the inability to love and relate to others, nor is it a denial of the opposite sex. Rather it is a special capacity and need to love and to express one's love for people of the same gender in all the meanings of the term "love." (p. 11)

In the more recent literature, a distinction is being made between male and female homosexuals. Lesbians, because of their femaleness, experience a different life course than do their gay male counterparts. And the dynamics of two women in couplehood are being seen as distinct from the dynamics of two men in couplehood, and from the dynamics of a man and a woman in couplehood (Roth, 1985). The process of coming out for a lesbian is also different from that of a gay man (deMonteflores & Schultz, 1978). Further, the more recent psychological literature takes into consideration the sociological and phenomenological aspects of gayness. That is, the personal experience of gay men and lesbians is being viewed as the most central aspect of describing gay existence, as descriptions move away from the purely behavioral.

Lesbians have received considerably less attention in the psychological, psychiatric, and counseling literature than have gay men, despite the recent changes to a more phenomenological and sociological focus. Only in the mid-1980s did such notions as a "psychology of lesbianism" or specific psychotherapy issues for lesbian clients begin to be seriously considered (see *Boston Lesbian Psychologies Collective*, 1987, for example). This is an important and much-needed change from the former treatment of lesbians by psychology, psychiatry, and medicine, which included such atrocities as aversion therapy, electroshock treatments, clitoridectomy, hysterectomy, lobotomy, and various drug and hormone therapies (Katz, 1976). Such methods were singularly aimed at asexualization or heterosexual reorientation, which invariably involved a negative value judgment of lesbianism.

All of these trends point toward the emergence of a new field of knowledge for psychotherapy, and especially for the practice of clinical psychology, psychiatry, counseling, and social work. This new field views lesbians and gay men in a positive manner, it does not seek to "cure" a pathology, it acknowledges minority status, and it considers the distinctly different experience of lesbians from that of gay men.

In spite of these changes, many myths, stereotypes, and misunderstandings prevail. Homosexuality is still largely considered immoral by religious standards, criminal by many state and civil standards, and sick or merely tolerated by many members of the psychology and medical professions.

Both a psychology of lesbianism and an understanding of clinical treatment issues for psychotherapy with lesbians are in a preliminary stage, and will require many years and many volumes of literature to be addressed adequately. I hope to make a contribution toward that end by providing a compilation of the literature on psychotherapy with lesbian clients—with women identified as lesbian and with women not identified as lesbian but as women whose lives encompass the love of other women. I have attempted to present both the literature itself and practical guides and clinical examples to offer therapists a resource for working with many aspects of lesbian issues.

TRAINING PSYCHOTHERAPISTS TO WORK WITH LESBIAN CLIENTS

Why the need for specialized training for therapists working with lesbian issues? As with any subspecialty in clinical psychotherapy (for example, alcoholism treatment, neuropsychology, treatment of survivors of sexual abuse, treatment of phobias, treatment of racial minorities), the ethical standards of most therapists require that therapists who are working with lesbian clients be appropriately trained and competent to do so. For example, guidelines 1.5 and 1.6 of the American Psychological Association's *Specialty Guidelines for the Delivery of Services by Clinical Psychologists* (1980) state the following:

> 1.5. Clinical psychologists maintain current knowledge of scientific and professional developments to preserve and enhance their professional competence; and
> 1.6. Clinical psychologists limit their practice to their demonstrated areas of professional competence.

Psychiatrists, social workers, and other counselors are under similar professional guidelines.

The American Psychological Association's Board of Professional Affairs has recently affirmed that psychotherapy with lesbian and gay clients is an "area of special competence" that calls for specialized training (K. A. Hancock, personal communication, October 30, 1986). At present, no specific standards for competence to do psychotherapy with lesbians have been developed. However, the Association's Committee for Lesbian and Gay Concerns plans to undertake such a project, setting standards that reflect a positive view of lesbianism and a more complete understanding of the lesbian's experience and based on previously forged informal standards (for example, Brown, 1984 and 1985; Schlossberg & Pietrofesa, 1978; Kingdon, 1979).

A 1984 study by Graham, Rawlings, Halpern, and Hermes demonstrated unequivocally the need for psychotherapists to be trained in counseling both gay men and lesbians. They collected data from 112 psychotherapist respondents in the Cincinnati area who worked in private or public inpatient or outpatient settings. A measure of therapist attitudes showed that the vast majority held positive attitudes toward homosexuality:

- 81% agreed with the American Psychological Association's and the

American Psychiatric Association's positions that homosexuality is not a mental disorder;

- 77% stated that homosexuals can be just as well adjusted as heterosexuals (those who did not think so placed blame on society's negative attitude rather than on the homosexual person); and
- 94% or more stated that homosexuals belong in roles such as teachers, parents, child psychologists, physicians, nurses, and religious leaders.

In contrast to these fairly positive attitudes, the therapists in this study demonstrated only a modicum of basic information about gay men and lesbians that is available in the scientific literature:

- Only half were aware that most homosexuals have had sexual experiences with members of the other gender;
- 62% incorrectly agreed with a statement that it is possible for therapy to change a person's sexual orientation; and
- 26% felt that helping clients to make other people aware of their sexual orientation was not applicable or never came up in therapy, despite the relationship demonstrated in the literature between psychological health and openness about sexual orientation (which will be elaborated upon in Chapters 4 and 5).

Eighty-three of the respondents stated that special training and knowledge are needed by therapists for counseling gay men and lesbians. They stated a need for:

- workshops to help them get in touch with their own feelings toward homosexuality (82%),
- knowledge of current research on homosexuality (66%),
- attendance at conference presentations on homosexuality (59%), and
- sensitization through contact with gay and lesbian groups (58%).

Although 63% of the respondents stated that they would attend such training if it were available locally, they in fact did not do so; on two occasions the authors of this study scheduled training workshops and both had to be cancelled due to lack of participants. The authors conclude that their findings raise serious questions about the quality of services that many gay men and lesbians apparently are receiving due to lack of training and inaccurate information on the part of therapists. They also point out that the many therapists who provide services to these populations and who are not trained to do so are acting irresponsibly. I have had similar experiences, where attendance is very low at "voluntary" continuing education training on lesbian and gay issues in therapy, yet trainings in "mandatory" settings, such as university classes and practicums, are well received.

Psychotherapists then must be trained before conducting psychotherapy with lesbian clients if ethical, and even humanistic, standards are to be met.

A very few references already exist for the therapist who wishes to gain expertise in doing psychotherapy with lesbian clients (Clark, 1987; Woodman & Lenna, 1980; Moses & Hawkins, 1982; Gonsiorek, 1982a; and Stein & Cohen, 1986). These are all high-quality references; however, they either do not address lesbians and gay men separately or they do not describe the lesbian's experience in a comprehensive way; thus they are lacking critical information for the psychotherapist about the distinctly different experience of lesbians. I hope to have supplemented these previous references by reviewing empirical and theoretical materials published since 1980 and applying these to psychotherapy with lesbians.

SOME PRELIMINARIES

There are six areas of knowledge that provide important adjunctive reading to this volume, especially for readers with limited exposure to lesbians. Suggested readings are provided in each area to offer background material.

1. *Demographics.* The recent literature has shown without question that it is much more accurate to talk of "homosexualities" than of "homosexuality." There is no single way to describe the typical lesbian. Demographically, she comes from all socioeconomic classes, education levels, career paths, sex-role choices, styles of upbringing, religions, and races. All facets of her life are highly individualized: sexual activity and techniques, types of partnerships sought, interfacing with the mental health community for professional help, the role of friendships, interfacing with the legal system, and the level of openness about her lesbianism to the outer world, among other things. Demographically, lesbians are just as diverse as their nonlesbian counterparts and therefore cannot be well described as a group. However, as further reading of this volume will indicate, certain pressures, self-representations, and environmental systems may be unique to lesbians as a group and can have an effect on their interaction with the mental health community.

For further information on the demographics of both lesbians and gay men, see Bell and Weinberg's (1978) excellent report of their 10-year study of nearly 1,000 gay people in the San Francisco Bay Area. *Lesbian/Woman* (1983) by Martin and Lyon is another fine descriptive work.

2. *Language*. Lesbians often have a jargon of their own, a jargon that changes with the times. For example, for some lesbians, it can be an important self-defining and political choice to use the word "lesbian" rather than "gay" to describe herself; for others this is not so. Some prefer not to use the word lesbian as a noun ("I am a lesbian"), but rather as an adjective ("I am a lesbian person"). Some use "dyke" or "queer" to identify themselves, but in a positive manner (by reclaiming and redefining a term that is pejorative in the language of nongays). Some eschew labels.

Lesbians also call their lovers by various terms: lover, partner, mate, wife, roommate, friend, and again, in reclaiming a nonfeminist term, girlfriend. Lesbians may talk about being "politically correct" (or "PC"), referring to having a high social consciousness, a feminist ideology, and a respect for all forms of life on the planet. They may refer to heterosexuals as "straight" or "het." They may speak of "bringing someone out" or of "being brought out" by someone, referring to one's initial introduction to lesbianism, either by acquaintance with lesbians or by a lesbian affair.

All such uses of jargon are idiosyncratic and geographical. Language that is commonly used among lesbians themselves may not be acceptable to them when used by a nongay person, a fact to which a nongay therapist should be alert.

The reader should also be familiar with such terms as:

"homophobia"—the fear of gayness said to be the root of the denial of civil and economic rights to gays.

"internalized homophobia"—the psychological acceptance of beliefs about oneself that homosexuality is inferior to heterosexuality. These beliefs can be conscious or unconscious.

"lesbian community"—a network of women who identify themselves as lesbians and who establish a broad range of activities (social, political, cultural, athletic, and so on) especially for lesbian participation. The lesbian community can be described locally within one's own town or region, or more globally as across the nation or worldwide.

"heterosexism"—the assumption that heterosexuality is in any way better than homosexuality.

"in the closet" (or *"closeted"* or *"a closet case"*)—being secretive about one's lesbianism, often due to external homophobia, internalized homophobia, or heterosexism.

"out" (or *"out of the closet"*)—being open about one's lesbianism to a particular person or in a specific situation.

"passing"—to look or talk as if one is not a lesbian (also called "passing as straight").

"separatism"—the ideological choice to minimize interactions with men, and women who relate to men.

This is only a small sampling of words and phrases used by the lesbian and gay community. Perhaps the best way to keep current with lesbian jargon is to maintain social interaction with lesbians and to read current lesbian newspapers and magazines, available at lesbian or feminist bookstores. It should be noted that only lesbians with some exposure to the gay community may be familiar with such jargon at all.

3. *The coming-out process.* In the lesbian literature, the process of coming out is now also being called the "identity formation process" more or less interchangeably, although the distinction between the two terms is sometimes significant. This is discussed at more length in Chapter 5. As background, it is important that the reader understand several things. First, the literature shows unequivocally that attempts to change a person's identity from gay to heterosexual, by whatever means, are very rarely successful, even when the client is highly motivated. Second, several theorists have described a stage theory of coming out (Woodman & Lenna, 1980; Lewis, 1984; Cass, 1979), whereas others describe a process model (Golden, 1987; Ponse, 1978; Gramick, 1984), but all theorists make the strong point that any stages are not fixed or sequential and that identity formation is an individualized phenomenon. Third, the literature has shown that there is a correlation between psychological health and degree of being "out" or open about one's gayness (Greene, 1977; Gartrell, 1984; Bell & Weinberg, 1978).

Clark's (1987) *Loving Someone Gay* is a sensitive guide to understanding what it means to be gay. I also recommend Cruikshank's (1985) *Lesbian Path*, a collection of interviews with lesbians about their lives.

4. *The effects of oppression and invisibility.* Two issues are important here. First, lesbians in most current societies exist in a hostile culture. This has a negative effect on many individuals that, when seen out of its cultural context, makes it look as though it is the lesbian herself who is maladjusted. However, the question is actually whether it is really the culture that is ill, rather than the lesbian. Ever since Hooker's (1957) acclaimed study, the literature has shown over and over that homosexuals are no less well adjusted psychologically than are heterosexuals. In Hooker's study, experts were unable to distinguish homosexual and heterosexual men on the basis of their Rorschach protocols, their responses to Thematic Apperception Test cards, or to the Make a Picture Story, leading her to conclude that homosexuality is a "deviation in sexual pattern which is still within the normal

range psychologically." More recent research on lesbians in particular has given results indicating that on several measures, lesbians appear to be psychologically healthier than their nonlesbian counterparts. These studies are discussed in Chapter 2.

Second, the effects that lesbianism will have on each individual woman are different and unpredictable. Psychotherapists know that a client who was raised by alcoholic parents, or a client who experienced incest, or a client whose primary caretaker in infancy was physically or emotionally unavailable to them will feel the effects of such experience in some way. However, both the depth of the effects and the actual manifestation of the effects are highly individualized, and, given the present state of the art of psychotherapy, are unpredictable. Unknown predispositions, fixed or malleable personality traits, resiliency, outside support, reactions of family and peers, the continuously self-modifying character of one's perceptual system, and other factors may all be involved in determining just how the effects are shown. So it is with lesbianism. The depth of the effects of her lesbianism (both negative and positive), the behavioral or psychological manifestation of those effects, and even the potential denial of those effects, are all individually determined, and it is up to the therapist to help investigate and explore them; there is no formula.

For good background reading on the effects of oppression and invisibility, I recommend Katz's *Gay American History* (1976). It is a large volume not meant to be read in one sitting. I suggest skimming through it for what interests you, paying particular attention to his introductions to each chapter.

5. *Sexuality and love.* Kinsey's work in the 1950s (Kinsey et al., 1953) forever changed the American public's notion of homosexuality as rare or as simply an adolescent phase. Kinsey found that sexual activity is best described on a continuum; he developed a 7-point scale ranging from "exclusively heterosexual" (a score of 0) to "exclusively homosexual" (a score of 6), based on self-reports of both arousal feelings and behavior. The concept of such a continuum is essential to the therapist's understanding of all human sexuality; humans cannot be simply categorized into two camps, heterosexual and homosexual (or with the addition of a third camp, bisexual), but instead can only be described in reference to a continuum of sexuality.

Masters, Johnson, and Kolodny (1986), Blumstein and Schwartz (1983), and Bell and Weinberg (1978) describe distinct differences between lesbians and gay men when it comes to sexuality and love. The most striking difference is that lesbians appear to prize a love relationship above all else in their lives, whereas many gay men (and nongay men) do not. (Although relationships are important to men, too, these studies find that they are not given the highest priority in life.) Love is frequently regarded as a prerequisite to sex for lesbians. These studies also report a somewhat lower frequency of sexual activity among lesbians than among other populations, but a higher rate of affection, caressing, touching, and nongenital sensuality.

Since the early 1970s, lesbians have more and more moved away from any kind of sex-role defined activities ("butch" and "femme"), both in the structure of their relationships and in the initiation and activities of making love. Many have had sexual experiences with men, a large percentage having been heterosexually married at one time. Lesbians are no more likely to have had negative or traumatic sexual experiences with men than are nonlesbians (Brannock & Chapman, 1990; Vance & Green, 1984). Also, more lesbians do not consider themselves unattractive (Bell & Weinberg, 1978).

For background, I recommend a good skim through all three of the books mentioned above, Masters, Johnson, and Kolodny's *On Sex and Human Loving*, Blumstein and Schwartz's *American Couples*, and Bell and Weinberg's *Homosexualities*. Further useful reading includes Hite's (1976) *Hite Report* and *Lesbian/Woman* by Martin and Lyon (1983). *Lesbian Sex* by Loulan (1984) is essential reading and is taken up in more detail in Chapter 7.

6. *Therapy issues.* The issues that lesbians bring to therapy are numerous and diverse. It is important that the therapist be able to do two things:

(a) The therapist must work continually to be conscious of her or his own homophobia, heterosexism, and especially her or his own personal feelings toward members of the same gender. Therapists must acknowledge their own limits of knowledge and awareness and be ready to refer or to obtain consultation or supervision when therapy oversteps those limits. The therapist must keep currently trained by attending professional workshops and by reading the literature, even if the therapist is lesbian herself.

(b) The therapist must be able to ascertain to what level lesbianism is a part of the therapy issues. Sometimes lesbianism is an overt part of the therapy issues presented, as in coming-out issues or working with the client's internalized shame or homophobia. Other times lesbianism may not be an overt part of the therapy issues, as in some instances where the therapy work centers around incest or addictions or adult children of alcoholics syndrome or personality disorders. However, lesbianism is *never* irrelevant to the therapy issues. Even when it is not at all part of the treatment "problem" or diagnosis, it is always an integral part of the context of that client's life. Lesbianism must never be ignored.

Good background reading includes Woodman and Lenna's (1980) *Counseling With Gay Men and Women*, Clark's (1987) *Loving Someone Gay*, Moses and Hawkins' (1982) *Counseling Lesbian Women and Gay Men*, Gonsiorek's (1982a) *Homosexuality and Psychotherapy*, and Stein and Cohen's (1986) *Contemporary Perspectives on Psychotherapy with Lesbians and Gay Men*.

Assuming now that the reader has obtained a solid background in the six prerequisite areas mentioned here, I turn your attention to a more detailed description of the lesbian and her world.

LESBIANS: WHO ARE THEY?

As the small but growing body of literature on lesbians unfolds, we are able to glean more and more information about this population. Several large recent studies have been undertaken that shed additional light on psychology's knowledge about lesbianism. These are described here.

Lesbianism has no universally agreed-upon definition or description. Some consider lesbianism only as a behavior. Others consider it an emotional bond (thus the word homophile is often used to replace homosexual). Some say it is a choice and other say it is a "given." Both researchers and lesbians themselves define lesbianism in diverse and idiosyncratic ways. We are thus dealing with a phenomenon that from the start is difficult to pin down, and by nature is phenomenological and idiosyncratic to the individual involved.

A description given by Kingdon (1979) exemplifies some of the fairly common aspects of a definition of lesbianism:

A lesbian is a woman whose primary emotional, psychological, social and sexual interests are directed toward other women. Lesbians come from all social classes, economic levels, educational levels, racial and ethnic groups. Lesbians are married, single, with and without children, and in every type of work. It is impossible to obtain an accurate estimate of the number of lesbians because so many lead totally hidden and closeted lives, and unlike other minorities, lesbians have no distinguishing characteristics. There are rough estimates of 11 million lesbians in this country—about one out of every ten women. (p. 44)

Little cross-cultural research on lesbianism has been done. However, one landmark study was done by Cavin in 1985. She studied 30 societies worldwide, including societies from Africa, the Mediterranean, Eurasia, the Pacific, and North and South America. She found that lesbianism crosses all world regions; it occurs across all industrial, preindustrial, and subsistence economies; it crosses all types of human settlement patterns, such as nomadic bands, compound settlements, neighborhoods, and hamlets; and it crosses most marriage types, family types, household types, and economic exchange systems. Cavin points to Margaret Mead's research in Samoa that showed a 68% frequency of lesbianism and a 48% frequency of heterosexual experience. Cavin also points out that among the Amarakaeri of Peru, lovemaking is almost exclusively homosexual, with heterosexual acts performed only two or three times per year at ceremonial rites.

Turning to this country, Cavin finds that Kinsey's (1953) estimate of a 2% frequency of lesbianism is the lowest estimate in the literature. Kinsey admits that his figures are probably low. Cavin points to research by Davis (1929) which found a frequency rate of over 50% among the 1200 women sampled of "intense emotional relationships with other women as adults," with 27% acknowledging "overt lesbian experience." Hite's (1976) nationwide study of female sexuality estimated an 8% frequency of lesbianism among her sample.

Although the Kinsey report on women (Kinsey, Pomeroy, Martin, & Gebhard, 1953) estimated that only about 2% of women are predominantly lesbian in behavior, these researchers also found that 26% of women reported being erotically aroused in homosexual situations and that half that number reported reaching orgasm with another woman by the age of 45. More recently, McConaghy, Armstrong, Birrell, and Buhrich (1979) found that over 40% of women report being erotically attracted to members of their own sex at some time.

Thus, depending on the definition of lesbianism, current figures estimate that approximately one-fourth of U.S. women experience lesbian sexual behaviors, and over half have had lesbian emotional experiences. For the sake of comparing numbers, note that Blacks constitute 12% of the U.S. population, Native Americans 0.6%, the elderly 11.9%, and Hispanics 6.6% (*Statistical Abstract of the United States,* 1986). Of course, lesbians are also Black, Native American, elderly, Hispanic, and members of many other minority groups as well. Lesbians are thus clearly deserving of the same minority status as these more readily acknowledged (and more visible) minorities. Lesbians are indeed a significant portion of the population at large, and likewise of the clientele that avail themselves of psychotherapists' services.

The recent work by Masters, Johnson, and Kolodny (1986) contains some important information on lesbians. In this work the authors review theories on the origin of homosexuality, including genetic theories, hormone theories, psychological theories, and learning theories. They conclude that all theories are lacking and that there is no agreement about what "causes" homosexuality (or heterosexuality for that matter).

Masters, Johnson, and Kolodny also shed light on other aspects of homosexuality, especially its diversity. The number of lesbians, they say, who have a "masculine" appearance is very small. Nor is there any occupational group that is purely homosexual. Further, there is no evidence that homosexuals are maladjusted—a fact that they point out is remarkable considering the prejudice in our society. Lastly, they point out that there is no such thing as a "homosexual lifestyle" that would accurately describe how most gays and lesbians live because there are endless examples of homosexual diversity.

Masters, Johnson, and Kolodny also discuss the differences between *discovering* one's homosexuality and *accepting* it. Because all U.S. children are exposed to almost exclusively heterosexual role models at home, in school, on television, and in books, and because in our society everyone is considered heterosexual unless "proven" otherwise, children grow up assuming their own heterosexuality. Lesbians must therefore at some time in their lives come to discover their nonheterosexuality and go through the beginnings of the coming-out process. Because of assumed heterosexuality, many lesbians who experience emotional or physical homosexual feelings do one of three things:

1. disregard their feelings,
2. fail to label their feelings as lesbian, or
3. consider their feelings just a phase.

An example of this phenomenon was seen in the 1977 report of the American Psychological Association's Task Force on the Status of Lesbian and Gay Male Psychologists. Among our own professional group, the progression of events in the coming-out process is as shown in Table 1, where the 270 APA-member respondents listed their ages for each event.

The reports of lesbians differ from those of the gay men. Lesbians were later in recognizing their homosexual feelings and they tended to have an intellectual understanding of lesbianism before acting on those feelings sexually, whereas the reverse is true of gay men. Lesbians reported a six-year lag between their first awareness of homosexual feelings and their first same-sex sexual experience, but for the men the lag is only two years. Perhaps the most telling feature in this study is the gap between first awareness of feelings and acquiring a positive gay or lesbian identity— approximately 16 years for both sexes. A gap of approximately 10 years for lesbians and eight years for gay men exists between first awareness and

TABLE I.
Age of Occurrence of Developmental Events in
the Coming-out Process for Psychologists

	Lesbians	Gay men
Aware of homosexual feelings	13.8	12.8
Had first same-sex sexual experience	19.9	14.9
Understood what "homosexual" was	15.6	17.2
Had first homosexual relationship	22.8	21.9
Considered self "homosexual"	23.2	21.1
Acquired positive gay identity	29.7	28.5
Disclosed identity to spouse	26.7	33.3
Disclosed identity to friend(s)	28.2	28.0
Disclosed identity to parent	30.2	28.0
Disclosed identity professionally	32.4	31.2

From "Removing the Stigma" by Task Force on the Status of Lesbian and Gay Male Psychologists. 1977. *APA Monitor*, p. 16. Copyright © 1977 by the American Psychological Association. Reprinted by permission.

labeling oneself as homosexual. For this group, coming out in a professional context did not occur until 18 years after initial awareness. Although the subjects were psychologists and may thus be a special subpopulation, the results point not only to some important differences between lesbians and gay men, but also to the fact that the awareness of homosexuality and the acceptance of it are two very different events in one's life.

Just as lesbians themselves are a diverse group, so too are the environments they inhabit. In some larger urban settings the lesbian community may be a full-fledged entity complete with lesbian bookstores, coffeehouses, bars, religious organizations, medical and psychological clinics, newspapers, recreational groups, support systems, and guides to lesbian merchants. In other areas, there is no organized community and a lesbian may live her entire life not knowing that any other lesbian exists within commuting distance aside from her lover.

As she interacts with the world outside her private community, the lesbian still faces many hurdles even in the 1990s. Lesbians are still banned from employment with the FBI, CIA, or the military (although they may now leave the military with honorable discharges in some cases and legal cases continue to challenge these policies). Lesbian mothers are becoming increasingly successful in winning child custody cases, but a clear danger of losing their children due to their lesbianism still remains. Although obvious employment and housing discrimination is on the decline, subtle forms of such discrimination remain; lesbian employees are now terminated more often by reason of false claims of inadequate work record rather than by directly stated anti-lesbian sentiment.

The 1983 study on American couples by Blumstein and Schwartz gives another overview of the world of the lesbian. These researchers analyzed questionnaire data from 12,000 couples, 300 of whom were intensively interviewed. A large cross section of the country's population is represented. Of the couples interviewed, 72 were married heterosexuals, 48 were cohabiting heterosexuals, 90 were lesbian couples, and 90 were gay male couples. Their results are divided into three major categories of importance to couples: money, work, and sex. Some of the findings relevant to lesbianism are as follows.

Findings on the role of money in relationships show that the amount of money earned by one partner compared with the other partner establishes relative power (such as financial autonomy and level of accountability) for heterosexual and gay male couples, but not for the lesbian couples in the study. The authors hypothesize that women do not judge worth by income and may make a conscious effort to keep relationships free of any form of domination. Lesbians, they found, use income not to establish dominance, but to avoid having one woman dependent on the other; they often attempt to equalize contributions to their joint financial responsibilities in spite of differences in income. They tend to stress independence and self-sufficiency for both partners, and only after individual strengths are established do they allow themselves to be dependent or vulnerable.

In terms of the role of work in relationships, it was found that in most lesbian couples both partners are employed outside the home. They also usually share many of their leisure activities, which is seen as an advantage by the authors, serving to conserve quality time together compared with many heterosexual couples who work and who spend time apart in separate playtime activities and who have little time left over for activities together other than the mundane and less enjoyable details of life and homemaking. For lesbians, having had an entire life of similar experiences as women, communication comes easier and a kinship is possible that is less easy to find with someone of the other sex.

Findings on the role of sex in relationships show plainly that being a woman shapes sexual opportunities, choices, and behaviors for lesbians. Lesbians, as women, are socialized not to be sexually initiative, have less genital sexual contact than the other couples studied, and do not have a compensating rate of sex outside the relationship. However, the lesbians studied prize nongenital contact and sexuality, such as cuddling and hugging, more than the other couples do, and more important, they see these activities as ends in themselves rather than as "foreplay" to genital sex. Another finding is that lesbian couples are the only couples that do not place a high premium on physical beauty as it affects their happiness. The researchers also found that sexual satisfaction for all couples studied correlates with sharing equal responsibility for initiating and refusing sex, which can be problematic for lesbians, who, as women, are socialized not to initiate sexual contact.

In addition to the breadth of information that Blumstein and Schwartz's (1983) study contribute to psychology and sociology, their study makes a major statement simply in its design, which gave credence and recognition to the importance of gay male and lesbian couplehood in the fabric of North American culture.

Bell and Weinberg's 1978 study has become a landmark study in the field of sex research carried on in the Kinsey tradition. The findings of their 10-year study are numerous and their book is well worth the reading. Their findings encompass such diverse areas as job satisfaction, religiousness, physical health, the role of friendships, how leisure time is spent, political affiliation and involvement, self-acceptance, loneliness, suicidal feelings, exuberance, and contact with professional counselors. Their most important contribution was twofold: (a) there is no such thing as "the homosexual," only "homosexualities" that reflect a diversity of lifestyles and make-up of persons who are homosexual; and (b) homosexuality (and heterosexuality) is inevitably intertwined with the social and the psychological spheres of life.

Bell and Weinberg developed a typology of gay and lesbian experience that is found to closely parallel heterosexual experience. Their five types are:

1. Close-coupled—a committed couplehood with few sexual problems and few or no outside partners. Eighty-one of their 211 lesbian subjects fit this type.
2. Open-coupled—a committed couplehood but with significant sexual problems or several outside partners. Fifty-one subjects fit this type.
3. Functional—a noncoupled person who scores low on regret over being lesbian. Thirty subjects fit this type.
4. Dysfunctional—a noncoupled person who reports a high level of sexual activity, rates herself as unattractive, reports numerous sexual problems, and scores high on regret over her lesbianism. Sixteen subjects fit this type. Although the fewest lesbians fit this type, it is apparently the type from which most early negative research on lesbians was drawn.
5. Asexual—a noncoupled person with few or no sexual partners and low sexual activity. Thirty-three subjects fit this type.

The researchers state that their respondents could be distinguished from each other on the basis of several factors: their involvement in a quasi marriage and their management of that relationship; the degree to which their lesbianism is problematic; and the extent to which they are disengaged from the explicitly sexual aspects of gay life. The authors call for a more comprehensive and discriminating typology in the future.

CONCLUSION

In summary, the literature describes lesbians as an extremely diverse and quite large population. All of the theories on the origins of homosexuality that have so far been developed are found to be lacking. The development of a lesbian identity is quite complex, with a distinct difference seen between becoming aware of one's homosexuality and coming to accept it. The lesbian's world can range from a state of isolation from a lesbian community to complete immersion in it; either way discrimination remains in our culture, and the lesbian must live in an outside world that is unfriendly at best and hostile at its worst. Self-disclosure is always potentially dangerous.

Because lesbians are first and foremost women, their socialization as women influences their sexual behavior, their management of their relationships, and many other aspects of living. Lesbians thus tend to equalize their relationships, spend more quality time together, and engage in more nongenital sensuality than other couples do. Lastly, at least one typology of homosexualities has been developed that indicates that lesbians may be categorized into types of relationships and singlehood that are similar to patterns seen in heterosexual lifestyles.

The psychotherapy literature of late has greatly expanded our knowledge of lesbianism. The following chapters magnify this knowledge, especially as it applies to the practice of psychotherapy with lesbian clientele.

2

PSYCHOLOGY AND THE LESBIAN EXPERIENCE

The foundations laid in Chapter 1 allow us to now focus in more closely on the subject of psychology and how it has interfaced with lesbian persons and with lesbianism in theory. Chapter 2 reviews the literature in three main areas. First, an overview is presented of the treatment of lesbians by psychologists and psychiatrists throughout the 20th century; also included here is the research of the last 60 years that has attempted to show what, if any, differences there are between lesbians and nongay women. Second, information is gleaned from the literature to show what makes doing therapy with lesbian clients distinct from doing therapy with nongay women. Third is a look at several models of lesbian-affirmative psychotherapy that have emerged in the literature, which serve as a guide for the knowledge and skills needed to provide lesbian-affirmative therapy.

PSYCHOLOGY AND THE LESBIAN: TREATMENT AND RESEARCH

In many cultures throughout history, lesbianism has been a fully accepted manner of life, and in some cultures, it has even been revered as a gifted manner of life with special status, privileges, and ceremonial duties reserved for lesbians (Grahn, 1984). However, in the last few centuries of Western culture in particular, lesbianism has moved from being considered a theological-moral phenomenon (a sin), to being considered a legal matter (a crime), to most recently being considered a medical-psychological phenomenon (a mental illness). At first, it may have seemed a humane advance to consider lesbianism an illness rather than a crime, but the medical-psychological community has done its share to continue the oppression of lesbians and to advance the notion that lesbianism is an inferior way of life.

Treatment

The list of "cures" and treatments of lesbians by psychiatric-psychological professionals is nothing short of horrifying. Surgical treatments have included removal of the uterus, the ovaries, or the clitoris. These practices still occur in some cultures today. Lobotomy as a means of treatment was performed as late as 1951. Drug treatments have included hormone therapy and administration of LSD, sexual stimulants, and sexual depressants. Electrical shock and chemical shock treatments, hypnosis to change sexual orientation, and behavioral aversion therapies are also found among clinical records from this century. Hospitalization was common in the 1960s and it still is not unheard of now.

It has been argued that lesbians entered these treatments voluntarily and thus must have wanted such treatments. However, Katz (1976) points out that gays and lesbians are socially pressured into feeling that they are "psychological freaks" in need of treatment, which in truth may have made entering treatment not a voluntary action at all. As further noted by Cabaj (1988), many lesbians fear the psychotherapeutic community and feel that in order to be treated—or even listened to—they have to present themselves as wishing to change their orientation, thus skewing the therapeutic community's conception of the actual reasons that clients may enter therapy.

One of the most widely used texts in the mid-1900s was Caprio's (1954) *Female Homosexuality: A Modern Study of Lesbianism.* Caprio describes lesbians as jealous, unhappy, possessive, emotionally unstable, immature, narcissistic, guilty, sadomasochistic, insecure, and suffering "a multiplicity of neurotic health ailments" (p. 179). He states, "Psychoanalysts are in agreement that all women who prefer a homosexual way of life suffer from a distorted sense of values and betray their emotional immaturity in their attitudes toward men, sex, and marriage" (cited in Sang, 1978, p. 81). By this description it is clear that lesbianism is seen as an illness primarily because it contradicts established attitudes about women's place in the realm of sex and marriage; maturity is defined as accepting the cultural sex-role stereotype and being married to a man. This is a commonly held view and points up the sociopolitical nature of lesbianism that has long been a central concern.

Even when the treatment of lesbians has not been overtly inhumane, psychology's view of lesbianism as less desirable than heterosexuality has subtly but deeply pervaded psychotherapy:

There was good reason for gay suspicion of the shrinks. Mental health professionals had long been responsible not only for stigmatizing gays but also for incarcerating, lobotomizing, castrating and generally abusing gay people who either sought help or were forced into treatment when their homosexuality was discovered. (Mach, 1987, p. 44)

As the gay and lesbian liberation movement began to explore these subtleties in the 1960s and 1970s, all psychology and psychiatry became strongly suspect by the gay and lesbian community, and therapists were often called "the-rapists," seen as rapists of a positive lesbian identity (Boston Women's Health Book Collective, 1973). Members of the Gay Activists Alliance in New York City, who were active in the early attempts to point out the damage done to gays and lesbians by classifying homosexuality as a mental illness, were nevertheless forbidden by the organization's rules to communicate with psychiatrists or psychologists directly because the mental health profession was considered "the enemy."

A personal case example is cited in *Our Bodies, Ourselves* (Boston Women's Health Book Collective, 1973:

Molly reports that she checked herself into a psychiatric hospital when she found herself drinking heavily and becoming increasingly unable to cope after the suicidal death of her long-term lover. She reports that her doctors were oblivious to her alcoholism and focused solely on her lesbianism. She writes that the doctors "... told me I was utterly dependent (love women), had anxiety neuroses (alcohol withdrawal), was borderline schizophrenic (failed to conform to their ideas of what a woman's life should be), and had a poor prognosis (I believed in myself more than in their theories about me)." (p. 64)

The lesbian literature of the 1960s and 1970s contains many personal reports of such treatment, which fanned the flames of suspicion of mental health professionals.

Although the diagnosis of homosexuality as a mental disorder was removed from the *Diagnostic and Statistical Manual of Mental Disorders* in 1973, a diagnosis called "ego-dystonic homosexuality" remained in the Manual until its 1988 revision. Under this category, anyone could be diagnosed with this "mental illness" who felt a degree of discomfort about her or his orientation, a discomfort that is essentially a given in an unaccepting society. The most recent version of the Manual, published in 1988, still has a category listed under "Other Sexual Disorders" describing "persistent and marked distress about one's sexual orientation." Homosexuality remains classified as a mental illness in the current diagnostic document that is used by physicians worldwide, the *Manual of International Statistical Classification of Diseases, Injuries, and Causes of Death* (9th Revision) (WHO, 1977). The illness model of homosexuality is dying very hard!

Even into the 1990s, many lesbians are suspicious of psychotherapy treatments and avoid entering therapy when other life factors might recommend it. When making a first therapy appointment with a client over the phone, I am occasionally asked if I take notes during sessions (I don't); others ask if I keep notes or a file (I do). And when I have worked in agencies, some lesbian clients have asked if I could somehow keep their files separate from the rest of the agency's files so that office workers and other therapists would not have any chance of seeing the file. These clients are worried that written records by a mental health professional could be detrimental to them. This is at least in part due to their unsavory historical encounters with the "helping" professions.

Many of my clients have recounted months or years of costly therapy that they have spent with therapists who subtly or overtly undermined a healthy exploration of lesbianism. Unfortunately, too many therapists (and nontherapist researchers and academicians) still approach homosexuality negatively: In the late 1980s, I was dismayed to see this ad carried by my local metropolitan newspaper:

The biological reasons why homosexuality should be considered a mental disorder so that it may be medically and psychologically treated and eliminated—*Evolution Versus Homosexuality*, the new book against homosexuality and feminism from one of the most talented evolutionary biologists of our time—Mark Warren Manhart.

Information on how to order the book followed. When a "talented evolutionary biologist" states that homosexuality must be "treated and eliminated," one can see why lesbians must still fear for their rights, may wonder whether they are indeed psychologically healthy, and may still avoid contact with mental health professionals.

In spite of their fears, lesbians have become quite heavy utilizers of mental health services in recent years; a survey of nearly 2,000 lesbians done in 1987 (NIMH, 1987) showed that 73% reported obtaining some form of counseling or mental health support during adulthood. Clearly, the need for lesbian-affirmative therapy is great.

Research

The history of research on lesbianism is no more favorable than is the history of therapeutic treatments. Early research was based on psychoanalytic theory and attempted to validate the belief that lesbianism was a symptom of arrested psychosexual development and overdependence upon the mother. This research was carried out by use of projective testing methods that were subject to nonsystematic content analysis only. (Today, analysis of content from projective tests is seen as secondary in importance to analysis of perceptual style.) Further, only patient populations were used.

Again citing Caprio's (1954) widely used text of its time, it was held that lesbianism was a symptom of a severe personality disorder, which was thought to necessarily be "caused" by negative experiences. The "contributing factors" were determined to be:

1. Poor parenting: Fathers who really want a son instead of a daughter or who are poor providers or alcoholics; or mothers who instill a fear of sex in their daughters or who are critical, dominating, unsympathetic, and distant.
2. Psychic traumas: Rape, incest.
3. Environment: Occupations such as prison matron, masseuse, lingerie sales, executive in a women's organization, and theatre.
4. Sociological influences: The feminist movement, women in traditionally male occupations and sports, smoking cigarettes, drinking alcohol, and wearing masculine tailored clothes.
5. Frustrations: Unhappiness or abuse caused by a man.
6. Homosexual seductions: "The experienced lesbian invites the innocent one to spend the night with her." (p. 143)

Hooker's (1957) study, mentioned in Chapter 1, broke this line of research by showing that trained professionals could not distinguish the projective test results of nonpatient homosexual men from those of heterosexual men. Her research has been duplicated many times over the years, with the same results, and has spawned a line of research that addressed homosexuality in both men and women as nonpathological.

In 1960, Armon studied projective test results for lesbian subjects, which showed no greater degree in overall pathology or in level of maturity among the lesbians than among nonlesbian women. In the conclusions, Armon states,

The failure to find clear-cut differences which are consistent for the majority of the group would suggest that homosexuality is not a clinical entity. . . . The absence of dramatic differences between homosexuals and heterosexuals on projective tests should influence the conception that homosexuality is necessarily associated with deep regression and concordant limitations in personality functioning. (p. 309)

Despite these results, studies have continued to be conducted to find out if lesbians are less well adjusted than other women. Throughout the 1960s and 1970s, a popular research method on lesbianism was to study the results of personality assessment tools. These studies looked for trends that would show lesbian samples to perform differently (that is, "worse") from heterosexual controls on such tests. These studies are reviewed well by Mannion (1981) and by Hart et al. (1978), which are strongly recommended reading for more thorough treatment than the brief summary I include here.

Hart et al. note the numerous methodological problems encountered in the research on homosexuality. These include inadequate operational definitions, selection bias (by definition, lesbian and gay research subjects either will be selected by the researcher on the basis of patient status, or will be self-selected when voluntarily recruited), improperly matched control groups, experimenter bias, and lack of use of clinical interview methods. The authors review only studies that avoid most of these biases. The studies used various measures, such as the Cornell Medical Index Health Questionnaire, the Eysenck Personality Inventory, the Maudsley Personality Inventory, the 16 Personality Factor Questionnaire, the Minnesota Multiphasic Personality Inventory, and the Adjective Checklist. The data overall show an inconsistent pattern of differences too minor to state reliably that lesbians are either better or less well adjusted than matched heterosexual women.

Those study results that do show unfavorable results for lesbians, as compared with nonlesbian women, indicate more likelihood to commit suicide, to have problems with alcohol, and to score higher on neuroticism scales and somaticism scales, among other results. However, for each study showing such trends, another study contradicts them. Still other studies' results indicate advantages favoring lesbians, which are suggested to be the result of the fact that lesbians are usually more socially and financially independent than are heterosexual women. Some of the favorable factors that have been found more commonly among lesbian subjects are goal-directedness, self-acceptance, job stability, job satisfaction, and self-actualization (Gartrell, 1981).

In Mannion's (1981) review of these studies, she comes to the same conclusion, that several studies' results have shown lesbians scoring more favorably than heterosexual female controls on several factors, such as interpersonal satisfaction and self-determination. She also notes that studies that show some differences between the two groups are unable to determine whether those differences are inherent in lesbianism or are the result of the lesbian's response to societal pressures that force her to become inner-directed, aware, sensitive, and self-reliant in meeting her physical and economic needs.

A recent study by LaTorre and Wendenberg (1983) is perhaps the first to ensure that both heterosexual and lesbian subjects have had both heterosexual and homosexual experiences, and to differentiate between a self-chosen label (of heterosexual, bisexual, or lesbian) and actual preference for sex of partner (determined by a numerical rating scale). It is interesting to note that the total agreement between self-labeling and actual sexual preference was 89.6%; agreement was higher among self-labeled lesbians (94.4%) than among self-labeled heterosexual women (90.6%) or self-labeled bisexual women (81.1%). (These percentages of agreement between self-label and actual preference point out the fact that lesbian identity is a complex and sometimes inconsistent phenomenon. This is discussed more fully in Chapter 5.) The measures used were the Extended Personal Attributes Questionnaire, the Body Cathexis Scale, and the Rosenberg Self-Esteem Inventory. Lesbians were found to very rarely score high on either masculinity or femininity, and instead scored as "undifferentiated" (suppressing both masculine and feminine attributes) or as "androgynous" (developing both sets of attributes). Lesbians further were more "agentic" (possessing more socially desirable masculine traits), more satisfied with their bodies, more satisfied with their sexual activities and their biological sex, and more satisfied with themselves and their abilities than were the heterosexual women.

Research on who is better adjusted has sharply declined in the 1980s and 1990s. As Morin (1977) states, "The question 'Are homosexuals as a group less or better adjusted than heterosexuals?' would be of interest only if one wished to form generalizations or stereotypes that would have little application to an individual case" (p. 634).

The most recent form of research to emerge on lesbianism is the use of biographical material. Whereas several of these studies have provided significant phenomenological information (such as Bell & Weinberg [1978] and Blumstein & Schwartz [1983] discussed in Chapter 1), unfortunately most are based on the notion that some factors in childhood cause lesbianism, either through experiences with parents or through inadequate role modeling. Mannion (1981) points out that the interpretation of this kind of data is formidable, and the results are of questionable validity. Causal statements cannot be drawn from post hoc material, nor can the respondents' recollections be presumed to be accurate. These studies assume that the direction of effect is from parent to child, which is also open to question. Aside from these methodological problems, the results of such studies are so mixed as to preclude identifying any trends whatsoever. Studies such as Bell and Weinberg's and Blumstein and Schwartz's, mentioned earlier, are more successful precisely because they are searching for descriptive diversity and not for causality based on the superiority of heterosexuality.

Nevertheless, the search for the "causes" of homosexuality continues. Studies such as those done by Saghir and Robins (1973), Erhardt et al. (1985), and Money (1988) attempt to link sexual orientation to prenatal exposure to, or adult circulating, sex hormones. This line of research bases its results on either (1) animal studies showing that manipulation of prenatal hormones can affect stereotyped mounting and lordosis behaviors, resulting in same-sex sexual behaviors, or (2) human studies correlating prenatal or adult hormone levels with homosexuality. Doell and Longino (1988) provide an excellent critique of these studies, claiming that not only do these studies confuse possible "correlations" with a "cause," but that the wrong biological model is being applied by these researchers. Doell and Longino argue persuasively that "there is a vast difference in character between the more stereotyped behavior of animals and many of the behaviors studied in humans, such as play activity, career choice, some higher cognitive performances, and choice of sexual partner" (p. 58). It is inappropriate to equate the "reflexive" sexual behaviors of rats (mounting and lordosis) with human multifaceted behavior that is to varying degrees an intentional action done in awareness of agency and consequences. Further, they say,

> In order to arrive at explanations of the more complex intentional behaviors of humans, we must treat that behavior in its entirety, taking into consideration influences such as self-perception and sociocultural restrictions, as well as biological capacities. ... In a fully interactional model of the complexity required to understand human behavior, the influences—biological, environmental, psychological— upon output affect central processing in ways that can alter not just output, but reception of external and internal signals as well. This processing thus cannot be either of a simple or complex linear

nature, but is of a continuously self-modifying character. (pp. 59, 72, & 73)

The most significant body of knowledge today about the psychology of lesbianism may be coming from the individual lesbian's sharing of her personal experience. Although long considered an invalid method of research by scientists, personal experience may well prove less biased than the more "objective" scientific methods; or at least the bias is a known one. As mentioned by Sang (1978), many lesbians are advancing the body of knowledge by personal testimony, correspondence, fiction, unpublished position papers, small and intimate groups, and large conferences. Such literature should be essential reading for the psychotherapist doing therapy with lesbian clients; it can be found by browsing through women's bookstores and subscribing to lesbian periodicals.

THE VALUE AND DISTINCTIVENESS OF PSYCHOTHERAPY WITH LESBIANS

A lesbian can find her way to a therapist's office for many of the same reasons that anyone else does. She may be depressed or anxious. She may experience phobias. She may be in prolonged grief. She may be suffering an adjustment reaction, or an eating disorder, or a psychosis, or a substance addiction, or a career problem. She might be experiencing negative effects of a personality disorder—or she might be chronically mentally ill.

However, no matter what brings the lesbian into therapy, and no matter how many times the therapist may have worked with the same presenting issue in a nonlesbian woman, the therapy is not the same when the client is a lesbian. The therapist may think, "An eating disorder is an eating disorder; I should treat it the same whether the client is heterosexual or lesbian." This simply is not the case. The lesbian lives in a different world, no matter how much or how little she is "out." She experiences stresses that are unique to her as a lesbian, and possibly are unique to her as an individual. These will affect her entire life functioning in some way. It is necessary that the therapist be aware of these experiences and stresses in order to provide therapy that is holistic. I do not mean to indicate that all lesbians suffer major negative effects of their orientation, rather that the fact of their orientation provides a special context within which all assessment and treatment must be viewed. The lesbian context will usually have both positive and negative impact.

Riddle and Sang (1978) and Riddle (1978) note many of the stresses that a lesbian experiences that make therapy with lesbian clients distinctive. The fear of repercussion and the pressure to come out or pass for straight are both constant and realistic. The cost of coming out can be very high—loss of family, job, housing, friends, and children. Continually not revealing things about oneself requires a constant monitoring and a careful restriction of thoughts, emotions, and responses. This self-constriction will generalize to other areas of the lesbian's life. It is very hard to maintain positive self-esteem when all messages from the outside world say that there is something wrong with you. This is especially true when you are forced to confirm that something is wrong with you by hiding some parts of you. As Riddle and Sang state, women are socialized to be sensitive to the acceptance or rejection of others and to translate that response into a comment on their own self-worth.

Lesbians are also unique in living life without a man. They are not defined by a man, and they live lives based on their own merits. (Some nongay women are seeing the benefits of this option and are attempting to maintain self-identity while in relationships with men.) Also, lesbians do not have social support for their relationships. Lesbian mothers experience the turmoil of placing their children in the position of being different and often ridiculed. Except when they are together with totally supportive friends, lesbians will always experience the tensions of mere tolerance from others, of fear, or of invisibility from the world.

Riddle and Sang also report that the vast majority of lesbians seem to opt for a lifestyle that combines feminine and masculine traits, resulting in better personal adjustment but more social censure. They state that

> lesbians are left with the unattractive alternatives of adopting traditionally feminine sex-role behavior, which implies a second class status and is inherently maladaptive, or adopting traditionally inappropriate sex-role behavior, which carries with it negative sanctions. Therefore, most lesbians, by virtue of choosing the second alternative, are struggling with the twin difficulties of learning to define themselves independent of others' reactions and learning to ignore and/or challenge the negative sanctions traditionally placed on inappropriate sex-role behavior. (p. 87)

Lesbians also experience unique stresses in regard to their sexuality. As women, they are socialized to be passive sexual partners, which can create sexual dissatisfaction problems. The stereotype is that lesbians are hypersexual, and this may concern the lesbian if she finds that it isn't true for her. Religious upbringing can create considerable guilt over sexual experimentation. Internalized belief in the superiority of sex with a penis, or of sex for procreative purposes only, can make a lesbian feel there is something missing from her sexual activity, even if she defines her own relationship as satisfactory. Considerable stress is also caused by socially imposed restrictions on expression of physical affection.

Hiding integral aspects of one's identity can be psychologically debilitating. Years of lying and hiding can substantially damage self-integrity. The absence of role models has a psychological effect, as does the absence of a visible cultural history.

Collier (1982) suggests other factors that make therapy with lesbians distinctive. She notes that many lesbians internalize society's censure not only about their lesbianism, but also about the necessary departure from traditional feminine stereotyped behavior that lesbianism calls forth (as noted in Riddle and Sang's quotation above). Clients may express the stress of such internal pressures at both conscious and unconscious levels. Conflicts may develop between various aspects of themselves in attempting to resolve the external disapproval caused by being internally syntonic. For this reason, lesbians must learn to define themselves independently from society's reactions, a difficult task for almost any human being—as an inherently social animal—to accomplish. Collier states that the lesbian

> may therefore live with a high degree of stress because few of her choices are automatic, run by the conscious and unconscious satisfactions of fulfilling the sex-role stereotype; deliberative choice is a quality which lesbianism necessitates, and this is a form of stress as well as a strength with which therapists need to work. (p. 245)

Collier further points out that lesbians carry an "extra burden," which is not their sexual preference per se, but rather the discrimination that that preference brings them. She states that the claim of lesbian women that they are subject to double discrimination—based on their gender and on their sexual preference—is justified, and that this must be attended to in therapy. As she notes, the therapist must also be aware that the research indicates that lesbians are more like heterosexual females than they are like homosexual males. Lesbians are much less likely than gay men to be promiscuous, to have had many sexual partners, to have sex with strangers, to separate sex from affection, to associate volume of sex with self-worth, or to see fidelity as a restriction on their independence. Thus, both sexes tend to fulfill their sex-role socialization, despite sexual orientation.

To return to the earlier example, if a lesbian client enters the therapist's office presenting primarily with difficulties relating to an eating disorder, an in-depth assessment is in order. The treatment for the eating disorder will have to be carefully evaluated and molded to fit the unique experience of the lesbian herself. It will be especially critical to sort out how her lesbianism may be interacting with the dynamics of the eating disorder, but to do so without implying that the lesbianism needs to be altered—although *how* she deals with her lesbianism may be a matter for change. The assessment must take into account the degree of hiding in the client's life, the costs of being "out," the costs of *not* being "out," the effects of lack of support (both environmentally and in internal self-representation), the degree and effects of possessing androgynous traits, and overall self-integrity.

Therapeutically, these assessment issues can be difficult to broach with some lesbian clients. In my experience, it is ineffective to wait for the client to bring up these subjects, as some models of therapy recommend; the majority of lesbians with whom I have worked (though certainly not all) are not fully aware of these issues on the surface and may thus not bring them up voluntarily. However, neither do I recommend insisting that all of these issues must have a deep effect on each client. What is called for here is a gentle leading approach that helps the client explore the complete impact of her lesbianism to her fullest ability. It is fairly common to hear me say to a client, "You know, many women who love women experience a sensation of suppression, or a painful feeling of never being fully accepted by some important people in their lives. Is that sensation a familiar one to your inner self?" Or I might say, "It seems that one of the more difficult experiences you are struggling with is how to feel right or congruent within yourself and yet at the same time contend with the messages you hear from the outside that your love is not good." These comments are intended to invite the client to examine her own inner experience in a way she may not have conceptualized it before, while at the same time leaving room for her to say she does not experience these things if that is so (or if her repression is strong).

On the other hand, some lesbians come to psychotherapy for reasons that have directly to do with their lesbianism. Sang (1977) notes some of these reasons:

1. Some women have been in a long-term lesbian relationship, but have not interacted with other lesbians for fear of being labeled "gay." When the relationship breaks up, no social support system exists and the lesbian may turn to therapy for support.
2. Some women come to therapy confused about their sexual identity. They may be physically attracted to men, for instance, but emotionally and also physically drawn to women. They may be in a hetero-

sexual marriage but have fallen in love with a woman. They may be in some other circumstance that makes them feel that they don't fit some stereotyped definition of lesbianism. They seek help to grapple with the effects of labeling or of categorizing themselves as lesbians.

3. It is not uncommon for a woman to have had homosexual feelings for a good number of years, but feel too threatened to deal with them. In talking to a therapist, she may be sharing her "secret" for the first time.

4. Because of the stigma, some women spend many years not seeking out lesbian relationships despite their clear awareness of their attraction to other women. Thus they can find themselves in their middle years, highly competent in many areas of life, but rank beginners at how to "do" relationships.

5. Because ways for lesbians to socialize and network can be hard to find, some lesbians become involved in a permanent relationship with the first person they meet. Although the couple may later find they are not a good match for one another, they may also fear the isolation of ending the relationship. Alternatively, the lesbian who has made a series of unsuccessful commitments may see herself as a failure; this is based on the unfounded but strong societal notion that *longer* relationships are *better* relationships.

6. If a woman begins lesbian relationships in her teens, it is not uncommon for her to have experienced ridicule and punishment. This can affect her present relationships.

7. Some lesbians find themselves having a series of relationships with women who leave them for heterosexual relationships. This may cause them to feel very vulnerable in entering new relationships.

8. The "mask" that the lesbian wears to cope with the heterosexual world has its effects on her personality. Before long, a lesbian who is used to monitoring her every word and passing for what is acceptable will be unable to determine what her own feelings really are.

Unquestionably, then, lesbians deserve access to a psychotherapy process that is attuned to their unique situation and needs, and that is provided by a knowledgeable therapist. Because all therapy is value-bound to some degree, the therapist must be well trained and very alert to each nuance of meaning that a lesbian client presents. The lesbian client brings both a special set of difficulties and a special set of strengths to her therapy sessions, each of which requires assessment.

To summarize, when a lesbian, or any woman wondering about love and attractions in her life, comes into your therapy room, your therapy plan with her must include awareness of these factors as possible interactive dynamics in the client's life:

- The effects of fears of (or actual) outside rejection or reprisal;
- The inner and outer manifestations of the client's identity issues: "What does this mean about me?";
- The sometimes dramatic effects of a constriction of expression and affect, since this constriction generalizes to other areas in her life;
- The pros and cons of living a life without a primary male companion;
- The effects of a lack of social support, both in terms of her identity and her relationships;
- The effects of socialization as women, which will influence relationships;
- The absence of a visible culture, of a history, and of role models.

MODELS OF LESBIAN-AFFIRMATIVE PSYCHOTHERAPY

It is evident that in order to be consistent with the present positions of the professional organizations of psychiatrists, psychologists, social workers, and counselors, therapists have to adopt a set of skills different from those previously required of therapists (Graham, Rawlings, Halpern, & Hermes, 1984). Rather than diagnosing homosexuality per se, attempting to determine causative factors, or attempting to change sexual orientation of lesbian clients, therapists are now directed to help their clients become self-actualized as lesbian persons. To that end, several authors have delineated models of lesbian-affirmative or gay-affirmative psychotherapy, which are presented here.

As Maylon (1980) says, lesbian- (and gay-) affirmative psychotherapy is not a technique; rather it is more clearly a "frame of reference." Lesbian-affirmative therapy encompasses an absence of heterosexual bias, but it is not based on a homosexual bias either, where homosexuality is seen as superior to heterosexuality. As Morin and Charles (1983) state, "Lesbian/gay-affirmative psychotherapies value diversity and the integrity of each individual" (p. 334).

One model of lesbian-affirmative therapy is Kingdon's (1979), which suggests the following recommended principles:

1. KNOWLEDGE
   a. Therapists know the definition, prevalence, theories, and myths about lesbians.

    b. Therapists are familiar with community resources for lesbians—
hotlines, coffeehouses, support groups, church groups, bars, and
bookstores.

2. SKILLS
    a. Therapists have skills to help clients explore and determine their
sexuality.
    b. Therapists have assessment skills to determine whether a lesbian's
problem is due to internal dynamics or due to society's reaction.
    c. Therapists have skills to help lesbian clients come out.
    d. Therapists have group therapy skills since lesbian groups can
help alleviate isolation.

3. ATTITUDES
    a. Therapists believe that society needs to change as well as the indi-
vidual.
    b. Therapists evaluate personal homophobia and heterosexism.

Gonsiorek (1982b) suggests criteria for the further development of
lesbian- and gay-affirmative models as follows:

1. Must be relevant to the life experience of gay men and lesbians in a
   society that to varying degrees is unsympathetic, uninterested, or
   hostile;
2. Must enhance the mental health of gay men and lesbians and assist
   them in meeting the challenge of the primary task confronting them:
   the creation of an equal, healthy, ethical, and useful place in society;
3. Must be clinically useful and must creatively assimilate those ideas
   from the mainstream of traditional mental health practice that have
   something to offer gay men and lesbians;
4. Must function over a full range of psychological adjustment and
   must be able to speak to the concerns and clinical issues of the
   healthy through poorly functioning gay men and lesbians.

Collier (1982) also contributes to the development of affirmative models.
She recommends that "therapists who see a lesbian preference as a sign of
illness or maladjustment rather than as a source of discrimination should
be aware that they are making a moral, religious, or emotional judgment
stemming from their own acculturation, not a professional decision" (p.
247). Such a therapist should refer a lesbian client, or any client exploring
relationships that are not exclusively heterosexual, to another therapist who
does not see sexual preference in such terms, and at the same time must be
professionally aware that such a referral in itself may be taken as a rejection

by the client. Collier summarizes and applies Clark's (1987) recommendations for training therapists to be able to provide psychotherapy from a lesbian-affirmative position:

First, therapists should receive training to develop comfort with and appreciation of their own homosexual feelings.

Second, therapists should receive training in skills to undo the client's negative conditioning due to social stereotypes of lesbianism; skills to reduce shame and guilt by supporting her feelings and thoughts; skills to help her expand the range and depth of her feelings; and skills to assist her in developing a system of personal values by which she assesses herself rather than relying on society's values for validation.

In a description of training needs for social workers, Gochros (1984) lists skills and experiences that therapists should have in order to provide lesbian- and gay-affirmative psychotherapy:

1. To be able to explore sources of discomfort and help reduce them;
2. Come to understand one's own discomfort with any gay feelings in yourself and any fear of "guilt by association" if others perceive you as gay or suspect you for showing interest in or support for gays;
3. Integrate conflicting social values, religious beliefs, laws, and clinical traditions about gays and lesbians;
4. Refrain from defining people by their sexual gender preferences and refrain from dichotomizing people into two camps—heterosexual and homosexual;
5. Become aware of the effects of the invisibility of homosexuality (such as underestimation of the size of the population, generalizing and stereotyping based on those individuals who are visible, lack of good and diverse models, effects of isolation on self-concept and relationship abilities, and the difficulties of coming out);
6. Understand both the pressures to label oneself and the pressures not to label;
7. Understand the effects of minority status, and if you are a member of the majority, make an effort to understand yourself as a member of a majority that oppresses;
8. Expose yourself to learning experiences, such as having direct contact with members of lesbian subcultures; conducting formal research; viewing educational or commercial films; obtaining information on the medical, legal, and religious aspects of lesbianism; and maintaining exposure to clinical treatment considerations by sharing knowledge and being politically active.

As mentioned before, lesbians are first and foremost women. Any adequate model of lesbian-affirmative therapy must therefore include our knowledge of the psychology of women. The newly emerging body of literature on the psychology of women over the past two decades has substantial relevance to the psychology of lesbianism and the development of lesbian-affirmative psychotherapy models, but this combination is an area of literature that has yet to be developed. Most volumes on psychology of women have a chapter or two on lesbianism, but as yet there has been little integration of theory. The application of psychology of women theories to psychology of lesbianism will be a happy union once its paradigm is established.

Lesbian-affirmative psychotherapy models developed to date cover a broad range of skills, knowledge, attitudes, and experiences. As with all subspecialties in the field of psychotherapy, it is a task that requires effort and conscientiousness to obtain adequate training in providing psychotherapy to lesbian clients, and to update that training over the years as our knowledge grows.

3

THE THERAPIST

In this chapter, attention is turned to the therapist herself or himself. As discussed in Chapters 1 and 2, the literature on models of affirmative psychotherapy states repeatedly that therapists who want to work with lesbian clients should do several things in order to be adequately prepared to work with this clientele including:

- Obtaining knowledge of the many aspects of lesbianism;
- Obtaining knowledge of lesbian resources;
- Gaining a thorough understanding of the special stresses associated with being lesbian in the culture;
- Being able to assess whether the lesbian client's problems are due to internal dynamics or to society's pressures (pressures that can come from both outside forces and internalized beliefs);
- Understanding both the pressures to come out and the pressures not to;
- Exposing oneself to the lesbian literature and to lesbian lifestyles; and
- Looking within oneself to examine one's own feelings about lesbianism itself and about one's own degree of homosexuality.

This chapter expands upon several of these themes. First, it looks at the current literature on homophobia and the various and subtle manifestations of homophobia in the therapist (whether the therapist is lesbian or not). It is important to note that homophobia may be operating in both the therapist and in the client; the present chapter discusses therapist homophobia, whereas Chapter 4 discusses internalized homophobia within the client. Second, a review of the literature is presented on the effects of the therapist's gender and sexual orientation on the therapy outcome with lesbian clients. Finally, an overview of the literature on ethical issues when working with lesbian clients is provided—a literature body that is unfortunately still extremely small and in need of expansion.

HOMOPHOBIA

Homophobia has been defined in several ways—as an unreasonable fear of homosexuality (in oneself as well as in others), as prejudice against gays and lesbians, as a hatred that is acted out by discrimination against gays and lesbians, and as a belief in the superiority of heterosexuality. It has been categorized under several different names: homoerotophobia, homosexphobia, homosexism, heterosexism, and homonegativism. As Herek (1984) points out, these various definitions and names reflect the multiple theoretical assumptions and political orientations that have characterized the literature on this topic. Whether or not it is the most accurate term, "homophobia" has prevailed as the most commonly used label for any sort of stereotyping or negative attributions of gay and lesbian people.

Homophobia exists in both lesbians and nonlesbians. Lesbians are raised in the same heterosexually dominant atmosphere as nonlesbians and thus they often develop the same beliefs and stereotypes about the inferiority of lesbianism as the rest of society. Homophobia can thus also exist in both therapist and client, whether or not the therapist is herself a lesbian. As Martin (1982) states, many therapists are offended by the suggestion that we may hold a prejudice, because we pride ourselves in our open-mindedness, our nonjudgmental approach to human choices, and our freedom from irrational biases. However, therapists too were raised with the prevailing cultural attitudes, and we can hardly expect old and subtle notions to be disregarded just because we want them to be.

A recent survey of 456 psychologists (Pope, Tabachnick, & Keith-Spiegel, 1987) asked about numerous ethical matters for psychotherapists. One question concerned whether these therapists ever treated homosexuality per se as pathological. Seventy-five percent said "never," 13% said "rarely," and 11% said "sometimes, fairly often, or very often." Further, only slightly over half (56%) viewed such a practice as unethical. I expect these percentages reflect a dramatic improvement from previous decades, but they still are far from adequate.

In another recent survey (Jensen & Bergin, 1988), 425 psychologists, psychiatrists, clinical social workers, and marriage and family therapists were asked about their values regarding mental health. In describing a mentally healthy lifestyle, over half of these therapists (57%) stated that their value of health included a heterosexual sex relationship.

It requires careful scrutiny and acknowledgment to become aware of our homophobia. It is assumed that unless a therapist has looked thoroughly within to acknowledge and work with her or his own homophobia, she or he cannot help a client do so. A therapist's homophobia is a counter-productive phenomenon that creates significant countertransference issues that potentially can do harm to clients.

During the 1980s, several authors contributed to the literature by offering examples of homophobia in therapy and suggesting corrective counter-measures. These are reviewed here. Most of these articles are descriptive rather than theory-based. The review begins with perhaps the only piece on homophobia that suggests a theoretical understanding of the phenomenon.

Herek (1984) proposed a theoretical model of homophobia that distinguishes three types of attitudes. These attitudes are founded upon the social-psychological functions they serve, thus explaining why some people can express similar attitudes as each other but for entirely different reasons.

The first attitude Herek describes is "experiential." A person with an experiential attitude is one who categorizes social reality primarily on the basis of his or her past personal experience. Thus, past experience with a lesbian woman, whether positive or negative, is used as the basis for generalization to all lesbians. Face-to-face interactions provide information that refute stereotypes and reduce ignorance, which Marmor (1980) identified as the most important source of reducing hostility toward homosexuals.

Herek's review of the research shows that people who know gays or lesbians are more likely to express tolerant attitudes toward them and to recognize stereotypes about them. However, because only about one in four adults in the United States reports having gay or lesbian friends or associates, three-fourths of the population is basing its attitudes toward homosexuality on other factors (Herek, 1984). This situation can improve as the social climate allows more gays and lesbians to disclose their sexual orientation to friends and family.

The second attitude Herek describes is "defensive." This concept is derived from a psychodynamic view that prejudiced attitudes serve to reduce tension aroused by unconscious conflicts. Thus, a person may respond to gays and lesbians by externalizing inner conflicts and thereby reduce the anxiety associated with them. The conflicts that are specific to homophobia presumably involve a person's gender identity, sexual object choice, or both. The defensive strategy permits people to reject their own unacceptable urges by rejecting gays and lesbians, who symbolize those urges, without consciously recognizing the urges as their own.

The third attitude is "symbolic." Symbolic attitudes express abstract ideological concepts that are closely linked to one's own notion of self and one's reference groups. This attitude is typified by the person who states that cherished religious values or social morals are being violated by gays and lesbians, and that homosexuals are making illegitimate demands to change the status quo. On the positive side, a person may have a favorable symbolic attitude toward gays and lesbians that is based upon the belief that discrimination and prejudice are themselves violations of the values of freedom and equality.

Herek suggests that each of these attitudes may require a different strategy to change it. In order to change a symbolic attitude from negative to positive, an appeal to the values consistent with the self-concept and supported by the person's important reference groups would probably be most effective. Experiential attitudes would be most easily changed by exposure to gays and lesbians, especially those from a broad range of diverse lifestyles. Defensive attitudes are possibly the hardest to change because of their psychodynamic roots and lack of conscious awareness. Herek suggests that a defensive attitude can probably be changed only when the defense is moderate, and that the method of change would be to arouse insight into the defensive process.

Herek also summarizes the qualities of those persons that research has shown to be most likely to hold unfavorable attitudes toward gays and lesbians. Compared with people who have positive attitudes, people with negative attitudes tend to:

1. Have less personal contact with gay men and lesbians;
2. See their colleagues and peers as also holding such negative attitudes;
3. Be male;
4. Be more likely to have lived in rural areas or small towns during their adolescence;
5. Be older and less well educated;
6. Be more religious, attend church more frequently, and subscribe to a conservative religious ideology;
7. Be more likely to express traditional, restrictive attitudes about sex roles;
8. Be less permissive sexually or manifest more guilt or negativity about sexuality; and
9. Manifest high levels of authoritarianism, defined as perceiving the world in a rigid, inflexible, black and white fashion.

Herek also notes that heterosexuals tend to have more negative attitudes toward homosexuals of their own gender than of the opposite gender.

As noted earlier, most writers on the subject of homophobia do not write from a theoretical base but rather from a descriptive position. Riddle and Sang (1978) wrote one of the frequently quoted descriptive pieces on the effects of bias in providing psychotherapy to lesbian clients. They hold that therapists tend to display their bias in one of three ways:

1. avowedly trying to "cure" lesbians,
2. believing their biases to be irrelevant, or
3. believing their biases to be nonexistent.

Those who believe that their biases are irrelevant, or that they do not have any, are less obvious and therefore can potentially do more damage.

The authors list several ways in which more subtle biases can manifest themselves in therapy sessions. One such way is to display covert suspicions about pathology. Questions about the origins of the client's lesbianism can imply lack of respect for the client's lesbianism and an assumption of a pathological origin. Also, careless or unknowledgeable answers to questions that the client herself asks about causation can contribute to any myths she may hold about the pathological origin of her lesbianism. When a client expresses to me a concern about the origin of her lesbianism, for example that she became lesbian because of a negative event such as rape or incest or absent parents or physical abuse, I will usually supportively reflect that fear at first and then explore its meaning for her. However, shortly thereafter I will describe the literature to her that has shown no differences between lesbians and heterosexual women in upbringing, sexual experiences, or traumas (Brannock & Chapman, 1990; Vance & Green, 1984; Mannion, 1981).

It is frequently therapeutic for the client to be able to tell her "coming-out story" to a caring, empathic professional who can affirm the strength the client displays in being able to listen to her own inner voice, even when it goes against society's pressures. In telling their stories, most lesbians consciously or unconsciously scrutinize the therapist's every response (or lack of response) for signs of judgment, discomfort, or acceptance. Watch for this.

Another manifestation of a therapist's subtle bias mentioned by Riddle and Sang is when the therapist emphasizes the positive aspects of any of the client's past heterosexual experiences and the negative aspects of lesbian experiences. Sometimes lesbians do have better relationships with men than with women precisely because they may feel so much conflict about the relationships in which they are more emotionally invested—those with women. This does not make their lesbianism invalid.

A third manifestation of bias is to expect superhuman behaviors. Some therapists expect, and imply in sessions, that the lesbian client should be able to always feel good about herself despite societal responses. This is unrealistic. It is also important for therapists to be able to assess when the client may be proffering a superhuman image due to her own internalized homophobia, by trying to appear "together" and failing to admit any difficulties for fear that the therapist or others will see her in a pathological light.

In response to their own list of biases, Riddle and Sang describe several alternatives. One such alternative is for the therapist to gain enough experience, training, or supervision to be able to effectively separate lifestyle concerns and stresses from personality problems. Another alternative is to place the stresses of gay life experienced by the client in a sociopolitical context. This can be done in part by encouraging the client to create a supportive environment for herself. Another alternative strongly espoused by the authors is the need for lesbian clients to be seen by therapists trained in feminist philosophy. This suggestion is derived from the fact that the problems experienced by lesbians are often related to female socialization. The authors describe additional alternatives including attendance at workshops and institutes that are geared to helping therapists look at their own homophobia; locating a lesbian therapist who can act as consultant or supervisor to the therapist, and even as a model to the client; using self-disclosure in a discretionary fashion; and using the nearest gay service center for consultation, referral, or some volunteer work for the therapist.

In her article on homophobia among mental health practitioners, DeCrescenzo (1983/84) provides a helpful list of expressions of homophobia of the less subtle sort. These include

> making comparisons in conversation between homosexuals and cripples as reflected in psychotherapy aimed at helping homosexuals "adjust to their condition"; being condescending toward homosexual clients, frequently characterized by pointing out all of the supposed lost life opportunities being homosexual carries (such as children and marriage); identifying homosexuality in an agency case conference as one of the "problems" presented by the client being discussed; not protesting when anti-homosexual jokes are told; denying one's own homosexual feelings (Clark, 1977, points out that the mental health professional who denies having homosexual feelings is akin to an analyst who denies ever dreaming); discouraging homosexual clients from disclosing their sexual orientation to family, friends and coworkers (an attitude which imposes tremendous psychic stress on the client leading a "double life"); and in any other way disconfirming or devaluing a homosexual identity. (p. 121)

DeCrescenzo also gives examples of "hidden agenda items" of which a therapist must be aware. For example, therapists who have a hidden agenda consisting of a need to establish themselves as liberal may find themselves assuring the client that they hold no negative views about lesbians, when such a discussion is not germane to the treatment of the client. Another example is a woman therapist whose hidden agenda is a need to reinforce her own desirability as a heterosexual woman. She may find herself behaving in a subtly seductive manner toward a gay male client. A last example is that of a woman therapist who is looking for validation of her own femininity, who may find that she has trouble working with a "masculine"-appearing lesbian and finds herself subtly pressuring the client to become more "feminine."

Martin (1982) is another source of examples of subtle homophobia. One example, as previously noted by Riddle and Sang (1978), occurs when the therapist inquires into the causes of the client's lesbianism. In the same vein, the therapist can reinforce the client's own homophobia in the situation where some childhood experiences are uncovered and the client states that these experiences might explain why she is a lesbian—and the therapist agrees. As Martin says, "We don't have any need to 'account for' someone's being heterosexual. We simply accept it as a given. By exploring the reasons why someone became homosexual we are failing to take homosexuality also as a given" (p. 343). In doing this we are treating it as a failure of heterosexuality.

Martin also suggests that when the therapist questions the lesbian client about her capacity to function heterosexually, homosexuality is again being treated as a failure of heterosexuality; therapists don't usually ask heterosexual clients about their capacity to function homosexually. Another example is when the therapist reinforces a client's own homophobia by accepting the client's statement that the topic of her lesbianism never comes up in conversation, so it's never a problem. The therapist must be aware that the client's lesbianism does indeed come up, and quite frequently, every time any conversation includes the topics of family, home, marriage, love, dating, or living arrangements. The therapist must—at a proper time—point out that the client is actively choosing not to reveal herself on these occasions, and that not revealing herself will have consequences, for herself and for others.

Martin stresses that the processes whereby homophobia may be inadvertently perpetuated are subtle and may involve no more than a failure to inquire about something the client says. There is nothing neutral about the choices therapists make concerning when to inquire, when to reflect, when to interpret, when to educate, and when to remain silent.

Gartrell (1984) shares a strong view held by some therapists that

homophobia is central to the coming-out process, that it is of high importance to come out of the closet, and that lesbians should be seeing only
therapists who are "out" lesbians themselves. This is an interesting contrast
to the views presented by Siegel (1985), who writes about how to learn to
work with lesbian clients from the perspective of a nonlesbian therapist.
Siegel suggests that it is important for lesbian and nonlesbian women not
to become polarized from each other, and that working together in a therapy relationship provides learning opportunities for both client and therapist. She names four modes of learning to be undertaken by the nonlesbian
therapist.

1. *Learning through therapy.* In one's own therapy, the therapist can best
   uncover the complexity of his or her feelings, both one's attractions
   and aversions to women and to lesbianism. Siegel recommends that
   one see a lesbian therapist, or a therapist who is extremely well versed
   in these issues.
2. *Learning from the literature.* A reading of the older literature is of limited use because of its heterosexist assumptions, but it can be important in understanding the history of how psychology and psychiatry
   have treated lesbians. The more recent publications are essential to
   remaining well versed in the psychology of lesbianism. In addition to
   professional publications, Siegel recommends reading the lesbian literature in order to remain aware of the richness of lesbian culture.
3. *Learning from lesbian colleagues.* Although acknowledging the risks
   of self-exposure (both the risks of being identified as a lesbian therapist in the heterosexual therapist community, and the risks of being
   identified as a nonlesbian therapist in the lesbian therapist community), Siegel pleads for more dialogue. Learning among colleagues, in
   consultation, in supervision, or at professional meetings entails
   engagement in a dialogue between lesbian and nonlesbian therapists
   that is essential to nonlesbian therapists' ability to work with lesbian
   clients.
4. *Learning from lesbian clients.* Siegel does not advocate using the
   client's therapy hour as a place to obtain information or to gain
   understanding for the therapist. However, she does advocate listening very carefully to lesbian clients, and asking for clarification
   when one is feeling confused or uninformed. This kind of listening has helped Siegel become aware of the nuances of her own
   homophobia and to understand her position of privilege as a
   married woman who can express her love openly and who is
   accepted by the culture at large.

Siegel also describes her own process of growth from a benign, liberal stance, through a stage of becoming envious and admiring of lesbians' strength, to finally realizing that idealizing lesbians was not the answer either. She states that mutual learning between lesbian and nonlesbian women is limited by the degree to which the nonlesbian's interpretation of lesbian reality comes out of the nonlesbian's own reality, just as a male's views of women are by definition self-limited. Her answer is to continue the dialogue, accept the differences and commonalities, and work toward deeper self-awareness and self-acceptance.

In my clinical practice, I have heard clients tell of quite a variety of homophobic responses from their prior therapists. I describe several of them here to help therapists avoid similar responses:

1. "The 'You're Not a Lesbian' Response"—this effectively shuts the client up about this subject and informs her that she is unable to read her own perceptions. I have even heard of therapists calling clients outright liars, claiming that the client only wants attention.

Elana described to me how she took several months to tell her previous therapist that she thought she had stronger feelings for women than for men, and that she thought that might mean she was a lesbian. Her therapist replied, "Oh, don't worry, you're not a lesbian." Elana never again brought up the subject during her subsequent year of therapy with this therapist. In her work with me, she had to sort through the effect of this lost time, time during which she might have been able to explore her lesbianism if her therapist had responded differently.

2. "The Lecture"—wherein the therapist delivers an unfounded description of lesbians as unhealthy, developmentally arrested, acting out, or otherwise pathological.

Early in her therapy with me, Rosa reported that she had been in therapy for more than two years when she built her courage to discuss her feelings toward women. The therapist delivered what was to Rosa a very frightening lecture on the immaturity of homosexuality and told Rosa that her feelings were evidence of her psychological arrest at an early stage of development. He told her that it was imperative that she stay in therapy and allow him to help her expunge her feelings. She did stay many more months, but she eventually came to believe in herself more than in this therapist, and sought help elsewhere.

Another client, Bobbi Jo, was hospitalized on a psychiatric unit early in our therapy for severe reactions to the loss of her lover of many years. In spite of my input about the precipitant of her behavior, the hospital staff insisted that lesbianism alone was at the bottom of Bobbi Jo's troubles and that she was simply acting out. The staff's treatment plan focused on her lesbianism, and did not at all address Bobbi Jo's feelings about, and reactions to, the loss of her lover. This caused Bobbi Jo a great deal of distress, for which the staff in turn medicated her with an antipsychotic agent.

3. "The Liberal Response"—wherein the therapist tries to treat the client "just the same as if she were heterosexual" or as if lesbianism has no meaning. This denies all the stresses and dynamics (as mentioned in the previous chapter) that the client may experience, and effectively bypasses much important therapy material, making it impossible for the client to leave that therapy experience as a more aware and expressive being.

Helga told me that she had come out to her previous therapist early in treatment. Her therapist had responded with comments about the positive changes in society's attitudes and the increased acceptance of lesbianism, saying that Helga should therefore find herself in a supportive atmosphere with little to worry about. Helga explained to me that at first her therapist's words made her doubt herself, thinking there must be something wrong with her for having any struggles with her lesbian identity and with telling others about her lesbianism. She said she later found herself trying to convince her therapist that her experiences of nonacceptance were indeed real.

4. "The Inadequate Response"—wherein lesbianism is treated with avoidance by the therapist.

A prospective new client, Raven, called me, saying she was searching for a new therapist. She said her current therapist would not talk with her in any depth about lesbianism. She said she had come out to her therapist long ago, but that the subject only came up if Raven herself brought it up, and that even then, the therapist fairly quickly changed the subject. Raven finally decided this was not a therapeutic situation for her.

My client, Guiseppina, wanted to attend a therapy group for survivors of incest as an adjunct to our individual therapy. She interviewed potential group leaders in our city on her own, and reported to me that on more than one interview with a leader, Guiseppina was asked to not mention her lesbianism to the group if she were to join. As she realized herself, not revealing her lesbian self would perpetuate secret-keeping, shame, and belief that there is something wrong with her—all strong dynamics of molestation in the first place. In such a group, she could not possibly heal.

At an initial intake session, many clients hold back any information about a spouse or lover, unless directly asked about it. Whenever such holding back occurs, it can be helpful to use the word "partner" in mentioning the topic to the client, and to refer to the partner with the phrase "he or she" no matter what the gender of the client. This lets the client know you are open to hearing about a lover, whatever the gender may be.

Homophobia, then, is subtle and pervasive, and in need of careful scrutiny before a therapist begins working with this population. In the American Psychological Association publication on homophobia, Hancock (1986) outlines four methods of eliminating homophobia: (1) legislative and educational approaches, including being involved in changing homophobic legislation and in retraining therapists and other professionals; (2) individual change, which might mean making an effort to expose oneself to lesbians if one is nonlesbian, or coming out whenever possible if one is a lesbian; (3) reducing internalized homophobia through support groups or therapy; and (4) taking steps to validate homosexuality as a normal variation of human behavior, which would mean encouraging one's church or civic organizations to remove the stigma from homosexuality, as the American Psychological Association, American Psychiatric Association, the National Association of Social Workers, and other mental health organizations have done.

Gramick (1983) makes a few additional suggestions for mental health workers: (1) to encourage agencies to provide speakers or in-service training on the topics of homosexuality and homophobia; (2) to participate in research endeavors designed to evaluate societal attitudes toward homosexuality; (3) to discourage jokes, hostility, or other homophobic actions in one's daily work environment; and (4) to create a nonthreatening environment in which clients and their significant others can talk about homosexuality and homophobia with nongay friends, parents, and relatives.

I invite readers to consider as many of these suggestions as are fitting for you.

GENDER AND SEXUAL ORIENTATION OF THE THERAPIST

Until the second wave of the feminist movement in the United States developed in the early 1970s, the biology and traits of the therapist were rarely considered relevant factors to therapy outcome. Chesler (1972) at that time was perhaps the first to take the stance that a woman therapy client could only be understood and helped by a female therapist with a feminist ideology. This argument spurred research that did show some trends that supported this perspective. According to Tanney and Birk's (1978) review of that research, women therapists made a difference in therapy in three arenas: increased self-disclosure on the part of the client, more women clients request women therapists than request male therapists, and women clients report more satisfaction with therapy outcome with a woman therapist than with a male therapist. However, those researching this subject soon found that the gender of the therapist was quite difficult to separate from other factors such as age, status, race, and experience level of both the therapist and the client. Nevertheless, the trends do stand: women clients tend to ask for women therapists if given a choice (especially if the reason for entering therapy is perceived as very personal), and they report more satisfaction with therapy outcome when the therapist is a woman.

In a more recent overview of the literature on the effects of the gender of the therapist, Mogul (1982) came to similar conclusions. She found that

> while there appear to be some demonstrable trends, under certain circumstances, toward greater patient satisfaction or benefit from psychotherapy with female therapists and no studies showing such trends with male therapists, no conclusion that certain patients should be treated by women appears warranted. (p. 2)

As was true for Tanney and Birk (1978), Mogul's review concludes that therapy outcome depends on many factors in addition to therapist gender, such as type and goal of therapy, length of therapy, client developmental level, and therapist sensitivity and value system regarding gender issues. Mogul notes that little attention has been given to the specific issue of lesbian therapists for lesbian clients, except by a few feminist and "out" lesbian therapists, and that further study is needed in this area.

A new direction in this research may be launched by the 1986 study of Petry and Thomas. Their study of 52 therapist-client pairs showed that the sex of the therapist was not as important as the androgyny of the therapist, that is, the ability of the therapist to move comfortably within both masculine and feminine gender behaviors and to avoid stereotypic gender-role limitations. The clients in this study reported more favorable relationships with therapists who had scored as androgynous on the Bem Sex Role Inventory, regardless of the degree of androgyny of the client. It is unknown how these results may apply specifically to lesbian clients.

The striking results of the now classic study by Broverman, Broverman, Clarkson, Rosenkrantz, and Vogel (1970) and the flurry of studies that followed it, demonstrated that clinician's judgments about the mental health of individuals differed as a function of the sex of the person being evaluated. This left a bitter taste in the mouths of the "activist therapy consumers" from the feminist movement and from the fledgling gay liberation movement. Because clinicians were found to hold different standards for each gender and to hold a set of sex-role prescriptions for each gender, it followed that a clinician's perceptions of gay and lesbian clients would also be affected, especially because gays and lesbians are characterized as sex-role nonconformists (Brooks, 1981).

The literature contains two types of material on the subject of whether the therapist for a gay or lesbian client should be gay or lesbian as well. I will first describe the research-oriented literature and then look at literature written from the personal and clinical perspective of lesbian therapists. Attention is turned first to Brooks's (1981) review of the literature that reflects lesbians' perceptions of therapy experiences in relation to the therapist's gender and sexual orientation.

Research on Gender and Sexual Orientation of the Therapist

Brooks (1981) discusses the results of research measuring the effect of gender on therapy outcome, and adds to the contributions of Tanney and Birk (1978) and Mogul (1982) mentioned previously. She states that sex biases of therapists have been measured rather abstractly and may not represent the most accurate indication of whether a woman will benefit more from a woman therapist than from a man therapist. One trend in this research is that premature termination of therapy seems to occur more often in opposite gender pairings of client and therapist. Brooks offers the explanation that more practicing therapists are male than female, and that more clients are female than male; thus the female client is simply more likely to encounter male therapists' sex biases. However, for women who complete therapy, the evidence is inconclusive. Some of the studies are contradictory and the results again suggest that controlling for variables other than gender of the therapist and client can provide more useful information for predicting beneficial outcomes that can single-variable studies that look at gender only.

Brooks was the first to report a study on the therapy outcome effects of sexual orientation of therapist and client. She received questionnaire responses from 513 lesbians indicating their preferences among therapists if they were to seek therapy, and from 257 lesbians indicating their assessment of their therapy experiences. Her data showed significant differences between heterosexual male therapists and all female therapists, whether lesbian or heterosexual. The subjects reported an unusually high positive therapy experience overall, with 77% indicating some degree of benefit. Two-thirds (66.1%) of those indicating that therapy was very helpful had a female therapist, either lesbian or heterosexual. In contrast, about three-fourths (74.1%) of those indicating that therapy was destructive had a heterosexual male therapist, although it should be noted that only 10% of the subjects reported destructive experiences. Overall results of lesbians' therapy experiences are reported in Table II.

Findings in relation to lesbians' preferences if choosing a therapist indicated that 70.5% would prefer a lesbian therapist, 10.3% would prefer a heterosexual female therapist, and about 20% indicated no preference in terms of either gender or sexual orientation. These results parallel the data that were obtained from 1,917 lesbians and reported in the *National Lesbian Health Care Survey* (National Institute of Mental Health, 1987). These lesbians reported their preferred characteristics of counselors. As to gender, 89% stated preference for a woman therapist, less than 1% preferred a man, and 10% said it didn't matter. As to sexual orientation, 66% preferred a lesbian counselor, 1% preferred a nonlesbian counselor, and 33% said sexual orientation did not matter to them. This survey also asked about preferred ethnicity of the counselor; 27% of the respondents preferred a therapist of their own ethnic group, 1% preferred a different ethnicity, and 73% said it didn't matter. It should be remembered that the subjects in Brooks's study and in the *National Lesbian Health Care Survey* were self-selected and were self-identified as lesbians; the results may not generalize to women with lesbian experience who do not identify themselves as such.

Brooks concludes that "a therapist's sex role ideology would seem to be considerably more relevant to the therapeutic relationship than his or her sex or sexual orientation per se" (p. 207). Research that controls for age, marital status, parental status, and presenting problem as well as gender and sexual orientation may further clarify the beneficial matching components, particularly in relation to the effects of modeling influences. The research suggests that modeling, or similarity of broad demographic variables, may be necessary but insufficient components of beneficial therapy.

TABLE II.
Relation of Therapists' Sex and Sexual Orientation to Therapy Evaluations by Lesbians

Therapists' Characteristics and Percentage	Lesbian Evaluations (in percentages)			
	Destructive	Not Helpful	Fairly Helpful	Very Helpful
Heterosexual	16.8	20.2	34.5	28.6
Male (46.3)	(n = 20)	(n = 24)	(n = 41)	(n = 34)
Homosexual	16.7	0	0	83.3
Male (2.3)	(n = 1)	(n = 0)	(n = 0)	(n = 5)
Heterosexual	6.9	4.6	41.4	47.1
Female (33.9)	(n = 6)	(n = 4)	(n = 36)	(n = 41)
Homosexual	0	2.2	20.0	77.8
Female (17.5)	(n = 0)	(n = 1)	(n = 9)	(n = 35)

Reprinted with permission from "Sex and Sexual Orientation as Variables in Therapists' Biases and Therapy Outcomes" by V. R. Brooks, 1981 *Clinical Social Work Journal*, 9(3), p. 206.

Another contribution to this body of literature was published in 1982 by Rochlin. He states that "most theories of psychotherapy give the person of the therapist a central place" (p. 22), and that among the therapist qualities that have been found necessary for effective psychotherapy is that of client-therapist similarity. Rochlin cites research that indicates the importance of modeling and identification with the therapist as a significant factor in facilitating change in the psychotherapeutic relationship.

Rochlin further cites research that shows that gay and lesbian clients usually report dissatisfaction with therapy experiences based on one or more of three things: the therapist's lack of practical knowledge about homosexuality, the therapist's lack of positive attitude toward the client's homosexual feelings, or the lack of being mutually disclosive with the client. He concludes:

> At present, research data on the effects of sexual orientation in client-therapist dyads are sparse but suggest that, when the therapist is openly gay, sexual-orientation congruence in such pairings facilitates effective counseling and psychotherapy for lesbian and gay male clients. (p. 25)

Clinical and Biographical Literature on Gender and Sexual Orientation of the Therapist

In a nonresearch mode, several authors have published their personal experiences as psychotherapists working with lesbian clients. These authors are all "out" lesbians. On the subject of the effects of sexual orientation of the therapist on therapy outcome with lesbian clients, these authors present personal opinions rather than quantifiable data, but these opinions are based on years of clinical work and careful observation.

As touched upon in the previous section on homophobia, Riddle and Sang (1978) and Gartrell (1984) both state quite strongly that a lesbian therapist is a must for a lesbian client. To this, Riddle and Sang add that the therapist should be feminist in ideology; Gartrell adds that the therapist must be out of the closet, based on the research literature that shows that psychological health is associated with a greater degree of being out about one's lesbianism, and the therapist must model this. To come to these conclusions, the authors cite the reports of negative experiences from clients with a prior therapy history, the therapists' estimation of the efficacy of outcome with their own clients, the efficacy of modeling, and the ability to understand and empathize with their clients.

A third author, Anthony (1982), provides a demographic description of her lesbian clientele, including presenting problems, coming-out issues, couple concerns, sexual problems, and problems of single lesbians. She also discusses approaches to therapy with lesbians and transference and countertransference issues that the reader may want to investigate. On the subject of the sexual orientation of the therapist, Anthony says:

> While my particular lifestyle gives me an advantage in understanding and establishing rapport with my lesbian clients, I think that the most important factor in therapy with lesbian and gay clients is not the sexual orientation of the therapist but, rather, the consciousness of the therapist: She or he must be aware of and sensitive to the threats to self-esteem and self-actualization that arise from societal prejudice and the status of gay men and lesbians as oppressed minorities. (p. 46)

In summary, the evidence is not clear-cut. It seems that many out lesbians report a preference for a lesbian therapist, and there is some trend toward lesbian clients faring better with women therapists than with men therapists. However, the trend is far from absolute. Additionally, a great many women clients could be struggling with a lesbian issue of some sort but are neither out nor in search of an "out" lesbian therapist. Further, thorough training in gay and lesbian psychotherapy issues is completely lacking in all but the rarest of therapist training institutions; thus, therapists well equipped to work with gay issues are probably self-selected and self-trained due to their interest and commitment to this field of psychotherapy. Such a therapist is likely to be lesbian or gay herself or himself, which could skew the results of these therapy outcome studies.

A final note concerns the lack of discussion in the literature about the dangers for the therapist who decides to be "out" enough to make herself visible to the lesbian community. She risks professional isolation and threats to her economic survival. She also may narrow her potential client pool within the lesbian community itself, because more "closeted" clients may not want to risk seeing an "out" therapist. Yet it is in the best interest of her own mental health that a lesbian therapist be as "out" as possible, professionally and personally. This is an unsolvable dilemma.

ETHICAL CONSIDERATIONS

A special set of ethical issues arises in doing therapy with lesbian clients. Very little discussion yet exists in the literature on this topic. Ethical considerations arise for all therapists working with a lesbian population, and additional issues arise for lesbian therapists.

Brown (1984) has written on some of the ethical issues encountered by a lesbian feminist therapist in private practice. She notes that is is important for many lesbian therapists to be involved in their own lesbian community, for their own personal health, to satisfy a need for community, and because of the philosophical advantage of being a practitioner who is not separate from the community she serves. However, this presents challenges to the ethical codes for psychologists and other therapists, codes that forbid dual relationships with clients yet require an awareness of community values and involvement in the community one serves as a professional. A lesbian therapist who lives among and connects with her community is also constantly in the view of her current and potential client population. Her relationship with that community can affect her prospects for economic well-being. The therapist may feel that she is constantly being watched whenever she is in the public eye of her community. Brown states that "lesbian therapists in private practice thus find that this thin line between personal life and professional credibility can limit their earning power or curtail their social activities" (p. 13).

The lesbian therapist in practice in her community is challenged with the management of the overlap between her life and the lives of her clients, and the overlap among the lives of clients, some of whom are bound to know each other in some capacity. The therapist must always be alert to the demarcation of what she knows in the confidence of the therapy room and what is publicly known about her clients. She may also be more aware of the interpersonal resources of her clients than is a more traditional therapist.

Especially in smaller cities, where the lesbian therapist is involved in her local gay community, considerable overlap problems can occur with personal life and professional life. Clients tend to refer each other, and a therapist can end up seeing several clients from a particular social circle, all of whom know each other; the therapist may thus hear information about other clients she is seeing at the same time. I experienced such an overlap situation when a professional colleague of mine with whom I also have a social relationship became a lover of a former client of mine—could I see them socially as a couple? In another example, a client whom I was currently seeing became lovers with my accountant—do I switch accountants? I can almost expect to run into a current or former client at large gay events and sometimes at smaller gatherings such as house warmings for acquaintances or workshops where I am teaching. These are difficult situations to address, although I always ask clients who attend lesbian community events whether and how they want to be greeted, should we run into each other. Most request a normal, cordial greeting. Others request no recognition or ask to take the lead by greeting me first, depending on who is accompanying them. I also inform them that I will not state to either their companions or mine where I know them from—that is up to them.

From a similar perspective, Berman (1985) discusses the ethical issues that surface whenever any therapist serves any subcommunity or is in a small-town situation—which describes many lesbian communities. Berman lists the potential problems of this situation: the therapist's misuse of power, breach of confidentiality, loss of the preexisting relationship, difficulties in transference, loss of privacy for the therapist, and criticism from colleagues. These issues must be weighed carefully by the therapist. She further notes that clients often may seek a particular therapist in a small-town atmosphere precisely because the client has considerable knowledge of the therapist and the therapist's values; in this case, the client's choice is an informed choice. Berman suggests that in each case of overlapping relationship, the therapist is defining himself or herself on a continuum that extends from intimate helping friend to professional distant stranger. She recommends that, to do this effectively with each client, the therapist use peer consultation and supervision and remain engaged in an ongoing process of clarifying his or her own values.

As yet, no literature exists on the ethical issues encountered by all therapists working with lesbian clients, whether gay themselves or not, although many questions need to be answered here. Also, no literature exists on the dilemmas encountered by lesbian academicians in therapist training institutes. Gramick (1983) notes that child custody and adoption issues for clients present a problem for clinicians, because of the potential dire consequences to prospective or biological parents as well as to a child who may be evaluated as actively or potentially homosexual. Other issues that are unaddressed include the following:

- the application of psychological assessment tools to lesbian populations. Test manuals do not state whether the sample population included lesbians, so the norms on which the test is standardized may or may not be appropriate.
- whether or not to record lesbian issues in the client file. Files can be subject to subpoena or to quality review. If lesbianism is noted in the file, damage could be done to the client; if lesbianism is not noted in the file (in order to protect the client), the therapist could be judged negligent.
- whether to inform a hospital staff of a client's lesbianism if hospitalization is required;
- and how to refer to a more well-trained therapist for lesbian issues without making the client feel rejected for her lesbianism.

For therapists who are themselves gay or lesbian and whose model of therapy includes discriminant self-disclosure, an important issue becomes how to address matters such as a query from a nongay client about one's spouse or how one spent a holiday; for a therapist to reveal her lesbian identity to a nongay client can result in loss of the client and the information is not always of therapeutic value to the client. Conversely, the client finding out that the therapist is lesbian from someone other than the therapist herself can also be damaging to the therapeutic relationship, leave the client feeling betrayed, or can result in loss of the client. And for therapists who are gay or lesbian and who want their clientele to be drawn from both the gay and nongay communities, it can be most difficult to maintain referral sources from the nongay sector without losing many potential clients should the clients or the referral sources learn of the therapist's sexual orientation.

These issues have no easy answers at present, and most professionals come to personal decisions about them. I have chosen in my practice to always indicate my sexual orientation when a client asks me directly (which gay clients almost always do and nongay clients rarely do). I do this because I believe it is therapeutic for the client to know this and because it facilitates modeling. But I will also ask the client to search out what meaning my orientation has for her or him—it's often useful therapy material. I do refrain from stating my lesbianism to clients who do not ask directly—that is if they are only asking how I enjoyed a holiday or how I have handled a similar relationship to theirs in my own life. Although I feel I make my choices to refrain from disclosure based on clinical therapeutic reasons, I also recognize a dose of homophobia within myself, in that I do fear (and have experienced) unpleasant losses of clients who may be unwilling or unable to stay long enough to work through their feelings about my orientation.

I am not fully content with these choices. Anytime I choose not to disclose this important aspect of myself, I feel I may be reducing my full presence with the client, possibly reducing my own authenticity, the very authenticity I am trying to teach clients to have for themselves. How can I demonstrate an optimal way of living in this world if I cannot do that myself in a therapy session? Yet it is inappropriate to self-disclose to clients information that they are not asking about or are not ready to receive, or that may result in some form of danger to me, either personal (hate mail, for example) or professional (unwanted exposure).

These probably will continue to be delicate professional problems as long as any sort of misinformation and nonacceptance of lesbians and gays exists within the culture that make it dangerous to be out of the closet.

II

THE
CONTENT
OF
THERAPY

4

CLINICAL ISSUES

Psychologists, psychiatrists, social workers, and other counselors are each trained in somewhat different aspects of diagnosis, assessment, and clinical expertise. Yet all of these disciplines share a belief in some method of helping others in which an appraisal is made of the client's life, and healing methods are applied to address the areas that cause the client undue pain or poor function.

The tasks of healing used by therapists have some commonalities that are applied to all clients. There are also many healing tasks that apply best to various individual clients depending on such specifics as age, race, values, gender, traits, history, and mental health diagnosis. When working with lesbian clients, both the commonalities and specifics come into play. In this chapter, we first look at the interfacing of lesbianism with mental health diagnosis, which can be very client-specific. Then we address what are perhaps more universal issues in lesbian dynamics, namely internalized homophobia and the effects of coming out.

MENTAL HEALTH DIAGNOSTICS

Probably the most widely used system in the United States for appraising a client to determine the focus of psychotherapy is the *Diagnostic and Statistical Manual of Mental Disorders (DSM)*, which is published and regularly updated by the American Psychiatric Association. The diagnostic criteria that I mention throughout this text are from DSM-III-Revised, which is currently in use. At the time of this writing, the DSM-IV is under development.

Using the DSM system of diagnosis can at times be especially complex when the client is lesbian. To date, only a few authors have written on this subject, yet it is a subject in need of a great deal of research, which we can hope for in the future.

In 1973, Saghir and Robins (Marmor, 1980) conducted one of the first

57

comprehensive studies of lesbians, comparing 57 lesbians with 43 heterosexual women. They studied several characteristics, among them the prevalence of DSM psychiatric disorders. They noted:

> When compared with matched heterosexual women, homosexual
> women do not seem to suffer from a greater degree of neurotic ill-
> ness, psychophysiologic reactions, affective disorders, psychosis, or
> other definable psychiatric problems in the form of hysteria, obses-
> sional neurosis, anxiety or phobic symptoms, or paranoid reactions.
> (p. 288)

Depression was found to be a common disorder among both the lesbian
and nonlesbian samples. The authors also found no differences in premen-
strual symptoms. The study further noted that close to one-fourth of the
lesbian sample reported patterns of alcohol use that are compatible with
problem drinking; this finding is the only difference found between the
two study groups.

The National Institute of Mental Health published the results of a mental health survey of 1,917 lesbians in 1987, called the *National Lesbian
Health Care Survey: Mental Health Implications* (NIMH, 1987). The survey
was conducted in questionnaire form in 1984 and 1985; participants were
lesbians from all 50 states and were from racial and ethnic backgrounds
somewhat approximating the racial and ethnic distribution of the United
States. They were located as volunteers through social and organizational
contacts (which, as in all lesbian research, makes them a skewed sample).
The age range was 17 to 80 years, with a preponderance of subjects in the
25-44 year age range. The sample was more educated and held more professional occupations than United States women in general.

One striking finding of this survey is the number of subjects who had
received some form of counseling or professional mental health support
either presently or in the past: nearly three-fourths (73%). An overlapping
36% had seen nonprofessionals for help, such as support groups and peer
counselors; one third of the sample had sought help from both professionals and nonprofessionals. The reasons for seeking counseling, although not
matching DSM categories, are given in Table III. Half of these subjects had
been in counseling for less than one year, 18% for one to two years, 11% for
two to three years, 7% for three to four years, and 14% for more than four
years.

The lesbians in this survey reported symptoms similar to those of other
high stress groups. For example, rates of attempted suicide were similar to

TABLE III.
Reasons for Seeking Counseling

Total N of Valid Cases = 1442	N	% of total sample
Feeling sad or depressed	952	50
Problems with lover(s)	836	44
Problems with family	685	34
Feeling anxious or scared	591	31
Personal growth issues	573	30
Being gay	401	21
Loneliness	407	21
Alcohol and/or drug problems	308	16
Upset at work	214	11
Problems with friends	191	10
Problems due to racism	55	3
Other:		
Emotional problems	61	3
Personal issues	45	2
Loss of significant other	27	1
Health problems	23	1

From *National Lesbian Health Care Survey* (p. 30) National Institute of Mental Health, DHHS Administrative Publication, Contract No. 86MO19832201D.

those of physicians. Twenty-seven percent of this sample had had thoughts about suicide sometimes or often, and 18% had tried to kill themselves.

Many subjects reported experiencing discrimination because of being lesbian. Fifty-two percent reported being verbally attacked. Eight percent reported losing a job because of being lesbian. Six percent reported being physically attacked. Four percent said their health care had been affected, and 1% reported discharge from military service for being lesbian.

The researchers of this survey comment on the high rates of suicide ideation, suicide attempts, discrimination, and seeking mental health support, saying,

it is troubling to recognize the extent of personal costs that may be exacted of gay women at least partially because of societal attitudes and legal restrictions that severely limit the personal expression of homosexuality. (p. x)

In addition to these difficulties encountered by the sample, several other diagnostically significant categories were approximately the same for the sample as they are for all United States women. These include the rate of physical abuse (37%), rape and sexual attack (41%), childhood incest (19%), the rate of eating disorders, and the rate of alcoholism in the older age brackets of lesbians compared with same-aged heterosexual women. Among the incest survivors, racial differences were seen: 29% of the Latina sample, 31% of the Black sample, and 16% of the White sample reported incest.

This survey, the largest of its kind ever done, supports the viewpoint that lesbians as a group may experience stresses, and therefore some diagnoses, that are more prevalent than among heterosexual women, such as suicidality and the effects of discrimination. At the same time, many diagnostic prevalences are probably the same for lesbians and heterosexual women, such as the rates of depression, eating disorders, and substance abuse. Also, given similar rates of rape and incest between the two groups of women, we can assume (although its not yet been studied thoroughly) similar resulting aftereffects, including generalized anxiety, phobias, adjustment disorders, dissociation, post-traumatic stress disorder, or exacerbation of a personality disorder.

In 1988, the *Journal of Homosexuality* published a double volume (Volume 15, Nos.1/2) on psychopathology and psychotherapy in homosexuality. In this volume, Smith provided a comprehensive examination of the DSM-III diagnostic categories as they apply to homosexuality, psychopathology, and internal and external manifestations of homophobia. Among the disorders usually first evident in infancy, childhood, or adolescence (which include retardation, attention deficit, conduct disorder, anxiety and avoidant disorders, eating disorders, and others) homosexuality can play a part according to Smith. For example, the conduct, anxiety, and avoidant disorders can occur more frequently in a young lesbian person who has a sense that "somehow I am different from other girls." Likewise, various reactive states can occur in youth and adolescence, arising from internalized homophobia and manifesting as depression, tics, stuttering, and identity disorder, or defenses such as denial and reaction formation. In the higher levels of mental retardation, a person with a homosexual adjustment who is interested in sexual activity may be interpreted as "acting out" rather than as expressing a legitimate need; this can confuse the treatment approach.

Substance use disorders, another category of DSM disorders, are reported to be increased among homosexual people as compared with heterosexual people by some researchers, including Smith (1988) and Saghir and Robins (1980). However, the *National Lesbian Health Care Survey* (NIMH, 1987) just described showed that rates of substance abuse were similar among lesbians and among heterosexual women, with a slight increase in alcoholism seen among older lesbians. Older lesbians, as a cohort, may have been more exposed to alcohol during their coming-out times than are younger lesbians, simply because 10 or 20 years ago, gay bars were one of the only places possible to meet other lesbians. This diagnostic area is more completely covered in Chapter 7.

Psychotic disorders probably do not occur with any greater frequency among gays than among other groups according to Smith (1988), but these disorders can be misdiagnosed. Paranoia in particular is prone to be over-diagnosed among lesbians. Diagnostic confusion concerning paranoia, hypervigilance, and reality-based fears must be sorted out. Clinicians must take care to examine with a client her fear about disclosure of her lesbian identity. Lesbians do lose family, jobs, children, housing, peer respect, and self-esteem in too many cases upon disclosure. Paranoid disorder should only be diagnosed when it is clear to the clinician that the client's fears are truly delusional; and paranoid personality disorder should be diagnosed only if it is clear that the hypersensitivity, restricted affect, and pervasive suspiciousness is completely unwarranted.

A psychotic lesbian client has special burdens to bear. She has two stig-matized identities—lesbian and psychotic—and because of her psychotic disorder, she has few coping mechanisms for handling these stigmas. It is especially unfortunate when such a client must interact regularly with legal, medical, and psychological/psychiatric institutions where neither stigma is understood compassionately.

According to Smith, affective disorders are another category in which homosexuality may have an effect. Chronic depression or dysthymia can result from the conflict between behavior and values that happens especi-ally among nondisclosed lesbians. Although there is speculation in the lit-erature that lesbians may experience depression at a higher rate than do nonlesbian women, Rothblum's (1989) research indicates that the rates are the same for the two groups. However, she postulates that the precipitating causes of some depressions may be different for the two groups, given what we know about risk factors and protective factors for depression in women. For example, there is indication that lesbians have less social support than do heterosexual women; lack of social support is associated with depres-sion. However, involvement with the lesbian community may protect some lesbians against depression by providing needed support. Marriage is also associated with depression, and many lesbians (not being married) are thus protected from this risk factor, although when a lesbian relationship does end, the lack of social recognition of the loss may increase the risk of depression. Raising young children is yet another factor associated with risk of depression. However, as fewer lesbians than nonlesbians may raise children, they are provided an element of protection here. When a lesbian is also a mother, societal disapproval or hiding her lesbianism from the children can be precipitates for depression. Finally, lesbians have a high rate of employment, and this is a protective factor against depression, but at the same time, lesbians may experience discrimination or feel it necessary to conceal their lesbianism on the job, which increase the risk for depression. Overall, the rates of depression from environmental factors may be similar among lesbians compared with nonlesbian women, but the protective and risk factors may differ for the two groups.

The anxiety, somatoform, and dissociative disorders, again according to Smith, are probably not overrepresented in the lesbian population, although increased anxiety or adjustment disorder may occur at times from internal or external homophobic conflicts in the life of the client.

Psychosexual disorders are a confusing category for some. Paraphilias and psychosexual dysfunctions are not overrepresented in the lesbian population, although when they do occur, they require a special effort on the part of the therapist to separate the real pathology from lesbianism itself. Gender identity disorder is often confused with a gay or lesbian identity itself. However, a gender identity disorder is an entirely separate phenomenon, describing persons who feel that their anatomic sex is inappropriate for them; occasionally, clients will adopt this diagnosis when what they are really struggling with is lesbian identity. Some lesbians may indeed also have a gender identity disorder, which would require thorough screening by the clinician to sort out. It can also happen that a heterosexual person will undergo cross-gender surgery and hormone therapy, and then become homosexual by virtue of continuing to be attracted to the same gender as prior to surgery. In either case, if transsexual surgery is undergone, the client may need help in adjusting to a new sexual identity.

In reference to certain other diagnostic categories, probably little or no difference exists in psychopathology between heterosexual and homosexual persons, again according to Smith; these include, organic mental disorders, factitious disorders, and personality disorders. However the latter, personality disorders, often present particular diagnostic difficulties in lesbian clients, because many clinicians see that these diagnoses are significantly overused and inappropriately diagnosed among lesbian and gay clientele.

Gonsiorek (1982c) has also contributed to the understanding of the interface of lesbianism (and gayness) by exploring the usefulness of DSM diagnostic concepts. Because the disease model of homosexuality has been of such little help (and has even done notable damage) to gays and lesbians, many gay- and lesbian-affirmative practitioners have developed an antidiagnostic viewpoint. However, Gonsiorek points out the importance of differential diagnosis in a sexual identity crisis, which is a common precipitant to entering therapy or to a psychiatric hospitalization. He further develops the notion of environmental impetus for certain characterological-appearing overlays to the personality structure.

Gonsiorek describes three areas of particular differential diagnostic difficulty. First, he points to the case of schizophrenia, especially the paranoid type. Some clients may be experiencing delusions about homosexuality that have little or no basis in a developed object choice; others may experience florid paranoid reactions to a genuinely reality-based homosexual orientation; and in a few cases, both of these may be present at once, as when the emergence of genuine homosexual desire precipitates a schizophrenic episode in a marginally functioning pre-schizophrenic person. Each of these instances requires careful diagnostics and different treatment approaches.

A second area of difficulty in differential diagnosis is the affective disorders. Some clients in a sexual identity crisis may respond with mood swings, hyperactivity, and impulsive behavior reminiscent of hypomania; or a hypomanic person may engage in unusual (for them) sexual behavior reminiscent of coming out. On the other end of the affective spectrum is a lesbian or gay client who has experienced a major life stressor, such as the ending of a relationship or the death of a lover, or a series of stressors, and may never have had the opportunity to work through the issues, which can look clinically like a chronic depression.

The third area of differential diagnosis is with borderline personality disorders. At one extreme is the client who appears to be coming out but is instead experiencing a characterologically based lack of ego differentiation and boundaries; she may be unable to distinguish acquaintanceship, friendship, affection, love, and sexuality, and thus has a chaotic rather than homosexual object choice. At the other end of the spectrum is the client who is experiencing a genuine sexual identity crisis and who may go through a period where such differentiations are poorly made. Again, treatment will differ according to the therapist's diagnostic assessment.

Borderline personality disorder is a particularly overused and misdiagnosed category among lesbian clients. This is certainly related to the lack of training in differential diagnosis of homosexual issues provided to clinicians in our training programs. It is probably also related to the strong overlap of criteria between borderline personality disorder and some of the "normal" effects of coming out as a lesbian. A client who is having a particularly difficult time coming out can look quite borderline temporarily, fitting the diagnostic criteria of impulsivity, intense anger, intense emotional relationships, and affective instability. Unfortunately, the criterion called "identity disturbance" among borderline criteria is often taken as the hallmark of the personality disorder, especially by nongay clinicians, who then misdiagnose and mistreat their coming-out client.

Jasmine entered therapy reporting extreme stress and loss of self-esteem over an ugly breakup with her lover. She had been hospitalized in a psychiatric unit previously for suicidal ideation and was there diagnosed with borderline personality disorder and treated with lithium carbonate, which she had quit taking after a time, noting that it made her feel worse rather than better. At the beginning of therapy, Jasmine appeared to be very fearful and to have a wavering sense of self, but she rapidly began executing some healthy plans for dealing with her hostile ex-lover and for taking better care of herself. After several sessions of evaluation and some psychological testing, it appeared to me that a much more useful diagnosis was drug abuse (interpreted by the hospital staff as "instability"—they did not screen for drugs) and histrionic personality traits. With this assessment as our base, therapy advanced quickly.

Another client, Sparky, came to therapy having seen three therapists in the previous six months whom she did not care for. All three of these therapists had diagnosed her with borderline personality disorder. (Although none had told her of their diagnosis, I couldn't help but wonder if their diagnosis had not naturally influenced their approach to working with her, which she had experienced in subtle ways that made her uncomfortable and made her feel not fully understood, precipitating her leaving therapy.)

I could see why these clinicians may have misperceived her at first. She was angry, intense, and threatened to hurt herself. But after a few sessions, her current crises waned, and who emerged was a person hypersensitive to rejection, fearful of relationships, socially withdrawn, in need of acceptance, and with low self-esteem; these are the criteria for avoidant personality disorder, so I asked her to do some evaluative testing. The results confirmed the avoidant diagnosis. As we continued to work together over the next several months, a hypothesis occurred to me that explained her apparent borderline behaviors. From Sparky's descriptions of her home life with her lover, it was plausible that Sparky actually learned such behaviors from her lover. Innumerable times in our therapy, my client described her lover as "two different people at once," and as "totally unpredictable; I never know who she'll be." These, in addition to other similar descriptions, may indicate a borderline personality disorder in the lover. Sparky's overidentification with her lover's personality style has produced some psychological fusion, which became an additional focus for treatment.

Zevy and Cavallaro (1987) report that they have also perceived over-diagnosis of some DSM categories for lesbians. They point out that many lesbians have spent a large portion of their lifetimes feeling invisible, invisible to themselves and to important others:

> The path to invisibility and deception produces the following traits: incongruent body language, cues, and signals; trouble establishing intimacy; and tremendous anxiety, woodenness, rigidity, or anger about revealing secrets about lesbian identity. Based on these traits, lesbians are often misdiagnosed as narcissistic or borderline personalities. Some have been misdiagnosed as schizophrenic. (p. 93)

Being treated as invisible can be a searingly painful experience for any person—and unfortunately, such treatment is quite common for lesbians. Many such clients respond with extreme withdrawal, which may be misdiagnosed as avoidant personality disorder, schizoid personality disorder, or social phobia. Other clients respond with "acting out" gestures unconsciously motivated to accomplish visibility; this can be misdiagnosed as antisocial personality disorder, passive-aggressive personality disorder, conduct disorder, or oppositional disorder. The degree of hiding that the client feels necessary to her life is always of primary importance in assessing the presence of such disorders. The hiding itself is often what is behind the seemingly pathological signs. When this is so, treatment and healing must address the hiding itself, rather than assign and treat for the "overlying pathology." However, this is not to say that true, diagnosable DSM disorders or dysfunctional personality patterns do not exist in lesbians; rather, the interplay of psychopathology and lesbianism must be very carefully distinguished.

Mitsuko was referred to me by another therapist who did not feel adequately trained in lesbian issues. Mitsuko had seen him for over two years, when she recently fell in love with a woman and was in a terrible quandary over whether to leave her husband and what to tell her grown children. Her situation looked like a pretty "normal" quandary process to me, with wavering back and forth between her husband whom she still loved, and her new lover, who was very closeted. Her lover's hiding was quite unsatisfactory to Mitsuko; nevertheless she felt more herself with her lover than her husband. She seemed to want to leave the decision of which lover to stay with up to one of them instead of making the choice herself, again a common dilemma in these situations. I might have simply supported her wavering process until she came to a choice, but, with her release, I spoke with her referring therapist, who let me know that the core of his therapy work with Mitsuko was an examination of her lifelong pattern of indecision and of leaving the responsibility for making choices to circumstances and to others. Her quandary was thus not just a lesbian dilemma, but a repetition of a relationship pattern, which changed the focus of our therapy.

The DSM is certainly not the only diagnostic system that therapists use. There is little literature to date on these systems, but it is tantalizing to speculate about the interplay of lesbianism with many other diagnostic and assessment systems. In many instances, it is the therapist's unseen homophobia or lack of it that can make a diagnostic difference. In conjecturing about these, I have come up with as many questions as answers.

1. *Psychodynamic defense assessment*: The traditional hierarchy of defenses discussed by Sigmund and Anna Freud and others is used by some clinicians to assess emotional maturity. Consider how lesbianism might interact with defenses such as denial, intellectualization, sublimation, and reaction formation. If a client were unconsciously (or consciously) denying her homosexuality, would the average clinician be trained to assess that, and would she or he diagnose this as a pathological repression? Is there a danger of the clinician assessing what might be an overuse of defensive mechanisms, and considering that as appropriate to a lesbian client, out of the therapist's discomfort with lesbianism?

2. *Object relations and developmental theory*: From the viewpoints of theorists such as Winnicott, Erikson, Mahler, Chodorow, and Gilligan, consider how a diverse array of lesbian clients might be evaluated as to developmental task achievement. Neo-Freudian theorists are particularly prone to assessing lesbianism as pathological, due to the theory's basis in the concept of "healthy outcome" as heterosexual. How would a therapist analyze "object choice" with a lesbian client?

In developmental theory, can society's response to lesbianism, or a client's internalized homophobia, increase likely diagnoses of developmental arrest? Consider how lesbianism might interact with Erikson's developmental stage of adolescence, where the psychological task is to develop identity versus role confusion; or the stage of young adulthood, where the task is to develop intimacy versus isolation. Or consider the effects of lesbianism on the three stages of moral development for women defined by

Gilligan. For example, could an especially lengthy or painful lesbian identity development process influence a woman's emergence from the initial stage, wherein a woman cares for herself over all others in order to ensure survival? Or the second stage, where a woman defines herself by the degree of responsibility and goodness she has toward others, often to the detriment of her own needs? Or the final stage, where a woman achieves a balance between caring for herself and caring for others? I also have wondered how the interaction of these stages with a lesbian identity formation process can influence lesbian relationships, where each partner may be working through differing aspects of development.

3. *Existentialism and humanism*: Therapists who follow these approaches to healing take the phenomenological view of the client, and may thus be able to see with greater ease just how the interactions of lesbianism with individual personality structure weave together. Yalom, Bugental, May, Rogers, and others take a "process" approach to healing rather than a "curative" approach, which is of distinct advantage with lesbian issues. Emphasis on self-definition, self-actualization, and analysis of individual existential meanings can promote a lesbian's psychological health.

4. *Systems theory*: This therapeutic style evaluates and treats the environment as well as the individuals in it. Consider how lesbianism may affect the social structure and system that it occurs within, in addition to how the system affects the individual lesbian. Consider how these interactions might differ with various degrees of disclosure on the part of the lesbian.

5. *Cognitive and behavioral assessment*: Again, consider how assessment and treatment might change when the client is a lesbian, or is trying to discover if she loves women. What would be appropriate behavioral goals, and who sets these? Likewise, what would be "rational thinking" in these instances?

6. *Jungian analysis*: Another interesting area for theory development is how a lesbian identity formation process might be influenced by the client's degree of awareness of her anima and her animus; or consider how archetypes may come into play. Bolen (1984) mentions some possibilities with respect to this in her book *Goddesses in Everywoman*, suggesting how a lesbian identity may be affected by the presence of a particular goddess archetype in the personality. Jungians also tend to address a client's deepest sense of spirituality (not necessarily religiosity), which affords an excellent pathway to evaluating internalized esteem problems. Jungians also assess "complexes," often with some useful attention to the balance of traditional masculine and feminine traits, which could provide a healthy environment for a budding lesbian to fully explore her orientation.

7. *Gestalt theory*: Gestaltists assess "contact disturbances" among other phenomenological processes. The "contact boundary" is the dynamic relationship occurring at the organism–environment boundary. Because Gestalt therapy thus relies heavily on aspects of the therapist-client "field" as it occurs in the therapy session itself, the therapist again (as in existentialism and humanism) has special access to a heightened awareness of the interplay of lesbian issues with the personality structure and with the environment. The therapy session, and healing itself, is often regarded to happen in each fully present moment, eventually giving the client an ever-changing dynamic understanding of herself, her needs, her motives. It would be important not to view lesbianism itself as a boundary disturbance.

8. *Feminist theory*: Feminist therapists are in the forefront of analysis of the effects of lesbianism on the client's environment and self-concept. A "psychoeducator" model is used whereby the client and therapist explore together the identification of problem areas, setting goals to address those problems, and evaluating outcomes. A feminist standpoint can be especially useful in assessing environmental effects and internalized beliefs.

To help me keep track of all the ways that lesbianism can affect the therapy process, I maintain a "Treatment Plan" in my clients' files. I make this treatment plan during the first few sessions of therapy and periodically update it as necessary. An example is shown in Figure 1 (p.70).

In the first section of the treatment plan, I state the goals of therapy as the client sees them, sometimes quoting her goals from the intake forms. The second section includes many potential ways of viewing the client's dynamics. These may include:

- Style of expressiveness
- Contact with an inner self or inner guide
- Boundaries, relationship quality, social interaction style
- Press for needs—conscious and unconscious
- Results of psychological testing or inventories
- Repertoire of coping mechanisms
- Flexibility, authenticity, consistent set of values
- Perception of self and of the world
- Degree of sex-role socialization
- Interface of lesbianism with:
     character style
     "stage" of identity formation process
     knowledge of self and expressiveness of that self
     signs and symptoms

internalized homophobia
generalization of constructions.

This section provides a thorough description of the various interpersonal and intrapersonal qualities I see, which, along with the client's stated goals, form the basis for the next two sections of the treatment plan.

The third section contains a diagnostic conceptualization, a sort of short-hand approach directly from the diagnostic literature. Listed here are appropriate concepts from the *Diagnostic and Statistical Manual*, from developmental theorists such as Gilligan and Erikson, from Jungian archetypeists such as Bolen, and from the three major schools of therapeutic thought: psychodynamic, cognitive-behavioral, and existential-humanistic. In this section a diagnostic interfacing with lesbianism is also described, such as the effects of stressors of being lesbian on personality or relationship dynamics, the degree of identity formation and its impact on the client's life, and the effects of social support (or lack of it) on identity and relationships.

The last section is the actual treatment plan. Delineated here are client strengths to be utilized in therapy, specific therapeutic approaches, any bibliotherapy or adjunctive treatments I might recommend (including medication referral, if appropriate), and any additional assessment needed.

When you as a clinician are attempting to make an assessment and treatment plan for your lesbian client, I would recommend the following guidelines:

- Make your usual assessment of clinical syndromes, personality traits, and the client's approach to her world. Then review each of these categories, asking yourself how the effects of a stigmatized identity might influence or exaggerate these signs.
- Always plan to spend a period of therapy time assessing with your client the effects of possible internalized homophobia. Examine with her what small doubts she may still harbor about the healthiness of her lesbianism, what stresses she encounters as a lesbian, what her beliefs are about lesbianism. Be alert to the fact that this may be very sensitive and unrecognized material for the client. Note and compassionately analyze any resistances encountered, rather than trying to simply push through the resistances.
- Look for unconscious processes that may be affected by lesbianism. To what degree does she have to constrict her full expression of herself, as a lesbian? And in what ways does that generalize? Does she appear to act "as if" she is basing her behavior on unspoken beliefs? Ferret out

Treatment Plan

Client: _Morgan_____ Date: _August 1, 1990_____ Plan #: ___1___

1. Client's stated goals and concerns:

"Stress management & sanity maintenance"
"Improve relationships with family, especially mother"
Improve social skills
Work on intimacy & meeting needs in relationships

2. Clinical assessment and observations:

Constricted. Fearful. Uncomfortable accepting empathy. Low expressiveness.
Boundary & contact disturbance with passive-aggressive or narcissistic flavor.
Dependency needs high — actively so, but unseen.
Crisis oriented. Lack of self-care & planning.
Few relationship skills.
Identity unsolid: both as a lesbian and an inner self/guide.
Values in conflict with repressed needs.
High anger & disappointment, unseen.

3. Diagnostic conceptualizations:

Personality traits: histrionic, some narcissistic.
Goddess archetype (per Bolen): Persephone.
ACOA syndrome.
In conflict re: degree of being "out"; affects relationships and career.
Low environmental support increases personality traits & dysfunction.

4. Treatment Plan:

Strengths to use in treatment: commitment; ability to examine
    transference, intelligence, desire to please, willingness to know herself,
        probable ability to integrate distancing behaviors with dependency needs.
Address lack of environmental support: on lesbian identity & sense of self.
Help define & legitimize needs. Then teach how to meet them.
Process & transference work for personality traits & boundary disturbances.
ACOA work.
Experiential healing of early wounds.
Build skills for intimacy, conflict resolution & tolerance, consistent values.
Bring internalized homophobia to consciousness; integrate with self esteem work.

Figure 1. Example of treatment plan created during the first few therapy sessions.

these beliefs, as they probably stem from unrecognized homophobia.

- Always examine together your client's "coming-out story." As with any good history taking, help her review the meaning of her first inner realizations; first behavioral expressions; reactions of peers, family, lovers, job supervisors, religious affiliates, and teachers; her sexual satisfaction and expression; her disclosure choices and restrictions; her present viewpoint on these factors; and her degree of satisfaction with her history and her current life. (Remember, she'll be watching you closely for every spoken or unspoken cue as to your understanding and acceptance.) Look for painful areas that appear as yet unresolved.

- Assess particular strengths that the client has developed that may have been enhanced because of her lesbianism, such as self-definition, interdependence, a set of values, stamina, or sensitivity. Support these.

- Whether or not your client identifies herself as a lesbian, distinguish for her among lesbian erotic interests, lesbian behavior, and love for women. These factors need not correlate, but your client's awareness of them can help her stabilize her identity or increase her degree of comfort with a fluid identity. Again, study how these processes could be affected by, or could affect, her personality traits or her approach to her world.

INTERNALIZED HOMOPHOBIA

To one degree or another, anti-homosexual attitudes become embedded in all persons who live in unaccepting cultures. This is of course true for homosexuals themselves as well. Everyone, including the "future lesbian" was most likely exposed to warnings, such as "Don't play with your brother's toys," "Don't hang around with 'those kinds' of people," "Why don't you show more interest in boys?" and "If you wear green on Thursdays (or yellow on Fridays) you're a queer." (The latter is a common grade school peer taunt, and the colors and days appear to differ across the United States.)

Likewise, most everyone, including the "future lesbian" was exposed to epithets such as "queer," "dyke," "bulldyke," "lezzie," "tomboy," "pervert," and "man-hater," all of which are considered to be quite derogatory. Myths also abound: "She must have had bad experiences with men," "It's her parents' fault," "Lesbians 'convert' others to their ranks," "Lesbians think of nothing but sex," and "It's a crime against nature."

These sorts of attitudes can have a profound and nearly unchangeable effect on some lesbians, and have very little effect on others. What causes this range of differences is unknown, but we can speculate that certain factors may play a role, such as characterologic make-up, the age of exposure to such detrimental information, the source of the information, and the individual's propensity to internalize information. One important therapy task then is to seek out the degree of internalization of homophobia, much of which will be unconscious, and to help reduce its effect where possible.

Gartrell (1984) has written about the widely held stance among lesbian-affirmative therapists that internalized homophobia is an inevitable focus of attention whether therapy is with a lesbian client, a client who has a friend or family member who is lesbian, or a client who is examining the meaning of an attraction to women but who does not identify as lesbian. Gartrell maintains that the therapist must understand the effects of "compulsory heterosexuality" (Rich, 1980) by studying the personal, economic, social, and political ramifications of homophobia.

Gartrell stresses that it is her clinical and personal experience that self-esteem and self-image increase in direct proportion to increasing visibility and openness about one's lesbianism. This view is supported by the research of Greene (1977); Rand, Graham, and Rawlings (1982); and Bell and Weinberg (1978) and is also reinforced by the clinical experience of many therapists, including myself. Gartrell gives a few examples of the therapeutic exploration of the risks and benefits of the client's coming out. One example is that of the closeted lesbian who has developed a system of defense that allows her to function as if being closeted were ego-syntonic. One common defense here is to deny that living in the closet requires any special effort. This client prides herself in her ability to lead a double life and to sidestep any questions about her personal life. She will also deny that her inability to be honest has any negative impact on her or on her relationships. This is a human impossibility. *Constriction generalizes.* In therapy, what is called for is an examination of these effects, perhaps in much more depth than the client is used to.

Another example Gartrell provides is the client who is in the process of exploring coming-out options. Obvious risks, such as personal and economic loss, are easily identified. In addition to clearly identified risks, some clients experience a generalized fear of coming out. Such a client may have reason to fear personal rejection, but the hopefully short-term effects of this rejection must be weighed against the long-term social and psychological effects of remaining in the closet. The constant need to lie or be on guard can be presented to the client as taking a toll on psychic energy and one's self-esteem.

Another example is the client who has decided she is ready to do some venturing out of the closet. Here the therapist, together with the client, must be able to develop some useful and thoughtful coming-out strategies.

Gartrell suggests a sort of hierarchy, where the client comes out first in areas that have lowest risk, and graduates to areas of more risk over time. Gartrell also reminds the therapist that it can take weeks or months to resolve any one coming-out experience. The therapist can also help the client decide which people in the client's life are worth taking the time and effort to educate and which may not be.

Zevy and Cavallaro (1987) discuss the internalization process of homophobia for lesbians in their writing about the relationship of invisibility, fantasy, and intimacy. In childhood, the authors say, a youngster who is aware of having interests that are outside of the norm often sets out unwittingly on a path of deceptive communication—deceptive both to others and to herself. She hides her real interests (interest in girls, interest in androgynous activities) and may attempt to perform only accepted behaviors. Or she becomes confused in attempts to meet both these needs. In adolescence, the deceptive communication style blossoms. To quote Zevy:

> Now the deceptive communication that I had practiced since childhood took on a frightening new twist. I could either avoid women entirely or assume very sophisticated communication strategies. Such strategies involved my providing cues and signals that would assume three ends simultaneously: First, I wanted the occasional woman who would be a possible sexual liaison to know I was interested. But second, my communication would have to be ambiguous enough to provide an out in case the woman was not interested. And third, I had to play the heterosexual game with no intention of winning; that is, I had to play the game without really playing, to appear genuine and interested in men for whom they appeared to be—perhaps colleagues and friends, but also potential mates—while still seeming unavailable for sexual liaison with the man who asked. . . . This is a very difficult game . . . for lesbians, who must play the game well enough so that everyone remains comfortable, but not *so* well that princess charming, should she happen by, would not recognize a potential love through the heterosexual disguise. (p. 87)

Zevy and Cavallaro then note that by adulthood, a lesbian must become master at further deceptive communication in order to maintain contact with heterosexual society. She must be able to engage in conversation with a man that appears "normal" for heterosexuals while also sending a strong-enough signal to a male that she is unavailable, and to a female that she may be available (but only if the other woman is available)! When this sort of deception is introduced into conversation, the deceiving lesbian is often viewed as ambivalent, tense, aloof, or indifferent, which may be quite inaccurate assessments of her true self and may negatively influence social interactions.

Lesbians who are attempting to hide their identity frequently succeed beyond their hopes. They then become physically and psychologically isolated due to lack of feedback from others about their identities, goals, needs, and perceptions. Further, intimate relationships are likely to be dramatically affected. Because both women in the lesbian relationship may have become experts at deceptive communication, chances are they may have never really communicated on a daily basis about their feelings, thoughts, and ideas. Zevy and Cavallaro further point out that intimacy involves the ability to disclose the essential, most inward parts of oneself to another person. They state, "If intimate aspects of oneself are withdrawn early in life through deceptive patterns of communication, then intimate relationships cannot be developed until the layers of invisibility are peeled away and the essential person emerges" (p. 91).

These deceptive communication effects do not happen for every lesbian, but lesbians may be most susceptible who are very closeted, isolated, or uncomfortable with their orientation.

Margolies, Becker, and Jackson-Brewer (1987) shed further light on the process of internalized homophobia with guidelines on "identifying and treating the oppressor within." They have developed a list of some of the less obvious expressions of internalized homophobia that is useful for a therapist's assessment. These expressions are:

1. *Fear of discovery.* This fear takes the form of either a need to protect oneself from rejection or to protect others from knowledge of one's homosexuality. Examples of the latter include "It will kill them," and "We never talk about my personal life, so there's no need to bring it up."
2. *Discomfort with obvious "fags" and "dykes."* This lesbian fears that association with more obvious homosexual types will give away her true identity.
3. *Rejection/denigration of all heterosexuals (heterophobia).* This is reverse discrimination. When a lesbian's homosexuality is ego-syntonic, she does not require everyone to share her values and lifestyle.
4. *Feeling superior to heterosexuals.* This may be a false embracing of differentness, yet may be a normal step in the lesbian identity formation process. Examples include: "We're better because we have a harder life" and "Our lives are more interesting, freer, more artistic, less encumbered."

5. *Belief that lesbians are not different from heterosexual women.* This belief rationalizes and minimizes a true difference in a probable attempt to avoid homophobia from others. It denies the social, political, and sexual context within which lesbian relationships struggle for existence—"Relationships are all the same, mine just happens to be with another woman" or "What we do in bed doesn't define us."

6. *Uneasiness with the idea of children being raised in a lesbian home.* "I believe children have to have a male parent." This perspective denies the reality that many children are raised by single mothers and also demeans the validity of lesbian relationships.

7. *Restricting attractions to unavailable women, heterosexuals, or those already partnered.* These connections never lead to a fully committed relationship and may be a way of restraining a full expression of one's lesbianism.

8. *Very short relationships.* In addition to avoiding issues of trust, intimacy, and merging, short-term relationships require less of a commitment to one's lesbianism, especially if the partners never live together.

These examples provide some clues for the therapist in looking for some of the more subtle forms of homophobia. Your style of therapeutic intervention will dictate how you actually approach your client with this information—whether you directly confront, reeducate, refute, lead, or process these observations.

Sophie (1987) adds further helpful suggestions to the clinician, stating that the goal of therapy "is not the achievement of any particular identity, but the reduction of internalized homophobia which enables a woman to accept her own lesbian desires and experience and choose her own identity" (p. 54). One of the most important events to watch for is the client's first disclosure of her lesbianism to the therapist. Although the disclosure of her sexual interests is apt to be of great significance to the client, the fact may be obscured by the manner in which she discloses it. *It is common for the client to disclose her lesbianism either defiantly or overly casually and then wait for the therapist's response before deciding if it's safe to continue on this topic.* And she may not let you know she is waiting. Further, a client may indicate that she has something important to say, but be unable to do so for several sessions or will do so at the very end of a session. However she discloses, this is the therapist's most significant opportunity to convey acceptance.

Once the disclosure events are resolved, Sophie, like many other therapists, feels that attention must at some time be turned to the effects of internalized homophobia. She suggests the following coping strategies:

1. *Cognitive restructuring.* This entails changing the meanings associated with lesbianism so that lesbianism takes on a positive, or at least non-negative, meaning for the client. Cognitive restructuring is the basic process that underlies the elimination or reduction of internalized homophobia and its replacement with a positive view of homosexuality. As such, it is probably the major process of coping necessary for self-acceptance. Negative stereotypes can be challenged by emphasizing the diversity that exists among lesbians, as among heterosexual women.

2. *Avoiding a negative identity.* Sophie's research has shown that those who avoid identifying themselves as lesbian, regardless of their experience, until after this identity has become a positive one, avoid negative identity and appear to be buffered from some negative self-esteem effects of lesbianism. Exposure to positive lesbian role models before taking on a lesbian identity oneself seems to be of benefit. The therapist may only have a certain degree of control here, depending on the client's history. For those clients who do not yet espouse a label, the therapist can discourage taking a lesbian label as long as that identity has primarily negative meanings for the client.

3. *Adopting an identity label.* As noted, it is useful to refrain from identifying as lesbian until that identity has taken on neutral or positive meanings for the individual; however, it is difficult, and possibly not healthy, to remain without a label of any kind for a long period. Doing so can impede further development, both identity development and emotional development. The lesbian label may have different meaning for different clients, and this too should be explored.

4. *Self-disclosure.* As has been noted before, self-disclosure to people who are important in one's life plays a crucial role in lesbian self-acceptance. Further, self-disclosure is necessary for intimacy in relationships, for confirmation of identity, and for self-actualization. Sophie recommends that therapy become a rehearsal ground for self-disclosure, where role plays and other techniques can help a client both practice and discover her fears.

Sophie also suggests some ways to evaluate the effectiveness of strategies used to reduce the client's homophobia. She says:

> Some behavioral indications that this goal has been achieved are: the client's comfort with her own feelings, relations with women, lesbian fantasies, and so forth; her comfort with, and respect and admiration for, other lesbians and gay men; her ability to form a meaningful relationship with another woman; positive self-disclosures; and her use of a homo-positive reference group (e.g., lesbians, gay men, pos-

itive heterosexual friends). Conversely, some indication of lack of success in the client's behavior would include her continuing discomfort with her own feelings, relationships, and fantasies; a preponderance of negative comments regarding gay people; potential relationships with women disturbed by the client's lack of respect for her partner, herself, or the relationship, or her inability to take the relationship seriously; her use of overly confrontational or apologetic self-disclosures; and reliance on a homophobic reference group. It is important to recognize that conflict with the heterosexual world—conflict with parents, old friends, colleagues, negative comments about the media, frustration with career or school—are not indications of failure to achieve self-acceptance and reduction on internalized homophobia. In fact, these external conflicts are likely to increase as internalized homophobia decreases, at least initially, as the individual becomes more aware of societal homophobia and its negative impact on her life. (p. 64)

Some examples from my own clinical practice may illuminate further the complex issues that can be interpreted usefully as internalized homophobia. For example, I have encountered clients whose physical disability or illness made them wonder if lesbianism was somehow to blame—perhaps a retribution from a vengeful god. Or a disability or illness can magnify the internalized fear that one is already defective as a lesbian, and is now doubly defective with the disability or illness.

Clients who have experienced rejections that are particularly meaningful to them have often internalized those rejections. I have seen this in particular when a lesbian client is told by an important person that she may no longer have any association with that person's children, or when a lesbian is rejected by her parents or her church. Many a client has read to me a scathing letter from family or a former friend that is invariably based on myth and that disallows the client from approaching the person to correct the mythical beliefs. It is common for a client to say "I got used to it" or "There's nothing I can do about it" to a degree that is a denial of her true hurt and rage; it may well be true that she is used to it or that there is nothing she can effectively do, but these conclusions are often made prematurely, bypassing the free expression of her feelings about the rejection. Expressions thus bypassed almost always fester. Setting a therapeutic environment for expressing her feeling experientially, not just describing them, often moves the client to either a different approach to the person who rejected her or a more comfortable resolution with the loss.

I take special note of a new client's use of lesbian terminology. An expression of internalized homophobia I've often seen is the client's avoidance of the word lesbian or gay in reference to herself. She can use the word itself, and say, perhaps, that she went to a lesbian poetry reading or that she reads a lesbian newspaper, but I may notice that she never *directly* identifies herself as a lesbian. These simple language contortions can be revealing.

Touch is another area to examine for internalization of negativity. A lesbian may express that she can freely kiss or hug her daughter and her best (married) friend in greeting, but fears that if she were to likewise kiss or hug her lover, her identity would be revealed for all to see. For this reason, many lesbians will go away for a weekend of skiing or hiking with a woman friend, but not with a lover, for fear that it would somehow be seen as "different" and would give them away.

Lesbians who have been very uncomfortable with their orientation have sometimes woven webs of deceit that they then must resolve as they become more comfortable with their lesbianism:

My client, Fiona, had spent some months in therapy with me exploring the meaning of her lesbian orientation. She had been in love with two other women prior to her present lover, but had not viewed those relationships as meaningful; they were "just exceptions, and I believed I would one day fall in love with a man, like I should." Because she had not fully legitimized the previous relationships, she did not lend them any credence as she noticed she was falling in love for a third time, this time with her then married neighbor. Fiona was determine to remain just friends with her neighbor, but their love grew. Her neighbor decided to leave her marriage to be with Fiona, which was what Fiona wanted too. However, Fiona found herself telling her new lover that there had been no previous women loves. This denial came out of her own discrediting of her past relationships and out of internalized homophobic fear that she would be seen as "one of those predatory lesbians who seduce married women." Every so often during their relationship, her new lover would mention how special it was to her that they were each other's first woman love. As Fiona's understanding of her past relationships and her comfort with her lesbianism grew, she wanted more and more to tell her lover of her past loves—but she feared that this disclosure would cause great damage to the relationship. She eventually decided to tell her lover, and we rehearsed in sessions. The couple weathered this disclosure very well.

Clients can mislabel their experiences in a way that takes some time for the therapist to search out:

Ruby came to therapy having diagnosed herself as having an "intimacy problem." She had heard that lesbians and that adult children of alcoholic parents often do have problems with intimacy and that was her own assessment of the difficulty in her relationship for which she took full credit. She reported that she never felt really loved by her partner, even when her partner stated her love or demonstrated it with little gifts or special times together. I asked her to describe the relationship, their usual types of interactions and their living arrangements, and from these reports I began to get the picture that theirs was a fairly closeted relationship, which my client expressed only slight displeasure about. Because Ruby saw the problem as one of being unable to accept someone's intimacy or love, I asked her to fill in this blank, "Assume your lover has just told you she loves you, and you say back, 'no you don't, because if you did, _____.'" My client surprised herself by blurting "No, you don't really love me, because if you did, you'd acknowledge our relationship to our friends and coworkers." She realized that her lover previous to this one had also been very closeted, and that in both relationships, Ruby had felt compelled to hide the meaning of her relationship with her "roommate" to the rest of the world. When she was able to work out this internalization of homophobia on both their parts with her lover, her "intimacy problem" disappeared.

Internalized homophobia is an aspect of therapy with any lesbian client that calls for the sharpest awareness possible on the therapist's part. There are so many subtle variations of it, and there is so much interplay with dysfunction or pathology, that I find I cannot expect myself to sort out or even notice every instance of homophobia. I recommend an ongoing peer consultation group, or supervision with a therapist trained in working with lesbians, as the best solution.

5

LESBIAN IDENTITY FORMATION

The process whereby a lesbian identity is formed and managed is one of the central features of lesbianism. It is often a critical aspect of psychotherapy as well, whether as an issue to be struggled with directly or as the context for other presenting features of the client. This chapter reviews the literature on lesbian identity formation, most of which has emerged in the 1980s. The concept of identity is addressed first, followed by a description of several models of identity development, a discussion of how a woman manages a lesbian identity, the fluidity of lesbian identity, and finally, the therapist's facilitation of the lesbian identity process.

LESBIAN IDENTITY

Prior to the 1980s, most literature on the formation of nonheterosexual identity focused on the etiology of the deviant identity. Looking for "causes" implied that what would follow would be a "cure." It is important to remember, as is described in Chapter 1, that no single theory about the cause of homosexuality has yet been supported by research. As awareness of homosexuality has increased in recent years, the focus of attention has changed from a search for etiology to an effort to describe a developmental process.

The construct *homosexual identity* first appeared in the 1970s, but as Cass (1984a) points out, no agreed-upon definition of the construct has yet been obtained. As the term is used, its diverse meanings include (1) defining oneself as homosexual, (2) a sense of self as homosexual, (3) an image of self as homosexual, (4) the way a homosexual person is, and (5) consistent behavior in relation to homosexual-related activity. In addition to this lack of specific definition, homosexual identity is usually written about in isolation from its parent literature on the general concept of identity.

As Cass (1984a) notes, some authors state that homosexual identity is equivalent to the concept of ego identity. Others see it as equivalent to sexual identity. Others see it as a group identity, and still others say that homosexual identity does not exist at all and is a figment of theorists' imagination. This last stance is based on the belief that it is dehumanizing to place a person in a stigmatized minority, and that a homosexual identity implies rigidity and permanence.

Cass suggests that homosexual identity may be best conceptualized as evolving "out of a clustering of self-images which are linked together by the individual's idiosyncratic understanding of what characterizes someone as 'a homosexual'" (p. 110). She agrees with those authors who distinguish between a behavioral construct, such as sexual preference or sexual orientation, and the cognitive construct of homosexual identity. Elliott (1985) likewise notes that because "the term 'lesbian identity' is fairly new to psychology, . . . it is worthwhile to differentiate such an identity from lesbian behavior and homoerotic tendencies, interests, and attachments" (p. 64). As will be seen throughout this chapter, these are important distinctions. *Lesbian identity, then, might best be seen as a cognitive or felt sense about oneself, or a belief about oneself, which can be more or less congruent with one's behaviors, interests, or affections.*

Despite the lack of clear definitions and clear theories, a good deal of information has come out of the recent literature. In 1978, de Monteflores and Schultz described some of the differences in the identity formation process between gay men and lesbians. They note in particular the effects of sex-role factors and sex-role violations. Sex-role factors are seen for example in the study of gay and lesbian psychologists described in Chapter 1 (see Table I, p. 14), where the ages for various aspects of identity formation (age of first same-sex experience, age of identity disclosure, etc.) differed between men and women. Further, studies cited by de Monteflores and Schultz show that in lesbian relationships, emotional attachment is emphasized over sexual behavior, whereas the reverse is true for gay men. As the authors summarize it:

Clearly these findings are consistent with the sex-role socialization of our society in general. Male sexuality is seen as active, initiatory, demanding of immediate gratification, and divorced from emotional attachment; female sexuality emphasizes feelings and minimizes the importance of immediate sexual activity. (p. 68)

The sex-role violations that de Monteflores and Schultz see as different for gay men and lesbians have to do with developmental issues. In a culture where the traditional route to full psychological development is for two complementary half-persons (for example, the man as "instrumental" and the woman as "expressive") to become whole by merging with each other, an alternative developmental route is ignored, which is based on the violation of these sex-role stereotypes. In this case, each individual comes to full development by becoming psychologically androgynous. It is this alternative that lesbians (and gay men) embrace. As the authors describe it:

> To the extent that homosexual preference is associated with sex-role violation, there will likely be an essential difference in the coming out process for lesbians and gay men, with gay men and women moving in opposite directions on sex-typed dimensions. (p. 69)

Sex-role violations, then, are seen to occur commonly among lesbians, along with the retaining of many traditionally feminine characteristics. Lesbians often undertake such traditionally male tasks as complete financial self-support, development of their physical bodies, and taking care of the "masculine" everyday tasks (car repair, yard maintenance) as well as the everyday "feminine" tasks (cooking, cleaning). The sex-role crossing also occurs in psychological realms: lesbians often become more agentic, active, and independent in their interactions with the world. Because lesbians develop some traditionally masculine traits, and keep many feminine traits as well, they may possess more psychological androgyny, which is considered a healthier position than either too much femininity or too much masculinity (Vance, 1984; Riddle & Sang, 1978). Although sex-role violations and androgyny are often seen as psychologically healthy, the lesbian pays the price of society's censure for acting against the sex-stereotyped norms.

De Monteflores and Schultz also note other factors that make the identity formation process different for men and women. One difference is the notion of a "political" lesbian identity which gay men do not share; some women consider themselves lesbian more for political ideological reasons than for sexual orientation reasons; that is, they feel a commitment to the enhancement of women's place in the political structure of the world, whether or not they form primary emotional or sexual attachments to women. Such a woman often calls herself a "woman-identified woman." Another difference is the impact of having legal custody of children. At present, many more lesbians are fighting custody battles than are gay men, probably because of the tradition that children stay with the mother (unless she is a lesbian) in a divorce.

Another writer on the subject of identity formation, Troiden (1988), offers a typology of homosexuality that applies to both men and women.

Troiden describes four types of homosexuality categorized according to the degree to which homosexual behavior is socially organized, interpreted by the individual as homosexual, and is perceived as significant. This typeology can provide a useful framework for clients who are trying to determine the meaning of their homosexual feelings and behaviors. Applied to women, the four types are as follows.

1. *Ambiguous homosexuality*: This describes the spontaneous decision of adolescents to engage in exploratory same-sex activities. Such activity falls outside organized group structures and is usually not interpreted as homosexual by the participant.
2. *Situational homosexuality*: This category describes special conditions such as prisons, the armed forces, or cultural arenas where homosexual behavior is not defined as such as long as it occurs only in the special circumstance.
3. *Clandestine homosexuality*: Here we see a person who feels that her homosexuality expresses a fundamental emotional need, and interprets her activity as homosexual, but does not involve herself in open aspects of lesbian life.
4. *Committed homosexuality*: This represents the deepest level of involvement in lesbian life. This person perceives herself as lesbian, and accepts herself as such, developing a lifestyle that permits a degree of openness and honors the significance of her homosexuality.

MODELS OF LESBIAN IDENTITY FORMATION

The development of a sexual identity happens for all humans, whether that identity is homosexual, heterosexual, or somewhere in between. This developmental process seems to consist of two parallel processes, the internal development of structures that define the self, called identity formation, and the more external development of behaviors and attitudes that are more or less congruent with the internal identity. The latter process is often considered the "coming-out process" for lesbians and gay men. In writing on the subject, authors have found that separating the two processes is very difficult, for the overlap is an essential part of the individual's development.

Several theorists have proposed models of identity development in recent years that consist of stages that the gay person passes through. Three of these are reviewed here. Notice the overlap between development in one's internal structures and external applications of them. Table V on page 100 summarizes these three theorist's models and provides suggested tasks for the therapist at each stage.

Coleman's (1982) model describes the coming-out process for both gay men and lesbians. His model postulates that identity integration depends on completion of tasks at earlier stages, and that individuals who experience identity integration are not static, constant, or stationary. Coleman names five stages:

1. *Pre-Coming Out.* In this stage, individuals are aware that their feelings are "different" from the norm, but that if same-sex feelings were acknowledged they would be subject to rejection and ridicule. Individuals thus protect themselves from clear awareness of their feelings through defenses such as denial, repression, reaction formation, sublimation, and rationalization. Because individuals at this stage are not consciously aware of same-sex feelings, they cannot describe what is wrong, and can only communicate their conflict through behavioral problems, psychosomatic illnesses, or other symptoms. A healthy resolution of this stage is to face the existential crisis of being different.

2. *Coming Out.* Individuals move into this stage when they acknowledge their homosexual feelings consciously, although they may not necessarily have a clear understanding of what "homosexual" means. Once same-sex feelings are acknowledged, the individual faces the task of telling others. This is a critical point, and reactions from others can have a powerful impact on self-esteem and on completion of all future stages. Coleman postulates that no one can develop self-concepts such as "accepted" or "worthwhile" all alone, and that individuals must therefore take risks to gain acceptance from others.

3. *Exploration.* This is the stage of experimenting with a new sexual identity. Exploration requires facing several developmental tasks. The first task is to develop interpersonal skills in order to meet and socialize with others. Second, some individuals need to develop a sense of personal attractiveness and sexual competence. Third, some individuals must learn that their self-esteem is not based on the stereotype of sexual conquest. Because most homosexual individuals were encouraged to follow a heterosexual path during their adolescence, they may not enter their own true adolescence until their chronological adolescence is long past. This can be puzzling or frightening for men and women who have matured in other ways.

4. *First Relationships.* After a period of sexual and social experimentation, the need for intimacy often becomes the center of focus. The developmental task of this stage is to learn how to function in a same-sex relationship, especially in a society where the norm is opposite-sex relationships.

5. *Integration*. Here individuals incorporate their public and private identities into one self-image. This is an ongoing process that lasts for the rest of the individual's life, as new feelings about the self will emerge, new labels and concepts will be discovered, and new relationships and social networks will be found. Individuals in this stage continue to face the other developmental tasks of adulthood, such as midlife and old age.

Lewis (1984) also postulates a five-stage identity formation process, but she addresses lesbians only. This is an important contribution, because, as noted previously, the coming-out process is different in some respects for men and women. Although Lewis does not state whether the process she describes is sequential, it is implied. She lists five processes that a woman goes through in developing a healthy, well-integrated lesbian identity.

1. *Being Different*. This manifests itself as a sense of knowing one is somehow different. The woman may be able to verbalize this difference as a child, or only in retrospect, or not at all, in which case the feeling stays below the level of awareness until adolescence or adulthood. In many cases, the client will be unable to verbalize what is going on within herself.

2. *Dissonance*. At this time a woman becomes aware that her emotional and erotic feelings are stronger in relation to women than to men. This acknowledgment often is accompanied by shame, anxiety, denial, or ambivalence. It is a time of great dissonance and inner turmoil, in which the woman faces the conflict between her socialization as a heterosexual and her own feelings that pull her toward wanting intimacy with other women. A grieving process often ensues, during which she may use denial or bargaining to lessen her dissonance and keep her from acting on her feelings.

3. *Relationships*. Because women are socialized to have and maintain relationships, sexual exploration and experimentation often take place in the context of a relationship. Early relationships lack social support and lack models for courtship and endurance, and can thus be stormy.

4. *Stable Lesbian Identity*. Here the woman feels a sense of settling down that is similar to finishing adolescence. Much of the earlier dissonance, fear, and anger gives way to self-acceptance. She often develops a "chosen family" of accepting friends to replace a less accepting biological family. Often during this time an ongoing committed relationship is formed.

5. *Integration*. At this stage, the woman finds ways to be positive about herself as a lesbian. Rather than looming large as it did earlier, her lesbianism becomes one aspect of her life and demands less time and energy. There will still be pain and anger, but rather than blaming herself, she will know that it is the culture that is oppressive. This is not a static stage, and a woman can be thrown back into a time of experimenting by the breakup of

a relationship or a move from a supportive environment to a less supportive one.

The final stage model of identity development presented is Cass's (1979).
Hers is perhaps the most widely used and widely quoted. It is also the only
model to date that has been subjected to verifying research (Cass, 1984b).
Her model is based on two assumptions: that identity is acquired through
a developmental process, and that the locus for stability of, and change in,
behavior lies in the interaction process that occurs between the individual
and her or his environment.

Cass's model applies to both gay men and lesbians, although sex-role
socialization will make some difference. Age, too, will make a difference,
because of the marked contrast in societal attitudes experienced by different age cohorts. At each stage, "identity foreclosure" is possible where the
individual may choose not to develop any further. Movement from one
stage to the next is motivated by the incongruence or dissonance that exists
in the individual's environment as the result of assigning homosexual
meaning to one's thoughts, feelings, and behavior. Cass's six stages are:

Stage 1: Identity Confusion. This stage is marked by a conscious awareness that homosexuality has some relevance to one's feelings and behavior.
The individual arrives at a self-definition as potentially homosexual, wondering, "Am I homosexual?" This confusion can be resolved in one of
three ways. The first approach occurs when the homosexual meaning
attributed to one's own behavior and feelings is found to be both correct
and acceptable; for this individual, the move to the next stage is automatic.
A second approach occurs when the individual perceives the meaning of
his or her behavior and feelings as correct but undesirable; this individual
may inhibit behaviors that are homosexual in meaning, may restrict exposure to information on homosexuality, or may deny that such information
has any personal relevance. These choices result in identity foreclosure, as
the individual rejects the self-portrait of a "potential homosexual." The
third approach is adopted when the individual sees the meaning of his or
her behavior and feelings as both incorrect and unacceptable; this person
redefines the meaning of his or her behavior as nonhomosexual and identity foreclosure again results.

Stage 2: Identity Comparison. At this stage, the individual begins to think,
"I may be homosexual." He or she begins to feel alienated from others and
has a sense of not belonging to society at large, to family, and to peers.
None of the guidelines, ideals, and expectations for the future that accompany a heterosexual identity are relevant any longer and they have not yet
been replaced by others. This alienation can be resolved in one of four
ways. The first approach is adopted when the individual reacts positively

to the notion of being different; this person must still grapple with the effects of his or her difference and will often cope by developing behaviors that allow her or him to pass as heterosexual. A second approach occurs when the individual finds a homosexual self-image undesirable and engages in methods to continue same-sex behavior without crediting it as homosexual. A third strategy occurs when the individual accepts her or his behavior as homosexual but views the behavior as undesirable; attempts are made to change actual behavior. The fourth approach occurs when the individual perceives both the behavior and the identity of homosexuality as undesirable and wishes to change both; behaviors are inhibited and homosexuality is devalued in favor of asexuality or heterosexuality. Identity foreclosure occurs with this fourth strategy, and the individual can be left with an extreme sense of self-hatred.

Stage 3: Identity Tolerance. At this stage, the individual has reached the conclusion, "I am probably homosexual," and views contact with other homosexuals as an important thing to do in order to counter isolation and alienation. The individual tolerates rather than accepts a homosexual identity. While alienation is reduced by the newly sought acceptance of other homosexuals, this accentuates the feeling of not belonging to the heterosexual world. The individual often copes by making careful choices about with whom to interact. The quality of the contacts made with other gays and lesbians at this stage is of critical importance; factors such as social skills, shyness, self-esteem, and fear can contribute to a negative experience, as can the responses of the other. Individuals who perceive their new identity and their behavior as desirable may also have different experiences from those who perceive their behavior as desirable but their identity as undesirable. Positive experiences will have the effect of making other gays and lesbians appear more desirable and of providing models for managing a homosexual identity. Negative experiences make them seem less desirable, and the individual may reduce contacts with homosexuals or inhibit behavior, increasing the risk of identity foreclosure.

Stage 4: Identity Acceptance. The individual now accepts rather than tolerates a homosexual identity, discovers a preference for homosexual social contexts, and develops friendships within them. The types of groups within the subculture that the individual associates with have an important influence on progression through the remaining stages. By Stage 4, "passing as straight," though with internal acceptance firmly in place, has become a routine strategy. The individual may also continue to cope with identity my minimizing contacts with heterosexuals who threaten to increase incongruency, such as families, and by selectively disclosing a homosexual identity to significant heterosexual others. The individual is primarily dealing with the incongruency of being acceptable in some places and not in others.

Stage 5: Identity Pride. In this stage, the individual finds that she or he can manage the incongruency between self-acceptance and society's rejection by revaluing homosexuals as more positive than heterosexuals. This becomes a characteristic immersion in gay subculture. There is a strong sense of pride in being gay. The individual not only accepts a homosexual identity, but prefers it. Because the individual is far less concerned now with how heterosexuals perceive him or her, disclosure now becomes a viable strategy for coping. Incongruency reemerges when the disclosure of homosexual identity brings about its inevitable reactions. Negative reactions may be expected that can lead to identity foreclosure. Positive reactions can be inconsistent with the individual's expectations, and attempts to handle this lead to the final stage.

Stage 6: Identity Synthesis. The individual enters this stage with the awareness that the "them and us" view previously espoused no long holds true. The individual becomes aware that some heterosexuals accept her or him, and comes to view them with greater favor. She or he is now able to integrate a homosexual identity with all other aspects of the self. Instead of being seen as *the* identity, it is now given the status of being just one aspect of the self. This awareness completes the homosexual identity formation process.

In most models of identity formation, the authors stress that the process is nonlinear. As Hess notes, "It is necessary to emphasize the process by which developmental change occurs, rather than the sequence of change or the specific content of a given 'stage'" (p. 70). Even though the three models presented are described in stages, Cass's and Lewis's do make allowances for a nonlinear progression, although their lack of emphasis on this matter is often a point of criticism. Most theorists, including the three described, conceptualize identity formation as an interactive process between the individual and the environment. In contrast to distinct stages, Ponse (1978) found among her lesbian subjects that the path toward a lesbian identity could start at any number of points. As summarized by Elliott (1985), these points are as follows:

- A subjective sense of being different and identifying that difference as a sexual-emotional attraction to one's own sex;
- An understanding of the "lesbian significance" of these kinds of feelings;
- Acceptance of such feelings and their implications for identity;
- A search for community of like persons; and

- Involvement in a sexual-emotional relationship.

Ponse calls these five events the "gay trajectory." Their chronology differs from person to person, but the first three elements are seen as primary and, once realized, exert a strain toward the remaining two. All the elements of a lesbian identity are seen to develop over time, regardless of the starting point.

Gramick (1984) has suggested a model of lesbian identity that is an alternative to stage models and trajectory models. Called an interactionist model, Gramick theorizes that a lesbian identity is adopted over time through a reciprocal action between individual and environment. Initial cues such as feelings, interests, same-sex attractions, and associations with lesbians, are continually reinterpreted and reevaluated. Homosexual meanings are constructed as the woman socially interacts with others. Gramick tested her theory on 97 lesbians, studying the importance on identity development of several events in the woman's life: feeling different, cognitive awareness of lesbianism, meeting lesbians, emotional attraction to a woman, physical/genital attraction to a woman, physical contact with a woman, and establishing a lesbian relationship. Gramick found that these events did not occur in predictable order. She further found that two of these events had the greatest impact on a woman's identification of herself as lesbian: physical/genital contact and the establishment of a relationship. The establishment of a lesbian relationship was the primary predictor of self-acknowledgment; physical/genital contact was second. These results support the theory that social interactions are of prime importance in the formation of a lesbian identity.

As the therapist constructs a system of identity formation development that applies best to his or her therapy style, it is important to remember to incorporate many factors into one's framework in addition to these models. Hanley-Hackenbruck (1988) describes it thus:

There are many variables influencing the coming out process. Individual variables account for vast differences and are related to personality or characterological make-up, age at first awareness of being different, overall psychological functioning, family rigidity (especially regarding sexuality), religious upbringing, and negative or traumatic experiences involving sexual orientation (especially in childhood). The other most common variables are: gender; race or ethnic group; locale, especially urban versus rural; and the values and attitudes of the society at that particular time in history. These variables tend to affect, at least, the timing, sequence and duration of experiences or stages in the process. (p. 30)

Although the models of lesbian identity formation can be quite helpful to the therapist working to facilitate the identity formation process with a client, it is important to keep in mind that the models are most effective when used as a general framework, and not as strict diagnostic categories. Many lesbians may find the models quite applicable to their lives, and many others will not.

MANAGEMENT OF A LESBIAN IDENTITY

The tasks of developing a lesbian identity must be undertaken at the same time that other developmental tasks are being dealt with over the life span. Burch (work in progress) has taken a look at the impact of lesbian identity on the developmental task of individuation. She notes that lesbian identity often emerges later in life and that a late change in identity may complicate matters of individuation. She suggests that the lesbian's experience of living in a world that she will never fully be part of will have an effect on individuation as well, both positive and negative.

Burch states that forming a lesbian identity pushes one deeper into oneself and into being able to stand alone, a process that both requires developmental strength and furthers it. Such a process requires a differentiation of self from others that one may otherwise be very close to, making the psychological boundary around oneself more sharply defined for lesbians than for other women. The lesbian's feeling of "differentness" from other people, if felt at an early age, may help facilitate differentiation from the mother, and thus serve the process of psychological individuation.

However, Burch states that the process of lesbian identity formation also presents hurdles to individuation. Girls who come out during adolescence can experience intense self-doubt, alienation, wounded self-esteem, fear, and guilt. On the other hand, changing identity after adolescence can be disruptive and painful, sometimes leading to a replay of an earlier developmental stage (such as adolescence) that must be worked through in a new way. As the lesbian finds herself using various strategies to ease the effects of her stigmatization (such as assimilation, ghettoization, or specialization), she could find that these very strategies delay integration of her identity into a fuller sense of self. Also, a supportive environment is generally not available for the lesbian who is establishing her identity, and she may find herself in a hostile, abandoning environment. Burch states:

Just as the young child needs to be able to move back and forth between mother and the world without fearing she will have to give up either, the "young" lesbian needs to be able to move out into the new world of lesbian identity and then perhaps retreat from it, back and forth until she has resolved enough of her conflict, fear, anxiety, etc. to feel ready to move on her own in that world. Instead of a "good-enough mother" who can tolerate the child's forays into separate, autonomous experience, . . . a lesbian usually has a family ready to abandon her at least temporarily if she individuates very far into lesbian identity. (p. 7)

In another vein, de Monteflores (1986) reports on the strategies that lesbians, like other minorities, use to manage their identity as "different." She describes four frequently adopted coping strategies:

1. *Assimilation*. The primary technique used in assimilation is passing as one of the dominant group. Assimilation promotes a strengthening of external skills (the dress, language, and organizational procedures of the dominant culture), but can lead to a profound sense of self-betrayal too, as one becomes disconnected from the values of one's subculture.

2. *Confrontation*. Confrontation occurs when one faces up to his or her difference, becoming visible first to oneself and then to others. Coming out is the primary technique of confrontation. Coming out involves the transformation of an apparent deficit into a strength.

3. *Ghettoization*. By choice or by circumstance, many individuals find themselves living a significant part of their lives within the geographical or psychological confines of their subculture. These individuals acquire credibility and protection within their group and may go to great lengths to prevent penetration by other modes of existence.

4. *Specialization*. Seeing oneself as special serves the function of believing one has unique, and therefore superior, qualities. Examples include being exotic (e.g., being the token lesbian at a heterosexual function), having special talents of the group (e.g., lesbians are unique because of their honesty and ability to challenge the status quo), being better for having suffered, and seeing oneself as belonging to a "chosen" or exiled group.

Each of these strategies has its apparent drawbacks as a managing strategy. Speaking of a more ideal method of management, de Monteflores says,

The mature identity necessarily includes a recognition of sameness as well as difference. The articulation of these attributes requires a certain flexibility in boundaries, which comes out of an inner sense of security about individual identity. (p. 79)

TABLE IV.
Behaviors Engaged in to Avoid Being Identified as Lesbian

Behavior	N	Percent
Introduce lover or partner as a "friend"	62	76
Avoid talking about living situation	54	67
Pretend to date a man	32	40
Use "he" instead of "she" to refer to lover or partner	27	33
Lie about living situation	23	28
Actually date a man	22	27
Invite a gay man as a "date" to social functions	21	26
Avoid being seen with gay friends	13	16
Pretend not to see a gay friend when with straight people	9	11
Pretend not to see a straight friend when with gay people	9	11
Actually get married	4	5
Get engaged	3	4
Pretend to be engaged	1	1
Pretend to be married	1	1

Mean number of behaviors engaged in = 3.64

Alice E. Moses, *Identity Management in Lesbian Women* (Praeger Publishers, New York, 1978), p. 108. Copyright © 1978 by Praeger Publishers. Reprinted with permission.

In 1978, Moses reported her cross-country study of lesbian identity management. Her data yielded a volume of information, two aspects of which are reported here. One aspect addressed the matter of whether lesbians felt they have any choice in the formation of their identity. To this question, the majority of the sample, 56%, felt that lesbianism was entirely their choice, and the remaining 44% felt that at least part of being a lesbian was something they could not help (although two-thirds of the latter group felt that lesbianism was "mostly" their choice). When asked whether they liked being lesbian, no one responded "never," 1% responded "seldom," 6% responded "sometimes," 10% responded "often," and 64% responded "almost always." Although the women in this study were self-identified lesbians, it is apparent that, at least for this group, lesbians report high satisfaction with their lesbianism and a sense of free choice about it, despite a strongly felt sense that their lesbianism was immutable.

Moses's sample reported a large degree of satisfaction with their orientation, and yet most report that they engage in behaviors to avoid being identified as lesbian. Table IV delineates these results and provides a sampling of commonly used strategies.

The three studies reported here represent some of the management tools used to cope with a lesbian identity and discuss possible effects on the individuation process. These topics are apparently just the beginning of a body of literature on a very complex phenomenon that future research and theory will, it is hoped, expand upon.

LESBIAN IDENTITY AS A FLUID CHARACTERISTIC

The literature on lesbian identity formation discussed so far implies that women are either heterosexual or lesbian, and therefore fails to address the fact that identity falls along a continuum rather than being a dichotomous division, as shown in Chapter 1. In her clinical practice, Golden (1987) reports noticing that her women clients defined themselves according to all possible permutations of sexual behavior and identity. She states, "The construction of a categorical definition of lesbian is bound to obscure the personal and variable meanings of lesbian identity as it is experienced by real women" (p. 5).

Among Golden's clientele who identified themselves to her as lesbian, there were some whose sexual behavior was exclusively lesbian, and some whose behavior was exclusively heterosexual or distinctly bisexual (some of the latter two groups also described themselves as "political lesbians"); in addition, some self-defined lesbians had had no sexual experience at all, and some women considered themselves to be celibate lesbians. Thus, among women who call themselves lesbians, a wide range of sexual behavior is evident. The same ranges were seen in women who identified themselves as either bisexual or heterosexual. Golden points out that one's identity is not always predictable on the basis of one's behavior, and, further, that the assumption that people strive for congruence among sexual feelings, activities, and identities may not be warranted.

Identity may therefore be fluid; it is not simply a matter of assuming that a person has attractions to one sex or the other (or both), that they act on those feelings exclusively, and that they eventually come to adopt the identity appropriate to their sexual activities. Further, both identity and behavior can fluctuate over a woman's lifespan.

In contrast to Moses's (1978) study cited earlier in this chapter, Golden's lesbian-identified clients show a distinction between those who felt their lesbianism was essentially beyond their control and those who felt it was consciously chosen. Following a similar phenomenon described by Ponse (1978), Golden categorizes these groups into two types: primary lesbians and elective lesbians. *Primary lesbians* appear to have had a conscious sense of difference at an early age based on their sexual attractions to the same sex, and do not perceive this difference to be based on any kind of choice.

In contrast, *elective lesbians* perceive their lesbian identity as consciously chosen.

The primary lesbians often referred to themselves as "born" or "real" lesbians, whereas elective lesbians often privately expressed speculations about whether they were "really" lesbians. Elective lesbians often interpret this speculation as a difficulty in coming out, an unwillingness to give up heterosexual privilege, or as internalized homophobia; it may in fact be simply a byproduct of a more fluid identity that is expressed in the context of the belief that a person must be either gay or straight, with no in-betweens.

Among the elective lesbians, Golden distinguishes two subgroups. Some of these women viewed their sexual attraction to women as a central, basic, and unchanging aspect of who they are. The others did not view their lesbianism as essential and enduring and did not experience dissonance in describing themselves as lesbians with heterosexual pasts. Among all the elective lesbians, some experienced their identity as essential and fixed early in their lives but had later in life come to view their identity as more fluid. Others reported the opposite, namely that their identity was more fluid in their younger years and had become more fixed over time.

The concept of primary and elective lesbians has also been studied by Vance and Green (1984). Their study distinguished self-defined lesbians from one another on the basis of the period of development that lesbian relationships first occurred. One group showed the following characteristics: they engaged in sexual relations with females during adolescence, they currently attributed to themselves more masculine traits, and they reported having been more precocious sexually at an early age (including engaging in heterosexual intercourse prior to adolescence). This group reported no emotional involvement with men prior to defining themselves as lesbians, despite the opposite-sex sexual activity. They currently defined themselves as exclusively homosexual.

The second group engaged in lesbian sexual experience for the first time in adulthood. They typically were involved emotionally in heterosexual relations prior to defining themselves as lesbians. Some members of this second group showed a tendency to maintain occasional bisexual activity, although they maintained a lesbian self-identity.

The groups were not distinguishable from each other on the basis of whether their first sexual experience was with a male, or in regard to the number of males with whom they had been sexually involved. Although the first group identified themselves as having more stereotypic masculine traits, both groups were high in the number of stereotypic feminine traits that they attributed to themselves. Vance and Green conclude that the later in life one adopts a lesbian orientation, the more likely one is to have been emotionally involved heterosexually and to retain interest in heterosexual activity.

It is critical, then, to remember that lesbian identity formation is a complex process that is affected by numerous social, biological, and developmental factors. Also, it is not necessarily a linear process, headed toward a fixed end-product. Finally, lesbian identity is defined by each individual woman.

THE THERAPIST'S FACILITATION OF THE IDENTITY FORMATION PROCESS

The complex nature of the lesbian identity formation process, and its diversely different meaning for each individual client, makes working with this issue in therapy quite an intricate matter for the therapist. The therapist must have a great deal of knowledge at her or his fingertips about general frameworks (such as stage theory, trajectory theory, and interactionist theory), coping strategies, the facilitation of developmental growth, and the fluidity of identity itself. Perhaps most important, the therapist must be able to listen with exquisite care to what the client herself is feeling about her own personal meaning about lesbian identity.

Sophie (1982) is one of the few writers to draw together information from the literature in a systematic way to help the therapist work with the lesbian identity process with a client; her work is therefore worthy of a detailed discussion. Sophie names three aspects of the process and gives specific suggestions for each aspect—recognizing and accepting lesbian feelings, coming out to self, and coming out to others.

Recognizing and Accepting Lesbian Feelings

Sophie calls attention to the flexibility of sexual identity or orientation and thus recommends that the therapist's first task is to help the client get in touch with her feelings without labeling or evaluation. To do this requires two things of the therapist: comfort with one's own well-examined sexuality and freedom from inaccurate theories and assumptions about lesbianism.

When a therapist is working with a client who is exploring lesbian feelings, Sophie suggests that the therapist discourage the client from premature self-labeling. As long as the woman believes the culture's negative stereotypes about lesbians, labeling herself as lesbian entails diminished self-esteem. Sophie cites research that shows that those lesbians who feel best about themselves usually do not identify themselves as lesbian, regardless of the extent of their lesbian experience, until they have begun to revise their image of lesbians to one that is positive or at least neutral.

If the client is seen in therapy before identifying as a lesbian, early self-labeling should be discouraged, while at the same time continuing to work to eliminate negative evaluations of lesbians in general and of her own lesbian feelings. If, on the other hand, the client is seen in therapy after identifying with a negative view of lesbianism, the therapist has the harder job of helping the client change her negative view of both lesbians and herself after her self-esteem has already been diminished.

Sophie states that some women can develop positive beliefs about lesbians based only on their own feelings, but that for most women, contact with other lesbians or with other sources of positive information is a requirement. The resources developed by the women's and gay/lesbian liberation movements can be very useful for this purpose, and the therapist must be aware of these resources. A feminist philosophy also can be useful to both therapist and client in providing understanding of a sociopolitical analysis of sexuality and sex roles in offering support for challenging traditional sex roles and exclusive heterosexuality.

Developing a Lesbian Identity: Coming Out to Self

The tasks of the therapist here are similar to the tasks just mentioned, but with a difference in focus; although premature self-labeling as a lesbian is detrimental, failure to eventually embrace a lesbian identity can also be problematic. The therapist should thus facilitate the client's acceptance of a lesbian identity appropriate to the client's feelings.

Failure to develop a lesbian identity is usually the result of—and often results in even more—isolation, self-denial, and suppression of feelings. Some women remain isolated on their own and others remain isolated in a couple. Isolation in a couple deprives the couple of needed validation and support, often putting so much stress on the relationship that it causes the couple to stay together too long or to break up too soon. When such a relationship breaks up, the women are confronted with the identity issue without support of a partner or of a community.

Sophie identifies two major requirements for successful lesbian identity development, based on the research literature: the first is social support from both homosexuals and heterosexuals, and the second is incorporation of a positive philosophy or ideology pertaining to lesbianism, usually accomplished within a particular lesbian subculture. These the therapist can facilitate.

Developing a Lesbian Identity: Coming Out to Others

Sophie cites research indicating that coming out to a fairly wide variety of others is important for self-acceptance. Revealing lesbian feelings to the therapist is in itself an act of coming out, and a positive response from the therapist can go a long way toward facilitating self-acceptance.

Hiding is very costly. It requires great effort and constant vigilance, and it greatly restricts what one can do. Learning to conceal a major part of oneself can lead to a general loss of spontaneity. Although there are probably very few lesbians who are "out" with everyone they encounter, hiding implies some acceptance of the devaluation of lesbians and thus of the self.

Despite the advantages of coming out, each decision to reveal one's identity must be weighed against the negative consequences that may ensue. This is the therapist's primary task here. A client who avoids self-revelation through complete immersion in the lesbian community may be enhancing her positive lesbian identity, but the cost may be a constriction of activities, both in personal life and in professional life. The other alternative, interacting in both the lesbian and nonlesbian worlds as an open lesbian, allows much greater latitude for career development and pursuit of interests, but the cost here may be lack of support from others and the need to deal often with negative reactions and ignorance. The therapist must keep in mind that this is an unresolvable conflict.

The therapist can also assist at this juncture by recognizing and helping the client to accept the turmoil associated with the process of developing a lesbian identity. The therapist also can explore with the client the advantages and disadvantages of coming out to each individual of concern to her, by role plays and discussion of the client's hopes and expectations. It is important to help the client find the right approach for her, revealing her identity as much as she is able, and not revealing where the cost is deemed too high compared with the benefit.

Woodman (1989) suggests engaging the client in the process of identifying the following:

- What is the worst that can happen in being out of the closet?
- What are the consequences of this worst event?
- Can you accept the consequences?
- How can you minimize the consequences?
- Can you turn the consequences into positives for you?
- Finally, what is the best that can happen?

The therapist may want to examine these questions with the client in regard to many or all people or places she is contemplating coming out to, as well as in regard to a decision about an overall life stance that she may be considering taking.

Other suggestions for the therapist come from Lewis (1984) and Coleman (1982) among their descriptions of the stages of coming out that were presented earlier in this chapter. Both Lewis and Coleman note that in the early stage of identity development, when the client is only vaguely aware of same-sex feelings but has not labeled them as such, the client may be unable to verbalize these feelings to the therapist. If the client is giving clues to this effect, a gentle exploration is suggested about homosexual feelings. This may help the client recognize her feelings more easily and help to resolve her confusion sooner. Although it is important to wait for clues from the client, it is also important for the therapist to open the subject up to a deeper level of exploration than the client is working from, a little at a time.

Lewis further mentions that the therapist can be of help during a stage of dissonance by encouraging discussion of that dissonance. The client's fears, ambivalences, and even the cost of not dealing with the dissonance should be verbalized and examined openly. Lewis also points out that many women experience considerable loss when coming out—of an easy sense of belonging with her family, perhaps, or of friends who no longer accept her, or of her own prior hopes and dreams about her future—which can cause a lengthy grieving process and can be worked through in therapy.

Coleman, in reference to his stages of coming out, adds that therapists can be helpful in discussing with a client those situations that are difficult because they involve risk-taking, but that might lead to an improved self-concept. Because of the vulnerability of the self-concept during a stage of coming out to others, it is important that therapists help clients choose carefully those people to whom they disclose their identity. Coleman also recommends encouraging clients to make the most of a period of exploration: meet others, be aware of their attractions, and experiment with a second adolescence.

In Table V, the identity formation stages described in the previous section of this chapter, Models of Identity Formation, are summarized. In this table the names given to each stage by Coleman (1982), Lewis (1984), and Cass (1979), which are described in that section, are listed in the first column. Sophie's (1982) three aspects of the coming-out process, just addressed, are also listed. The tasks and experiences of the individual client that are described by the theorists are listed together in the second column. The third column delineates some of the therapist's tasks at each stage recommended by all four authors.

Table V can serve as a general guide for the therapist. However, it is important to remember that these theorists' stage descriptions are only models of the identity formation process. Most individuals will proceed through the process in their own unique way, some fitting the model fairly closely and others barely fitting at all. A particular client will, therefore, not fit neatly into stages, and she will not proceed in a linear fashion through the stages in a prescribed order. The elements of each stage overlap with other stages.

Cohen and Stein (1986) also offer helpful suggestions for therapists working with clients in an identity process. They point out that the effects of the pressure toward a required and exclusive heterosexuality must be dealt with in detail in therapy. Because lesbians lack a personal framework for their feelings as they enter an identity formation process, what are considered normative developmental tasks may become developmental hurdles, such as the growth toward intimacy rather than toward isolation. They state,

> Although a simultaneous and parallel development in several aspects of identity, including sexuality, capacity for intimacy, and generativity, can occur throughout life for gay men and lesbians, their development will necessarily involve not only the same vicissitudes encountered by any individual who grows and changes, but also the special effects arising from stigmatization and discrimination. (p. 37)

Cohen and Stein also remind therapists that "the transference and countertransference reactions to homosexuality will have a powerful influence on both the development and the evaluation of the gay or lesbian identity that emerges" (p. 32). As Krajeski (1986) points out, almost no discussion whatever of countertransference in the treatment of gay men and lesbians yet exists, an unequivocal gap in the literature.

Brown (1989) describes common patterns lesbians may use to juggle the problems of identity and coming out, particularly to their families of origin. These patterns are:

1. The lesbian maintains a rigid geographical and emotional distance from the family. She avoids coming out to the family altogether by reducing contact to a bare minimum (for example, sending cards on holidays only). She may feel estranged and she may still suffer a sense of rejection or loss.
2. The "I know you know" pattern in which there is an unspoken agreement that no one will talk about the lesbian's personal life.

TABLE V.
Summary of Identity Formation Process and Therapeutic Tasks

Stage	Client Experiences and Tasks	Therapist's Tasks
Pre-Coming Out (Coleman) Being Different (Lewis) Identify Confusion (Cass) Recognizing and Accepting Lesbian Feelings (Sophie)	Vague and defended awareness of difference; may be unable to articulate source of confusion; beginning to wonder, "Am I lesbian?"	Help client understand causes of her conflict; help her verbalize what she is feeling and thinking and what that means to her individually; help her realize that lesbian feelings and behaviors are acceptable; discourage suppression or repression; discourage premature labeling.
Coming Out (Coleman) Dissonance (Lewis) Identity Comparison (Cass) Coming Out to Self (Sophie)	Acknowledging lesbian feelings; telling others; coping with turmoil; facing conflict between socialization as heterosexual and her own pull toward women; thinks, "I may be lesbian."	Provide acceptance; work through shame, anxiety, denial, ambivalence; facilitate grieving process; work through alienation; help develop new guidelines, ideals, and expectations for nonheterosexual life; help her value lesbianism and revise image of lesbianism as positive; provide information, resources and readings; self-esteem work; provide sociopolitical analysis of sexuality and sex roles.
Exploration (Coleman) Relationships (Lewis) Identity Tolerance (Cass) Coming Out to Others (Sophie)	Sexual and social experimentation; "second adolescence"; exploration of relationships; finding a community or sentiment that is supportive; thinks, "I probably am lesbian"; choosing whom to interact with and come out to.	Help develop interpersonal skills, sense of sexual attractiveness, and competence; help her understand and enjoy second adolescence; provide support; provide models for courtship and relationship endurance; assist through potentially stormy early relationships; help develop a support network or community with high quality of contacts, both lesbian and nonlesbian; encourage acceptance of a lesbian identity appropriate to client's feelings; incorporate positive philosophy or ideology of lesbianism; self-esteem work and intimacy work.

TABLE V. (cont.)
Summary of Identity Formation Process and Therapeutic Tasks

Stage	Client Experiences and Tasks	Therapist's Tasks
First Relationships (Coleman) Stable Identity (Lewis) Identity Acceptance (Cass)	Learning to function in a same-sex relationship; settling into new identity; develop a "chosen family"; developing relationships that match own values; valuing lesbianism; establishing a place in the subculture; choosing whom to be out to; learning how to pass as heterosexual and where to do so.	Continue intimacy work; educate couples in communication skills and in getting support for the relationship; help establish self-acceptance and outside support; help with establishing and maintaining relationships; help with decision making about coming out to others; help with incongruency about being accepted in some places and not in others; facilitate awareness of the costs of hiding; help develop coping strategies for responding to others' negative reactions.
Identity Pride (Cass)	Valuing homosexuality as better than heterosexuality; immersion in gay subculture.	Continue assisting in decisions about disclosure; facilitate expression of feelings about negative and positive responses received.
Integration (Coleman) Integration (Lewis) Identity Synthesis (Cass)	Incorporate public and private identities into one self-image; accomplish other developmental tasks of adulthood, midlife, and old age; lesbianism recedes into other aspects of identity and demands less energy.	Assist with ongoing adaptation to identity; help with accepting costs and advantages of client's chosen degree of self-labeling and disclosure; help with ongoing development of social networks and personal relationships; facilitate view of lesbianism as one of many aspects of the self.

Based on Coleman (1982), Lewis (1984), Cass (1979), and Sophie (1982)

When she interacts with her family, she may include her lover, but everyone (including the lesbian) treats her lover as just a roommate.

3. The "Don't tell your father" scenario in which the lesbian is officially out to one parent or a sibling, who responds with support but on the condition not to tell father, mother, aunt, or some other family member. This scenario is similar to the second pattern, but with the added notion that "This will kill your father."

Brown says of these patterns:

The lesbian or gay man who is presenting to therapy with one of these scenarios in place may manifest distress and symptomatology that has at least some of its etiology in the hidden agendas that guide such plots. This will be true even though the fact of not being out to the family will not usually be identified as the source of the problem by the client. . . . The acceptance of such an arrangement as a norm reflects her or his own internalized homophobia (i.e., we must take for granted that we will be rejected and accept that with grace). He or she may manifest self-esteem difficulties which stem, in part, from acting out the message that "I cannot be loved for who I am even in (or especially in) my family." (p. 69)

Coming out to families can evoke a range of emotional responses in your client. Some lesbians fairly breeze through the events and their aftermath, whereas others are devastated. I have known clients to wait until their parents are deceased to pursue their lifelong preference for women. Most lesbians, though, do come out to their parents, according to a study done by Garrison (1988). Among her 105 subjects, 63% had written or spoken to their parents about their sexual identification and 26% had not informed their parents, but believed that their parents knew. Of these, one-fourth had told their mothers only, and less than 1% had told their fathers only. Approximately one-third of the subjects felt fully accepted, and another one-third felt accepted but with a degree of discomfort. Kahn (1988) reports in her study of 81 lesbians that one family dynamic that can have a big effect on the lesbian's degree of openness is the level of intimidation she experienced growing up: intergenerational intimidation was negatively correlated with freedom in discussing sexuality, including discussing it in therapy. Kahn makes the point that the family, as a major socializing institution in this culture, might have a profound effect on the development and disclosure of lesbian identity. The therapist might well

TABLE VI.
Enablers and Inhibitors of Disclosure: Rank-ordered by Response Frequency.

Rank	Frequency	Enablers
1.	92.6%	Thinking the person to whom I was considering disclosure would be accepting of me.
2.	91.2%	Believing people deserve to be what they want.
3.	91.2%	Having a strong sense of identity, pride, and strength.
4.	90.3%	Wanting someone I care about to fully know me.
5.	88.9%	Wanting to be free of the burden of hiding.
6.	88.2%	Meeting strong wimmin who were out and comfortable being out.
7.	87.5%	Feeling good and confident about who I am as a lesbian.
8.	87.5%	Wanting a friendship to go deeper and thinking it couldn't unless I self-disclosed.
9.	86.1%	Feeling like I can only be completely myself by being open about my identity as a lesbian.
10.	86.1%	Having positive experiences in self-disclosure of my lesbian identity.
11.	86.1%	Meeting other lesbian professionals.
12.	84.7%	Believing that no matter what follows from my disclosure, I'll survive.
13.	84.7%	Hearing the person I will be interacting with express an awareness of the existence of other lifestyles and/or make mention of lesbian/gay friend.
14.	84.7%	Hearing or seeing music, plays, and writings that affirm lesbians and wimmin's culture.
15.	83.3%	Being with friends I could trust and who seemed to care.
16.	83.2%	Hearing positive things about lesbian/gay lifestyle.
17.	80.3%	Being in an intimate relationship with a womon. It's easier to be open with her support.
18.	76.4%	Finding the exhilarating experiences of a womon lover outweighed the hardships.
19.	75.0%	Being in openly gay environments like Provincetown, San Francisco, Wimmin's Music Festivals, and wimmin's bookstores.
20.	75.0%	Participating in all wimmin's events like wimmin's coffeehouses and wimmin's dances.

look for relationships between family dynamics and the client's present dynamics.

It can also be useful for the therapist to know what factors lesbians consider helpful and not helpful in their choices to reveal their identities. In her study of 72 lesbians, Ort (1987) developed a rank order of events that were reported as either "enablers" or "inhibitors" of disclosure. Table VI presents the top 20 ranked enablers and inhibitors from her study. Notice the diversity of perceptions utilized by these lesbians to make their decision about disclosure: they look for inner information about themselves (wanting to be fully known, fear of self-awkwardness), for information about the culture in general (living in a patriarchal culture, hearing positive things about lesbianism in general), for information from specific others

TABLE VI. (cont.)
Enablers and Inhibitors of Disclosure: Rank-ordered by Response Frequency.

Rank	Frequency	Inhibitors
1.	91.0%	Being afraid my disclosure would make myself and others feel awkward and uncomfortable.
2.	88.9%	Interacting with someone for whom I didn't think sexuality was an appropriate topic of conversation.
3.	88.9%	Interacting with people who have limited exposure to different types of lifestyles.
4.	86.1%	Hearing people around me, such as family, friends, or co-workers, tell homophobic jokes.
5.	85.9%	Fearing repercussions on my job, i.e., loss of job, loss of chances for advancement.
6.	81.9%	Interacting with people who are close-minded, ridiculing, prejudiced.
7.	80.6%	Wanting other peoples' approval and fearing I'd lose it by sharing my lesbian identity with them.
8.	80.3%	Feeling fearful of the changes that would come in my relationships with friends if I disclosed to them.
9.	79.2%	Fearing loss of respect of family, friends, and co-workers.
10.	77.8%	Feeling afraid of being rejected by straight friends by disclosing to them.
11.	77.8%	Fearing those at work who knew I was a lesbian would ostracize me.
12.	76.4%	Living in our culture, which is clearly patriarchal.
13.	75.0%	Being afraid if I told someone who seemed safe to tell, they'd tell someone and the information would spread to people who do not seem safe to me.
14.	73.6%	Not wanting to hurt my parents.
15.	70.8%	Fearing I or my lifestyle would be belittled by the person to whom I might disclose.
16.	70.8%	Hearing people around me, such as family, friends, or co-workers, use words such as "queer," "fag," and "lezzie."
17.	69.4%	Feeling anxious about others knowing I was lesbian.
18.	67.6%	Being unsure there was enough time to fully process my sharing of my lesbian identity with someone.
19.	66.7%	Being fearful that I might be verbally abused if I were identified as a lesbian.
20.	62.5%	Feeling reserved about myself in general.

Reprinted with permission from *Enablers and Inhibitors of Lesbian Self-Disclosure* by Janice D. Ort, 1987, unpublished paper.

(hearing that person express a positive attitude, hearing that person use derogatory language about gays or lesbians), and finally, for information from the lesbian culture (attending lesbian or gay events).

As Golden (1987) remarks, it is not uncommon to hear psychotherapists talk about women clients in the process of coming out, or who are having difficulty coming out, as if the therapist knows what the "right" result should look like. She suggests that therapists should question not only whether there is a "right" way to come out, but whether there is some search for authenticity, rather than assuming a fixed sexual identity that the therapist will help her discover.

In summarizing the literature on lesbian identity formation, Elliott (1985) states that writers agree on the following points:

1. It is important to distinguish among lesbian erotic interests, lesbian behavior, emotional attachments to women, and lesbian identity. A strict correlation among these factors does not exist.
2. The formation of a lesbian identity is a developmental process.
3. The time required to complete an identity process varies (assuming it can every really be considered complete).
4. Social interaction, both homosexual and heterosexual, is important to the identity formation process.
5. It is not possible to resolve the identity problem to the mutual satisfaction of society and the individual.

As our culture's attitudes toward homosexuality improve and reflect more tolerance of human diversity, the identity formation process also will change. As this happens, resolving a lesbian identity will become a less formidable task.

6

LESBIAN RELATIONSHIPS

Many similarities exist between lesbian relationships and heterosexual relationships. However, differences also exist that must be taken into account in both couples therapy and individual therapy with lesbian clients. These differences are many, but it can be useful to view them as arising from just two main sources: one is the lack of support and recognition of the lesbian relationship as a valid entity; the other is the fact that two women make up the couple, and that each brings with her the psychological dynamics of her gender. With this simple pair of sources, the therapist can evaluate most issues that lesbian relationships present.

This chapter begins with a brief overview of some of the factors of relationship quality in lesbian relationships as compared with heterosexual relationships. Attention is then turned to those issues that are seen as unique to lesbian relationships and that emerge from the two main sources noted above. These include issues of separation-individuation, socialization as women, power and equality, stigmatization, and lack of external validation. Finally, the focus turns to the therapist's tasks in working with lesbians as couples and in working with a lesbian client in individual therapy when the relationship is at issue.

RELATIONSHIP QUALITY FACTORS IN LESBIAN RELATIONSHIPS AS COMPARED WITH OTHER RELATIONSHIPS

Just as people in opposite-sex relationships do, people in lesbian relationships have to struggle with making a living, decide whether one or both work outside the home, plan vacations and holidays, and decide where to live. All couples may struggle with differences in religious or socioeconomic backgrounds, deal with illness, make decisions about children, cope with aging parents, and make choices about friends, social activities, and finances. Perhaps most important, all couples struggle with how to be intimate enough and yet separate enough to keep a healthy balance between attachment and autonomy. Yet the differences between lesbian relationships and other relationships are also salient.

The similarities and differences between same-sex and opposite-sex relationships have received little attention from researchers to date, but the literature is now beginning to report a few studies in this area. The large-scale studies of Blumstein and Schwartz (1983) and Bell and Weinberg (1978) are discussed in Chapter 1, both of which showed that the diversity of all relationships is enormous, that the similarities between same-sex and opposite-sex relationships were greater than had been thought, and that many of the differences that were found were related to the stigmatized identity of a same-sex relationship and its composition of two same-sex people.

A direct comparison of lesbian couples and heterosexual couples was reported by Schneider in 1986. She studied three factors of relationship quality—durability, interdependence, and equality—in 10 cohabiting lesbian couples and 10 cohabiting heterosexual couples. Her data showed significant similarities in most of the subfactors that went into the three main factors, and differences in a few. For example, the durability factor was measured by three subfactors—length of time cohabiting, importance to the individual that the relationship be permanent, and perceived likelihood that the couple would remain together in the future. The couples differed on the first and third subfactors; the heterosexuals had been living together longer and expressed greater confidence that their relationships would continue into the future (M = 4.76 on a scale of 1 [no confidence] to 5 [very confident]) as compared with the lesbians (M = 4.22). It is important to note that both groups did express a high degree of optimism despite the statistically significant difference (note the closeness of the Means). The interdependence factor was measured by 13 subfactors, such as recreational time spent apart and together, importance of monogamy, several legal and financial matters, joint purchase decisions, willingness to relocate for a partner's career, and perception of themselves as a family. The couples differed on only three of these subfactors: banking practices, wills, and life insurance arrangements. The third factor, equality, was measured by three subfactors: (1) division of labor for household chores; (2) division of cost for joint purchases, recreational expenditures, and household expenses; and (3) degree of influence in decision making. The couples differed only on the matter of household chores, with the lesbian couples dividing the chores more equally than the heterosexual couples. Also, when the chores were not divided evenly, the lesbian couples divided chores by personal preference, whereas the heterosexual couples divided chores more often by traditional gender roles. Schneider concludes that the lesbian relationships tend to be slightly less durable and less interdependent, but more equal.

In a study of relationship quality using a larger sample, Kurdek and Schmitt (1986) chose a different set of factors to measure: (1) love for one's partner, which tapped affiliative needs, dependence, predisposition to help the other, absorption, and exclusiveness; (2) liking of one's partner, which tapped favorable evaluation and respect and perceived similarity between self and partner; and (3) relationship satisfaction, which tapped agreement in dyadic matters, satisfaction with sexual and affectional relations, degree of tension, frequency of considering ending the relationship, activities shared, and favorable attitude toward the relationship. The researchers studied 44 married, 35 heterosexual cohabiting, 50 gay male, and 56 lesbian couples. Results indicated that cohabiting heterosexual partners had the lowest scores on all three measures, whereas the scores of the other three types of couples—lesbians, gays, and married heterosexuals—did not differ from each other.

Peplau, Pedesky, and Hamilton (1982) studied factors that were associated with relationship satisfaction in 127 lesbians, without making comparisons with other types of couples. Their data showed that lesbians reported a high level of relationship satisfaction, closeness, love, and liking. Further, higher satisfaction was associated with two factors: equal involvement and commitment in the relationship, and equal power in decision making. A less strong association was found between relationship satisfaction and perceived similarity of the partner; this is in contrast to research on attraction in heterosexual couples, where partner similarity has been found to be one of the strongest factors associated with relationship satisfaction.

In a study of 23 lesbians, Vetere (1982) made note of the role that friendship plays in the development of early lesbian relationships and in the continuation of present ones. She found that for 78% of her subjects, their first love relationship with another woman grew out of a friendship with her. Seventy-eight percent also reported that they were friends with their current lover before they became lovers. Only two of these reported that the friendship feelings interfered with their romantic feelings toward their partner; the rest said that it enhanced their romantic feelings. This study clearly suggests that for lesbians, friendship is a strong factor in initiating and maintaining relationships and that lesbian couples can be best friends and lovers at the same time.

Overall, these studies show strong trends in some relationship issues for lesbians. Relationship satisfaction is reported to be high, along with closeness, love for partner, and liking of partner. Durability is on the low side, a matter that is often seen as an indicator of pathology of the relationship, although no evidence exists to support this interpretation; I believe it is a misguided notion that longer relationships are better relationships. Friendship is a major factor in both developing and maintaining most lesbian relationships. And, finally, the equality of lesbian relationships is seen as very high and is seen as a dominant factor in relationship satisfaction.

CHARACTERISTICS OF LESBIAN RELATIONSHIPS

The literature on lesbian relationships describes several themes of difference between the lesbian couple and other couples. These themes are divided here into five categories: (1) issues of merger and separation-individuation, (2) the effects of socialization as women, (3) issues of power and equality, (4) issues arising from living with a stigmatized identity in a nonsupportive environment, and (5) other issues that have received less attention in the literature, such as children, sex, family of origin, lack of gender roles, and differences between the partners in the degree of coming out. These are each addressed in turn.

Merger and Separation-Individuation

Beginning with the works of Peplau, Cochran, Rook, and Pedesky (1978) on attachment and autonomy in lesbian relationships and of Krestan and Bepko (1980) on fusion in lesbian relationships, a significant number of clinicians have focused on the issue of merger in lesbian relationships (Burch, 1985, 1986; Lindenbaum, 1985; Eichenbaum & Orbach, 1983; and Kaufman, Harrison, & Hyde, 1984, among others). Merger (also called fusion) is seen as the tendency for two people to be as close together as physically and psychically possible. The concept is based on the work of Mahler (1975), who described the psychological process whereby an infant moves from its early symbiotic state with its mother or caretaker through stages of increasing awareness of itself as a distinct and separate individual. This process is termed "separation-individuation" and is thought to occur in the first three years of life. In psychodynamic theory, it is considered to be a critical aspect of ego development. The opposite of separation-individuation is merger or fusion.

The more recent works of Chodorow (1978) and Gilligan (1982) have expanded on Mahler's work and have proposed that the process of separation-individuation occurs differently for young girls than it does for young boys. Chodorow and Gilligan state that a boy's task is to individuate from an opposite-sex parent, his mother, which is an easier task than the girl's individuation from a same-sex parent. This will cause a more diffuse individuation process for girls than for boys. The fact that a mother will identify more with a daughter than with a son, because the daughter is female like herself, will also cause the daughter to have a more complex and prolonged state of merger than a son. A boy, then, will develop his sense of self in terms of *separateness from others*, whereas a girl will develop her sense of self in *relationship to others*. The sense of herself as a separate person is less rigid and her boundaries are less firm. She sees her worth in relation to caring for others, and her capacities for empathy and intuition are enhanced.

Given these theories, we can speculate how a relationship between two women may have different dynamics than a relationship between a man and a woman or one between two men. In a lesbian relationship, both partners have a strong capacity for identification in relationship with less psychic boundary between them than is true of a man and a woman, in which the woman often provides the relational capacity and the man provides the boundaries or separateness. Merger thus is thought to occur more easily in lesbian relationships. Whereas lesbians appear to be prone to too much merger, gay male relationships appear to be prone to too much autonomy and nonintimacy (Krestan & Bepko, 1980; Elsie, 1986). Thus, both lesbian and gay relationships seem to embody the prime characteristics of the separation-individuation process for each gender. Socialization as a female or male continues throughout one's life, thus these dynamics are repeatedly reinforced.

The difficulties that can arise from too much merger in a lesbian relationship are many (Burch, 1985; Kaufman, Harrison, & Hyde, 1984). Some couples will recognize it and name it to their therapist, saying that they feel too close or trapped. Some couples show confusion about their individual feelings and, in some cases, even about their identities, because the partners do not see themselves as separate from each other and hold an unconscious expectation that they should always feel the same way as each other. On the other hand, the couple may find that they take opposite stands on everything, thus becoming two opposite parts of one whole. Lack of conflict or the opposite, a great deal of conflict, may also suggest fusion or an attempt to reduce it. An outside sexual affair or a lack of sexual expression in the relationship can also signal merger. An overall lack of differentiation of each partner's emotional, territorial, temporal, or cognitive space is the hallmark of merger.

Often, couples describe themselves as going through a cyclic pattern of closeness and distancing that can eventually lead to breakup of the relationship because the couple is unable to find any other solution to their needed autonomy. Lindenbaum (1985) describes this cyclic pattern as beginning with the lesbian couple's initial enjoyment of merging and "primal intimacy" that comes quickly and passionately early in the relationship. The merging occurs both sexually and nonsexually, and eventually, a tremendous fear of the loss of self may evolve. The couple commonly sacrifices sex as a way of compensating for the loss of self, which creates some of the needed separateness. Sex is easily sacrificed because the pain of loss of self is great and because the couple has heard time after time that it is wrong to love a woman. Merger continues, however, in nonsexual ways, especially by maintaining oneness in such areas as feelings, opinions, values, interests, and time spent together. A fear of differentiation predominates that comes out of the continued need for merger, and any felt differences are seen as a threat to mutuality. However, merger continues in these nonsexual ways, a loss of self as a separate individual also continues. The pain of merger, and the pain of difference, can become too much to handle, and the couple arrives at the conclusion that the only way to solve the dilemma is to end the relationship, which provides the needed distance. As Lindenbaum says, "The women separate 'in the name of difference,' but the relationship ends precisely because so few real differences have been allowed to exist" (p. 97).

A variety of causes for merger in lesbian relationships have been suggested in addition to the psychodynamic explanation of the development of separation-individuation. For example, Krestan and Bepko (1980) give a comprehensive list of contributing factors to fusion:

- lack of support for the relationship from the outside world;
- pressures to come out and limitations on full participation in social situations in the outside world;
- lack of recognition of the relationship by the partners' families of origin;
- lack of sanction for mourning the losses brought on by coming out that are looked upon by society as simply the deserved consequences of deviant behavior;
- women's socialization to deny the self in relationships; and
- the enmeshment of the lesbian community itself that is caused by the closed nature of the system.

All of these factors may cause the couple to turn inward onto itself for protection and solace, thus contributing to too much merger.

Although all of these suggested causes have some validity, Elsie (1986) argues that the most important of all causes is women's sex-role socialization, which emerges from the dynamics of the childhood separation-individuation process. Thus, Elsie says, merger is a gender issue and not a homosexuality issue.

It is important to keep in mind two things: one is that overmerger patterns will not occur in every lesbian relationship; the other is that merger in itself is not pathological. Chodorow (1978) points out that the female's more permeable boundaries are both an asset (an ability to relate) and a liability (a difficulty with autonomy). Many lesbians consider the capacity to merge in their relationships as one of the best aspects of loving another woman. Elsie (1986) also believes that merging is not necessarily dysfunctional and that it is a healthy aspect of any relationship, and therefore a special strength of lesbian relationships. Mature intimacy, Lindenbaum (1985) says, "requires that the partners move comfortably between more merged and more differentiated relational positions" (p. 87).

Burch (1985) notes that in our culture, separateness and maturity are seen as synonymous, but that given the works of Chodorow (1978) and Gilligan (1982) just described, it can be seen that this notion is a male-oriented value—males move toward and value separateness, whereas females move toward and value relationships. Burch states, "Under the conditions of patriarchy, the needs of women are pushed aside. The predominantly female capacities for relatedness, emotional attunement, and nurturance are devalued" (pp. 102–103). It follows then that a lesbian would feel conflict about her relational capacity, because on one hand, it feels comfortable and easy to be able to relate to another person in such a close fashion because it is the characteristic of the prolonged separation-individuation process for her gender; on the other hand, these relational capacities are devalued by society, and the lesbian is likely to have internalized this evaluation of her capacities and thus be ambivalent about the favorable aspects of them.

Valuing separation over connectedness is not only a male bias, it is also heterosexist bias. It is important that therapists not expect lesbian relationships to mirror relationships that are determined by male values. It is equally important to remember that class differences and cultural differences exist that affect standards of autonomy and merger. As Burch (1986) states,

> The observation that merger is frequently a problem in lesbian relationships is relatively recent; yet it has proved to be so useful that it is already in danger of being overworked. We much remember that merger is a concept, a metaphor, not an empirical reality. . . . Lesbian relationships are often closer than other coupled relationships. This is a natural, even predictable, outcome of women's desire and capacity

for emotional connection. Lesbian relationships will look and feel different from other relationships. Their emotional intensity may be misunderstood or interpreted pathologically if we assume they should reflect the norms of heterosexual relationships. (p. 69)

Effects of Socialization as Women

Further information on the socialization effects of females comes from the literature on moral and psychological development, as do the theories on merger just described. Gilligan (1982), Peplau et al. (1978), and Vargo (1987) are primary contributors here.

The Peplau study examined lesbian couples' attitudes toward "attachment" (defined as needs for intimacy and dependence and orientation toward the other) versus "autonomy" (independence, self-assertion, and drive for self-actualization). These traits are traditionally seen as opposing ends of a continuum, but the couples in this study did not see them as such. Instead, they saw them as two parts of a dynamic balance, which they made efforts to maintain in equilibrium. In Vargo's application of this finding, she notes that this balance between autonomous and intimate behaviors suggests a different inner sense of self than may be true of nonlesbians, a sense of an autonomous self within the assumption of a relationship to others. This may influence the clinician's assessment of the source of dysfunction in some lesbian relationships: "Issues around intimacy and autonomy might be resolved not by lessening one person's attachment or the other's distance in the relationship, but by helping each individual to balance her needs for intimacy and autonomy" (p.167).

Gilligan describes a female process of conflict resolution, again applied to therapy by Vargo. This model describes a typically male mode of conflict resolution as one of applying moral principles to situations in order to produce judgments about right and wrong. In contrast, a female mode of conflict resolution takes into account the particular people involved in the situation and places priority on (1) maintaining the relationship, and (2) assessing the needs and vulnerabilities of the individuals involved and seeking a solution that will do the least to harm those in most need. A woman's own needs can then suffer whenever others in the conflict are perceived as more vulnerable, more deserving, or more in need than the self. Lesbian couples, then, may resolve their conflicts most often by assessing the needs of both individuals, yielding to the most "needy," and maintaining the relationship.

This pattern has definite pros and cons. On the positive side, this style of conflict resolution encourages the couple to stay together during conflicts and to respect both individuals' needs. On the negative side (and this is commonly seen in couples therapy), one or both parties may be too prone to sacrifice her own needs for the other, depending on her perception of each person's needs or on self-esteem. And when one or both parties are not aware of their needs on a conscious level, they are unable to respect each other's position or to maintain a healthy balance of needs. Much of my work with lesbian couples involves bringing the needs behind their behaviors to a conscious level. Vargo (1987) says this well:

> That two women in a relationship may consider their own and the other's interests in maintaining the relationship could well be the result of successful socialization and not indicative of any individual pathology. Therapeutic work on fusion issues with a lesbian couple will look very different if it is based on an understanding of these dynamics common to women, rather than a hypothesis about the individuals' ego weaknesses or hypotheses about communication patterns in the couple. . . . Therapeutic work with these couples must involve recognition of the normal developmental processes in lesbians of balancing needs of self and others and the effects on their relationships. (pp 167 & 172)

Power and Equality

Equality is often mentioned as an asset in lesbian relationships (Schneider, 1986; Blumstein & Schwartz, 1983; Kurdek & Schmitt, 1986). The majority of lesbian couples appear to make an effort to share their resources as equally as possible, share household chores equally, share decision making equally, and share living expenses and recreational expenses either equally or according to an individually designed system that takes each partner's income into account. Lesbian relationships are sometimes viewed as embodying the feminist ideal of equality in relationships.

Although this equality is a definite asset, the other side of the coin is power, and power is a concept that fits only uncomfortably into many lesbian relationships. Because the social power ascribed to men in this culture is absent in the lesbian relationship, many lesbians assume that power struggles will not exist in their relationships, and thus have difficulty recognizing them and dealing with them directly. The built-in power differential of male-female relationships (where the man is likely to have higher earning potential, access to networks for career support, and decision-making power for the couple) does not exist in lesbian relationships, and women who are unfamiliar with feelings of power can become fearful of its expression in the relationship. Some couples can find themselves in an ever-escalating cyclic competition as each partner tries to maintain at least equal footing with the other. Partners may be disillusioned with each other and angry that the power struggles seen in heterosexual relationships can also exist in their own relationships. This disillusionment is often a topic in therapy (Rothberg & Ubell, 1985; Sharratt & Bern, 1985).

Because many lesbians place high value on egalitarianism, their relationships may be enormously strained when the partners earn widely discrepant incomes or have other discrepancies in access to monetary resources, such as when one partner is in school full time or receives child support payments or an inheritance. Often, the couple will describe this strain in terms of its violation of philosophical equality, but less frequently will they recognize the concomitant disappointment about unmet dependency needs (Roth, 1985). Many lesbians sometimes develop elaborate financial arrangements to avoid monetary power imbalances. Few models exist for managing resources in equal or nontraditional ways that permit both financial pooling and legal protection for each partner, and most lesbians therefore have to meet this challenge individually.

> Azalea and Carmen came to therapy requesting assistance with their frequent conflicts about money. Carmen held a job that paid a considerably higher salary than Azalea's did. Carmen had bought a home in which they both lived, and paid for almost all of the pair's vacations, theatre events, restaurant meals, and household furnishings. Carmen often complained to Azalea that she wanted Azalea to be more appreciative, and Azalea complained that she felt that Carmen didn't understand her feelings of financial entrapment. We worked with this issue in therapy, developing systems for the couple to handle their finances that met their needs better. But for deeper resolve to occur, we had to also address issues of differential power and lack of equality; it was critical for this couple to focus on ways to help each partner feel more understood and respected by the other for each one's position. Carmen and Azalea eventually came to see their situation as "givens" for each partner's available life choices, and they have developed a sincere playfulness about it.

Whether you are seeing a couple or an individual, it can be very useful therapy material to inquire about your lesbian clients' financial arrangements with a partner, about decision-making power, career dominance, financial discrepancies, competitiveness, and dependency. The therapy goal here is to help your clients become able to name their values and needs about these matters and to develop a way to talk about them with each other to work toward a mutually satisfying solution that respects each person's position.

Lack of Support for the Relationship

One of the more prominent features that makes a lesbian relationship different from most heterosexual ones is the lack of support and validation for the relationship itself. Krestan and Bepko (1980) hypothesize that when a lesbian pair attempts to define its own validity and boundaries, it is usually met with either the absence of response from others or a response that communicates a negative or illegitimate status for the relationship. The pair often counterresponds by making its boundaries more rigid, which contributes to fusion within the couple. The couple may spend excessive amounts of energy on defining their boundaries in order to maintain relatedness in the face of countervailing forces; because no outside force, such as a socially and legally sanctioned marriage, exists to encourage the couple to stay together, the commitment to stay together is generated entirely from within the couple. This can be exhausting. Any attempts at individuated behavior within the relationship may thereby tip the balance toward dissolution.

If the lesbian couple is viewed as a subsystem functioning within the larger system consisting of co-workers, family of origin, and friends, it becomes clear that a model of satisfying relatedness must involve the formation by both the couple and the larger system of boundaries that are clear, respected, and flexible (Decker, 1983–84). This rarely occurs for lesbian relationships. It becomes difficult for the partners to retain their unique identities and at the same time keep the outer boundaries well delineated, so that clear lines become hard to draw between the partners and their children or parents or friends.

The lesbian couple has no marker events that define changes in status from dating to "going steady," to intention to become a couple, to making a commitment to couplehood. Lesbians have no marriage ceremony, which would legitimize the relationship legally, socially, and sometimes religiously. A marriage for heterosexuals legitimizes the boundaries of the relationship, declares public expectation of continuance of the relationship into the future, and assists young adults in separating and differentiating from their families of origin. Lesbians instead experience invalidating responses from others, such as when others choose to ignore the relationship, render it invisible, or disqualify it as not genuine, or when they see it as a phase, or as evidence of pathology.

Lesbians also experience more direct forms of invasion of the relationship boundary. These can include a failure to invite the partner to family holidays or functions, giving the partners separate rooms during visits to families of origin, depriving a partner of decision making during a time of illness, and denying partners legal protection in mutual ownership of property or in survivorship unless the couple takes special legal actions. (More and more lesbian couples are making durable powers of attorney to address some of these problems, in those states that recognize these documents.) These bond-invalidating activities may motivate couples to seek therapy early in their relationship, when it is possible that what the couple needs most from the therapist is not so much deep therapy work as just a witnessing and validation of their coming together, a function that no rabbi, minister, judge, nor priest has done for them (Roth, 1985).

To counter some of these invalidating forces, many lesbians create their own marker events. Some actually marry, within those religions that honor lesbian relationships as valid, although such marriages are not recognized legally in the United States at this time. Others create a ceremony to celebrate their commitment and invite friends and sometimes family. Some choose to have a private ceremony. Many lesbian couples take an important date in their relationship as their anniversary date and celebrate it yearly. The more the couple is out about their lesbianism, the more options they have in finding ways to validate their relationship externally. The therapist can encourage couples to find ways to validate their relationship that have meaning for them.

Other Characteristics of Lesbian Relationships

Lesbian relationships can be different from heterosexual relationships in the following ways: how the family of origin responds, the presence of children, different degrees of being out between the partners, the presence of ex-lovers, lack of gender roles, and breaking up.

The first of these differences, how the family of origin responds to the couple, has already been addressed to some extent in terms of its influence on the degree of support for the relationship. However, the issue is broader than that. In almost any therapy with a lesbian couple, the matter of dealing with families of origin is common (Rothberg & Ubell, 1985). This is often a painful and unresolved matter both for the individual women and for the couple as a pair. A lack of understanding from both partners' parents can create great pain and is often resolved by avoiding contact with the families. A lack of relationship with the families may be the best choice in many cases, but unresolved pain will linger and more pressure will come to bear on the relationship itself to provide a needed sense of family. When a relationship is maintained with families despite lack of acceptance for the relationship, the issue becomes how to manage this uncomfortable state of affairs. It also can be particularly painful if one partner's family is accepting and the other's is not.

Murphy (1989) offers suggestions for the clinician to address the impact of parental reactions to the lesbian relationship. She suggests that the therapist:

1. Always ask about self-disclosure to parents, especially as it affects the couple itself;
2. Focus on the implications of decisions about secrecy and disclosure to parents;
3. Provide specific help and preparation to each member of the couple when one partner decides to come out to her parents;
4. Help the couple grieve over the loss of "heterosexual privilege" in the family of origin;
5. Encourage the couple to challenge the ways the couple tolerates or perpetuates parental homophobia;
6. Help the couple to affirm their couple boundaries during interaction with their parents, whether or not the couple is out;
7. Recognize the need of lesbian couples to build and validate friendship networks; and
8. Review the course of therapy scrupuloulsy to check for signs of homophobia from within the therapist.

The second matter, that of the presence of children in the relationship, also has characteristics unique to lesbian couples (Rothberg & Ubell, 1985). Many lesbians are mothers already when they enter a relationship, and the couple faces all the strains that come with reconstituting a family, such as issues of co-parenting, dealing with ex-husbands or ex-lovers, the children's acceptance of the new lover, and other problems of blended families. The issues will be different when both women are mothers than when only one is a mother. Issues will also vary according to custody arrangements that have been made with other biological or legal parents. The nonmother partner has no models for developing an appropriate level of parental responsibility for her partner's children, a matter that can cause considerable conflict in the relationship; questions arise concerning whether the biological mother should be solely responsible for the children or whether the partner should be involved in parenting too, and to what degree. Also, if the couple breaks up, no guidelines exist for maintaining a relationship between the children and the nonmother partner. Other problems come up when lesbians adopt children or choose to have children either singly or within the couple. In any such arrangement, roles are difficult to develop, and, again, few models exist.

The third factor reflects the fact that the partners in a lesbian couple may be at different levels of being out about their lesbianism. Partners may be at different levels in the identity formation process (as is described in Chapter 5) or one partner may have decided on a different degree of being out than her lover. These variables can cause enormous tension in the relationship. Some women can be in a relationship with a woman for many years and never self-identify as a lesbian. In such a case, the individual identity issues enter the heart of the relationship if a deepening sense of commitment is felt. When the partners are moving according to their own timetables of developing a lesbian identity at different rates, the "slower" movement of one partner may be experienced by the other as a devaluation of the relationship or as a rejection or lack of commitment. At the same time, the "faster" movement by one may be perceived by the other as threatening to her own sense of self and her safety from stigma and ostracism. Any time that movement occurs in either partner, upheavals will be felt in the relationship.

When these matters are at issue in therapy, it is important for the therapist to work through with the clients the fact that whatever choices each partner makes will result in loss: they can end the relationship to reconcile their differences over the identity issue; the "less out" partner can declare her lesbian identity and experience all the loss that accompanies that declaration; or they can both remain less out than the more forward moving partner desires, which results in the loss of being more fully known by important others and in personal grief for the partner who wants to be more out (Roth, 1985). Nevertheless, many couples do find a comfortable balance.

Friendships with women present another factor that can affect lesbian relationships differently than nonlesbian ones. In a lesbian relationship, every woman could be a potential lover, whereas in heterosexual relationships, friends of one's own gender are not only unthreatening, but expected and healthy. Also, in heterosexual relationships, women friends can embrace, touch, and regard each other warmly without such behavior having romantic implications; when lesbians are affectionate with their nonlover women friends, boundaries for each relationship may become hazy—lover versus friend (Sang, 1984). Further, a great many lesbian relationships begin as nonlover friendships, increasing the threat that what is now a friendship may have the potential of damaging the couple relationship farther down the road. It is important for lesbians to have women friends in addition to their lover, and the therapist may be called upon to encourage this and to help define boundaries, behaviors, and values about monogamy.

> Dana described behavior she had witnessed on the parts of her lover Peaches and Peaches' ex-lover, which she defined as threatening. Dana had seen them engaging in long kisses and caresses of eroge-nous areas. Peaches saw these gestures as affection and insisted that Dana had nothing about which to be threatened. In treatment, we took the focus off of whose definition of the behavior was correct, and worked instead on helping the partners hear each other's concerns and respect each other's needs.

The lack of gender roles, another factor of special importance in lesbian relationships, is both an asset and a liability. As an asset, the absence of pre-determined roles that each partner is to play allows couples to define and decide their own roles and tasks in the relationship, which can be done creatively and in accordance with the preferences of the individuals. From this standpoint, the lack of predefined roles can be experienced as very lib-erating. On the other hand, it can be experienced as confusing or over-whelming. Difficulties can arise when the partners have different interpretations of what constitutes an appropriate and desirable interaction. Often any ideas that the partners hold about how this should be done are left unspoken, resulting in confused disappointment when one's expecta-tions are not met by the other. Also, because this is uncharted territory for many couples, there is a tendency for romantic ideals to prevail, which may again lead to disappointment (Decker, 1983–84). And finally, the task of each couple's developing its own guidelines can be exhausting. As a client of mine once said, "I'm so tired making every little decision about how we live; won't someone please draw us a map?" The recent books on lesbian relationships, listed in Appendix B, have provided help with such "map-making."

The final characteristic, breaking up a relationship, is also a matter with aspects that are fairly unique to lesbians. Some of the factors that can encourage a relationship to break up were addressed in the discussion of the lack of support for lesbian relationships and in the discussion of the dif-ficulties in managing merger. Some relationships break up early; others may hold on past the point of mutual satisfaction. There are many reasons for this holding on, but one of the most common is that women experience the act of breaking up a relationship as a violation of the female ethic to care for others, and as a violation of the social injunction to nurture and work at a relationship. Others stay in relationships in order to prove wrong the view that lesbian relationships do not last. Couples may also stay together out of recognition of the difficulties in finding another partner in a limited and largely invisible population.

When a lesbian couple has been co-parenting, the decision to separate may be complicated by the lack of legal protection of the parenting bond for the noncustodial parent. Couples sometimes seek therapy at the time of a breakup to establish a climate for negotiating visitation arrangements and property distribution. If the relationship was a secret, the partners are denied the aid and comfort that is usually available to heterosexuals, and the therapist may perform the essential function of bearing witness to the loss. In the lesbian community it is common for former partners to become friends after the immediate pain of the breakup has subsided; this offers opportunities for continuity and connection that are very valuable, but it also provides opportunities for triangulation of a former lover into a new relationship that can be difficult to manage (Roth, 1985), or for incomplete separation so that neither individual is completely emotionally available for a new relationship.

The therapeutic tasks in all of these situations are diverse. In establishing those tasks, and a treatment plan, I find it useful to do two things. First I review the issues discussed above to arrive at an assessment of what are the most salient dynamics to address. Then I discuss this assessment with my client(s) and reformulate according to the response. I am often awed by the fact that after such a presentation, even when the dynamics I assess are quite unconscious, the client seems to "resonate" to those aspects, conscious or not, that have relevance to her. This establishes our goals.

THE THERAPIST'S TASKS IN WORKING WITH RELATIONSHIPS

Most of the writers who have discussed the notion of merger in lesbian relationships are clinicians, and their writings include suggestions and guidelines for the therapist, which I summarize here. Kaufman, Harrison, and Hyde (1984), for example, list some clinical indicators of the lesbian couple that is struggling with issues of merger. Here are some signs you can look for:

1. The couple attempts to share all recreational activities with one another and do everything together;

2. Social activities and contacts are limited only to those they share;
3. Each is isolated from individual personal friends, and neither has a best friend unless that person is shared by both;
4. They are isolated from friends in the lesbian community;
5. They share professional service providers such as physicians, dentists, or therapists;
6. They often have the same employer, and, if not, regular telephone intrusions into the workday link the dyad during business hours;
7. Contracts for space and possessions are nonexistent, and there is no separate drawer space, individual clothing, or chair of one's own, and no clarity regarding shared and separate money; and
8. Communication patterns often include attempted mind reading and assumptions about the other's needs or wants, and behaviors directed at meeting imagined needs or wants; sentences started by one partner may be completed by the other.

The authors point out that many of these behaviors are reinforced by cultural descriptions of idealized romance, the isolation of the lesbian couple, female socialization, and the scarcity of role models.

Therapist intervention is directed toward helping clients create more "space" and separateness by such methods as teaching assertiveness skills, acting as a role model, encouraging individual evaluation of personal space needs, and suggesting referrals to organizations or resources where the couple can meet other successful pairs. Kaufman, Harrison, and Hyde continue their description of the therapist's tasks by describing six areas of the relationship where space needs should be evaluated:

1. *Territorial space.* For example, a room of one's own, separate places for personal belongings, one's own chair, clothing that is not shared, or an established side of the bed.
2. *Temporal space.* This includes spending time together but doing different activities, time spent with separate friends, and time spent separately on vacations, business trips, or weekends away or alone.
3. *Financial space.* Separate money and accounts, legal agreements to manage major assets, and making contributions to a common household management account.
4. *Cognitive space.* Interests, reading material, and ideas of one's own, and support for unshared fantasies and secrets.
5. *Emotional space.* Recognition of feelings and desires of one's own, and a therapist of one's own.
6. *Environmental space.* Promotion of social networks, reduction of iso-

lation, increasing exposure to role models, and separate hobbies and activities.

Naturally, these recommendations will have to be tailored to your client's personal tastes and abilities. Also, sex role socialization predicts that fusion will be problematic for many women, and therefore for many lesbians, but this is certainly not universal. The personality traits of some individuals may not fit this pattern at all, which you will have to assess. Although most may need to be taught some autonomy skills, others may need to learn more intimacy skills. Remember, it's a balance between autonomy and intimacy you are working toward, not simply the elimination of either fusion or independence.

Lindenbaum (1985) also makes a strong argument for helping partners in the overmerged couple to find their separate selves. She recommends instilling the relationship with some healthy competition between the partners to accomplish this. She does not suggest that the therapist promote envy or disrespect, wherein one partner gains something at the expense of the other, but she does suggest the encouragement of a kind of competition whereby both partners win something, and the competition is experienced by the couple as a form of relating. Examples include having a contest to see which partner can compliment the other most often, or who can arrange the best "date" for the other, or being cheerleaders for each other to help each partner achieve a desired goal in an individual hobby or sport. In this process, Lindenbaum reminds the therapist that creating this separation is not an easy task, and that time must be spent working through clients' resistances and deep fears of separation.

Burch (1985, 1986) recommends that the therapist be female for individual clients, which will allow the merger dynamic to develop in therapy. The therapist must be able to let merger occur between her and the client, and to tolerate the client's fears as she goes back and forth between merger and separation feelings. This therapy work will stir the therapist's own related issues, sometimes very deeply.

Burch also notes that in couples therapy, the therapist often will see the partners playing the opposite sides of the polarity. One plays the more merged role, the other plays the separated role. The more separate partner says she would change her role if only her lover would begin acting more separate. This is not an issue of individual pathology in many cases, but a dynamic balance of the relationship. The therapist's task is not to establish a permanently separated state between the partners, but to help them understand the process and its underlying meaning for them individually.

Both partners must come to accept their own passivity and dependence as well as recognize their needs for autonomy. Exploring either of the polarities of separateness or merger will engender fears of both abandonment and engulfment; they are opposite aspects of the same experience. These fears of engulfment and fears of abandonment are not necessarily signs of pathological disturbance or borderline states, as might be suggested, but again they are the dynamics of female socialization and ego development. Burch (1985) says,

> Merger is not destructive per se; only when a relationship is fixated in merger has the process gone awry. For women, connectedness to others is an important part of the sense of self. Therapy requires facilitating the ongoing process of merger and separation, both of which will continue to recur at their own pace. The task is finding one's self in all phases of this process, both in connection with the other and in separateness, alone with oneself. (p. 108)

Further recommendations from Burch (1986) include the following. She says the work of the therapist is to help the individuals differentiate, given their diffuse internal and external boundaries. At the same time, the therapist must recognize the boundary around the relationship and help the couple get outside recognition where needed. The therapist then serves two functions, one in helping the couple move toward identifying the sources of the external strain for the relationship and altering some of them, and the other in mirroring back to the couple the legitimacy of their relationship, which is denied in other places. During the initial exploration and assessment, the therapist is communicating what may be new information: that emotional distance can be a very good thing. The therapist can help the clients at this point to perceive the strength of their pull toward union, while underscoring that unity is not always important and that it is essential to be able to disagree. The therapist can discuss and support differences in feelings, values, and opinions, and observe for the clients the nature of the contact boundaries between them when disagreement occurs. Role reversal is sometimes beneficial for the couple. Also, the therapist can help each woman set limits, say no, and listen to the difficult feelings of her partner without attempting to take care of these feelings or change her own. This sort of psychological boundary separation is fundamental to the success of many relationships.

McCandlish (1982) offers a few additional notes for therapists. She reminds traditionally trained therapists who have not experienced lesbian relationships themselves to guard against the tendency to view a lesbian client's closeness to her partner as pathological or immature. Likewise, a feminist therapist might have to guard against idealizing or romanticizing the couple's embodiment of some feminist ideals, such as closeness and egalitarianism. Lesbian therapists themselves might also be on guard for tendencies to overidentify with the couple or become invested in the therapy outcome. The therapist might also have to be careful not to attribute all of the couple's problems to homophobia and its resulting self-hatred, and remain able to assess how the couple may perpetuate their own difficulties. McCandlish reminds therapists that:

> obviously, the therapist's attitude towards the lesbian couple's difficulties in maintaining separateness greatly affects the success of therapy. Traditional therapists see these difficulties as indicative of intrapsychic problems. Yet, to a great extent these issues are characteristic of normal lesbian relationships. (p. 78)

It is important to point out that all of the authors who are writing about merger in lesbian relationships are seeing a client population, and their view may be influenced by this fact. This is not to say that lesbian merger is not indeed a describable phenomenon, but that its apparent high degree of occurrence may be a product of seeing it in client populations.

Regardless of the specific issues a lesbian couple brings to therapy, many couples may find it useful to view their relationship strengths and weaknesses in a framework of relationship stages. Clunis and Green (1988) describe a six-stage model of lesbian relationships that can provide a rough map for couples experiencing turmoil or who need a "vision."

1. *Prerelationship Stage*—the "getting to know you" stage
2. *Romance Stage*—the time of greatest merger, of putting one's best foot forward, of neglecting friends and autonomy needs
3. *Conflict Stage*—differences in temperament, values, or goals surface; conflict resolution skills are needed; a common breakup time
4. *Acceptance Stage*—a time of stability, deep affection, and respect for differences; merger and separateness find a balance
5. *Commitment Stage*—the relationship is seen as dynamic and changing; contradictions become challenges rather than threats; each takes responsibility for her own needs and choices
6. *Collaboration Stage*—focusing on something bigger than the couple to share with the world, such as a political achievement, a shared dream for business or home, or raising children

A therapist may find that some couples can use the concept of stages to help them through hard times, to give them a focus for the present that is less overwhelming than the common urge to "make everything perfect immediately," and as a guide for deciding about the viability of the relationship.

Several books have been published in recent years that make good bibliotherapy for your clients. These include *Lesbian Couples* by Clunis and Green (1988), *Permanent Partners* by Berzon (1988), *Gay Relationships* by Tessina (1989), *Unbroken Ties: Lesbian Ex-Lovers* by Becker (1988), and *Lesbian Passion: Loving Ourselves and Each Other* by Loulan (1987). These volumes are described in Appendix B.

7

SPECIAL ISSUES

This chapter discusses six special topics relevant to psychotherapy with lesbians: lesbian mothers, lesbians of color, sexuality and sexual dysfunction, alcohol and drug use, youth and aging, and effects of the AIDS epidemic. Only a small body of literature is yet available on each of these topics, and working with most of these issues requires specialized training for the therapist. However, they are important topics to any clinician who wants to understand the many facets of lesbian life.

LESBIAN MOTHERS

A substantial percentage of lesbians are mothers. They became mothers for a variety of reasons. Many were unaware of their lesbian feelings until after they had married and had children. Others suppressed their lesbian feelings and hoped that marriage and children would dissuade them, but found they were dissuaded only temporarily. Others consciously rejected their lesbianism in favor of the more respectable roles of wife and mother. Still others chose motherhood after they were aware of their lesbian feelings, either with the help of a male (willingly or unknowingly) or with assisted insemination. Kirkpatrick, Smith, and Roy (1981) found that the desire to have children is no different between lesbians and heterosexual women. However, it is speculated that lesbians may actually have fewer children as a group than do heterosexual women (Rothblum, 1989).

The Wyers (1987) study of 34 formerly married lesbian mothers indicated that the three most common reasons lesbians give for marrying are personal and social expectation that they should marry, love for the spouse, and pregnancy.

Bell and Weinberg's (1978) study indicated that between one-third and one-half of all lesbians were married at one time and that approximately 50% of these marriages produced children. Studies have yielded estimates of between 200,000 and 3 million lesbian mothers in the United States

(Kirkpatrick, 1987). Further, most studies show strong similarities between lesbian mothers and single heterosexual mothers.

Lesbians experience all the joys of child raising that nonlesbians do. However, when a woman identifies as a lesbian (to whatever degree) and is also a mother, she is faced with a significant number of questions and stresses. Should she stay in a heterosexual marriage or obtain a divorce? Should she remain single to prevent stigmatization of herself and her children, or should she establish a lesbian relationship? How should a lesbian partner be introduced into the family unit, if at all? How much of a co-parent should a partner be? How much should the children be told? Do the children need a male role model?

The lesbian mother has few places to turn for help in answering these questions. Support for lesbian motherhood is not forthcoming from the heterosexual society at large, and sometimes it is not available from the lesbian community either, where women who have no children may prefer not to be involved with someone else's children. Lack of role models and lack of support take their psychological toll. Many cities now have various support groups for lesbians with children and for their partners, and several books are now available that speak to these issues for lesbian mothers (see Appendix B).

An abundance of myths places pressure on the lesbian mother and can make her question her capability as a mother (Moses & Hawkins, 1982; Loulan, 1986b). There is the myth that the children of gays and lesbians will also be gay or lesbian, although no evidence exists to support this notion. There are myths about skewing the child's gender development and about the supposed damages of growing up in a "deviant" home where the children may be harassed by peers who know of the children's lesbian mother. It is often true that children of known gay parents are ridiculed by peers, but the same is true of children who come from other "deviant" homes—mixed-racial parents, poor Appalachian parents, divorced parents, or parents with physical impairments or differences—and this is hardly considered a reason to remove a child from the parental home (Moses & Hawkins, 1982). There are myths that lesbians and gays molest children, despite evidence that over 95% of reported child molestation is perpetrated by heterosexual males, and that gays and lesbians are as careful about sexual indiscretion in the home as are nongays (Moses & Hawkins, 1982). And there are myths about the "dire" effects of the mother's coming out, although Lewis (1980) found that children express more difficulty with their parents' divorces than with their mother's lesbianism. These myths can affect the lesbian mother by making her feel inadequate as a parent, even though the problems of lesbian motherhood are not inherent to the individual mother but rather to society's reaction to her.

Custody is also a looming issue. In many courts across the United States, mothers who are found to be lesbian are denied custody of their children, or in some cases only allowed custody on the condition that they do not live with a lover. Progress is slowly being made in this arena, as it is in the areas of qualification for adoption, for foster parenting, and for assisted insemination as a single woman, but the threat of loss of custody keeps many lesbian mothers in fear and turmoil. A significant number of lesbians experience the trauma of divorce, the strain of coming out, and a custody battle all at once, which places tremendous strain on their emotional resources, and may be an impetus to bring them into a therapist's office.

For various reasons, some lesbian mothers choose not to keep custody of their children, and they, too, suffer society's indictment that any mother who does not keep her children is a bad mother. In instances where a lesbian couple chooses to have children together (one woman becoming the biological parent), many similar difficulties arise. The family unit is still not legitimized and legal adoption by the nonbiological partner is difficult.

Wyers (1987) studied 34 formerly married lesbians who had children, and found that slightly over half (53%) of the children lived with their mothers on a full-time basis or had done so during their younger years. Twenty-four percent of the mothers reported that the custody-determination process had been difficult for them. Nearly all of the children knew about their mother's lesbianism, and they had learned about it at the average age of eight; more than half had been told by their mothers, 30% figured it out for themselves, and 10% were told as a hostile gesture by angry former spouses. Most of these mothers reported that their children's knowledge of the mother's lesbianism had a positive, enhancing effect on the mother-child relationship, and about one-fourth reported a negative impact on the relationship. More than half of the children experienced relationship problems with other people because of their mother's lesbianism, especially censure and ridicule by peers and confusion about how to appropriately discuss their mother's lesbianism with others. The mothers also reported that having children made their own coming-out process complicated and difficult, and that they feared loss of custody of their children. The mothers in this study were also economically disadvantaged compared with gay fathers who were also subjects of the study.

Falk (1989) reviewed most of the literature to date on how lesbian mothers and their children are faring, and concluded the following:

- Lesbian mothers are at least as psychologically healthy as other people in general. There is some correlation between the ability to express her lesbianism and increased psychological health.

- In comparing lesbian mothers with heterosexual mothers, lesbians score higher in traits of self-confidence, dominance, and exhibition. Heterosexual mothers score higher in self-abasement and deference.
- No differences exist between lesbian and nonlesbian mothers in parenting ability or child-raising style, except that lesbians might actually be more child-oriented.
- No differences exist among children of lesbian and nonlesbian mothers in measures of emotional, behavioral, and relationship health. The children are similar in terms of peer-group relationships, popularity, and social adjustment.
- Children themselves believe that the breakup of their parents' marriage was more traumatic than learning of their mother's sexual orientation.
- No differences exist between the children raised in lesbian and nonlesbian homes with respect to their gender identity, sex-role behavior, sexual orientation, or sexual identity.

Loulan (1986b) reviews the literature on lesbian motherhood, and concludes that lesbian mothers share most of the same concerns that nonlesbian mothers do. Lesbian and nonlesbian mothers have similar reactions to child-rearing events, use similar systems of support from extended families, encourage similar types of sex-role behavior from children, share similar expectations of their children, and show similar knowledge or ignorance about child raising.

Loulan's review also revealed some of the differences between lesbian and nonlesbian mothers. Lesbians are more concerned about providing male figures for their children, are far more concerned about loss of custody, live in a lower socioeconomic stratum, and report being significantly affected by discrimination against them because of their lesbianism. Lesbians also must untangle the complications of establishing a lover's role in the parenting process and of managing a relationship (or nonrelationship) with the biological father. Additional studies on the subject show that lesbians have a more congenial relationship with their ex-spouses than nonlesbians do. Also, lesbian mothers are more concerned about providing opportunities for their children to develop good relationships with adult males than are heterosexual mothers (Kirkpatrick, 1987).

Loulan points out that just as a lesbian mother has the same concerns that most other mothers do, she also shares the concerns of most lesbians. She states, "The two roles of lesbian and mother combine, however, to cre-

ate some very special problems. . . . But the single most significant stress
faced by lesbian mothers and their families is the lack of legitimacy given
to the family structure itself" (p. 189). Loulan notes that many lesbian families conceal their family relationships outside the home, which results in
a sense of invisibility to the outside world and a feeling that the home is
the only place where they can safely acknowledge their relationships. This
can create tremendous pressure for each member to act within strictly prescribed behavioral limits that do not threaten the stability of the family—
and because of this, therapists will then be dealing with a family system
that is structurally rigid and closed.

When working with an individual lesbian mother, Loulan (1986b) recommends that a general frame for therapy should be a continual assessment of the relationship among the client's role as a mother, her identity
as a lesbian, and the interactions between these and other aspects of her
character. It is also important to remember that most lesbian families are
also blended families and will have the same assets and strains as other
types of blended families. Therapists must also be alert to the possibility
that when a lesbian client experiences concerns about raising her children
that are common to all mothers, she may be likely to attribute her concerns
to a conflict about her lesbianism. Other clients may discount or deny
interpretations about the effects of their lesbianism on the family dynamics,
for instance, insisting that whether or not one is out to her children is irrelevant to her relationship with them.

Loulan also alerts therapists to common transference problems. Because
the therapist may be one of the only sources of support for the client, a
particularly powerful base exists for the development of intense feelings
toward the therapist. A client whose primary support is her therapist may
be subject to triangulating her relationships with her lover and the therapist; she may project the therapist as a perfect coparent and lover, resulting in disappointment with her "imperfect" actual lover. Dependence and
independence issues may also come to the fore if the client sees her therapist as the perfect, accepting nurturing parent. Countertransferences are
also ripe for the making. It can be easy to find oneself siding either with
or against the mother, or feeling strongly that the mother should be open
with her children about her lesbianism, or feeling irritated by the mother's
relationship with her lover and the coparenting she does or does not allow.
Loulan concludes:

> Of all these considerations which affect the therapist working with
> lesbian mothers, perhaps the greatest form of assistance is the pro-
> vision of general support. Giving the lesbian family a sense of legit-

imacy as a family structure is an immeasurably powerful and important intervention. The client receives this endorsement from very few sources, and its role cannot be overstated in therapy. (p. 201)

Family therapy may be indicated for some lesbian mothers; if the mother is living with a lover, the lover should be part of the therapy. In these cases it is necessary for the clinician to have training in the usual areas for working with families, such as knowledge of child development, knowledge of developmental stages of families, and ability to teach parenting skills. If couples therapy is called for, it is necessary for the therapist to be trained in that specialty as well.

Virtually all of the literature on the subject strongly advocates that lesbian mothers come out to their children, and the sooner the better (e.g., Moses & Hawkins, 1982; Loulan, 1986b; Berzon, 1978). Protecting the children from stigma is the usual reason lesbian mothers give for not doing so, but, as mentioned earlier, many children come from stigmatized homes and that in itself is not a sound reason to remain hidden. The more important issue is helping the children understand with whom they can share this information, how to do it, and how to withstand negative reactions from others. Asking a child to keep a secret from significant others should be weighed very carefully.

Moses and Hawkins (1982) treat this subject very well. They give several arguments for coming out to children. First, trying to keep sexual preference a secret puts a strain on the entire family, both when the mother is sharing living quarters with a lover and when she is frequently absent from the home in order to spend time with a non-live-in lover. Second, attempting to avoid the issue fosters communication problems and confirms the negative impression that children receive about gayness from other sources. Third, if the mother does not bring up the subject, the child may hear it from another source and be too afraid to discuss it with the mother (which the mother has modeled), thus reconfirming negative impressions. Finally, the strain of keeping a secret undoubtedly will result in a constraint in the adults' relationship, possibly leading to resentment of the children.

The role of secrets in the lesbian family may contribute to family dysfunction, and may be reflection of dysfunction in a particular family as well; therapists are called on to help sort this out. Children are often able to understand more than adults think they can, and the unspoken messages they receive can have a long-lasting effect. Honesty may sometimes make life more difficult, but lack of honesty will always take a toll on self-integrity.

LESBIANS OF COLOR

In the literature, lesbians of color are referred to by various terminologies, such as third-world lesbians or minority lesbians, and by particular groups—Black lesbians, Hispanic or Latina lesbians, Native American lesbians, or Asian lesbians, for example. To facilitate understanding and evaluation in therapy, it is often important to consider subgroupings as well, such as whether your client is first, second, or third generation (or more) in the United States, and which country her heritage is most identified with. For example, if she is Hispanic, it can be important to consider whether her cultural roots are Cuban, Mexican, Puerto Rican, Argentinian, and so on.

In psychotherapy with lesbian clients, ethnic or racial influences must be woven into your understanding and assessment of the whole picture of the client's life. This will vary with each client. Some clients will be very identified with or influenced by their cultural roots, and others less so; some may experience a strong degree of attachment to their culture's beliefs about homosexuality, and others may not; some will have grown up exposed to a great deal of cultural heritage, whereas others may be just beginning to discover their roots.

Among Caucasians, it can also prove important to discern the degree of presence of cultural norms, because different European and related cultures have various views on homosexuality. Scandinavians tend to have a different outlook than, say, Sicilians, Slavics, or Germans. In addition, the common religions of each race and each country may have significant impact on the individual client's evaluation of her own homosexuality.

In assessing the effect of culture on your client, a good starting point is to consider that many women of color experience an identity-formation process regarding their culture that has many parallels to the identity-formation process entailed in being lesbian (Epsín, 1987; Chan, 1989). For both one's lesbianism and one's color or culture, an identity-development process occurs that includes embracing a stigmatized or negative identity. This process moves gradually from an often rejected or denied self-image to an identity that has been redefined as positive. People of color will often move through "stages" of acceptance of their culture similar to the stages of coming out as a lesbian described in Chapter 5, moving from self-hatred and negative beliefs to questioning and rejecting the dominant culture's values, to immersion in one's culture, to an integrated concept of one's cultural identity (Atkinson, Morten, & Sue, 1979). You may want to compare this with some of the stage models presented in Chapter 5.

Each person will allot relative importance to the different components of the self—as a woman, as a lesbian, and as a person of her culture. This allotment can change over the life span. It can be helpful for the therapist to evaluate with the client the interaction of her identities by assessing approximately where the client currently stands in the stages of development of both her cultural identity and her lesbian identity. But keep in mind that stage theories are only models, and it is a rare person who fits the stage progression exactly.

There are several others factors to consider that may have an impact on the interplay of lesbianism with culture and race. One is that many cultures consider homosexuality a North American phenomenon, as a "sickness" that can be caught from American culture, and they do not understand that homosexuality exists in approximate equal percentages across all cultures. Native American and lesbian writer Paula Gunn Allen says, "The lesbian is to the American Indian what the Indian is to the Caucasian—invisible" (p. 84). This is true of most racial and ethnic cultures. This belief puts the lesbian in a position of being pitted against both her individual culture and the dominant culture, belonging to neither. One of the most painful decisions for many lesbians of color is whether to remain more identified with their minority culture, where there is less acceptance of homosexuality and they may therefore have to remain closeted, or to identify more with the dominant culture, which is a bit more accepting of homosexuality but where they will lose contact with their culture.

In Epsín's (1987) study of Cuban lesbians, most women chose the second alternative, that is, to be involved in the larger lesbian culture of their cities even though that meant living among people unfamiliar with Latin culture. But this choice was made with great difficulty, with anger and with pain. It is always a painful human experience to have to decide between parts of oneself. When asked what was more important for them, being Cuban or being lesbian, most responded that they were of equal significance. Some women in this study did choose to stay more immersed in their Latin culture, and Epsín concluded that it is not possible to determine that one aspect of their identity is more important to them than the other. As in so many studies of lesbians, the subject pool may be a skewed one, in that it is very hard to reach the lesbian who does not hold lesbianism as a foremost aspect of her identity. This fact further supports Epsín's belief that we cannot determine which aspect of the identity is most important. The therapist's task is to help each individual first identify and articulate for herself the dual identity and its inherent dilemma, and then make these balances and integrations personally.

Chan (1989) conducted a study of 19 Asian lesbians (as well as 16 gay men), similar to Epsín's study. Chan notes that, as in many cultures, in

Asian cultures being lesbian is seen as a rejection of the most important roles for women—those of being a wife and a mother. In addition, the parents are seen by implication to have failed in their role and to have violated the primacy of familial obligation. Chan describes her study outcome:

> These results suggest that, when a choice of identification is required, more respondents identified themselves as lesbian or gay than as Asian American but that others refused to choose because it would mean denying an important part of their identity. It is likely that each person determines for herself or himself, depending upon the stage of identity development she or he is in, whether it is more comfortable to be Asian among lesbians and gay men or lesbian-gay around Asians or whether both are intolerable and she or he must be acknowledged as both Asian and as lesbian or gay by everyone. Because identity development is a fluid, ever-changing process, an individual may choose to identify and ally more closely with being lesbian or gay or Asian American at different times depending on need and situational factors. (p. 18)

More factors to consider in discerning the interplay of lesbianism with an ethnic minority status are outlined in the research of Tremble, Schneider, and Appathurai (1989). They investigated the influence of ethnicity on the relationships of gay and lesbian youth and their families in Canada. The subjects' cultural backgrounds were Asian, Portuguese, Greek, Italian, and Indo-Pakistani. The researchers found that a number of variables may be predictors of culturally based attitudes toward homosexuality, and these include demographics such as rural versus urban experiences, the number of generations in North America, education, degree of assimilation or biculturation, and religion. Further, those subjects who were in the most conflict with their cultures came from cultures where religious beliefs are orthodox, where there exists a strong expectation to reside with the family until marriage, where marriage includes strong expectations to have children, and where gender roles are strongly polarized and stereotyped.

The researchers noted that strong kinship ties, conformity to traditional gender roles, and the personal duty to continue the ancestral line through marriage and procreation are cornerstones of social and family life within these groups. None of these values are very different from prevailing North American attitudes; the difference lies in the strength of adherence to these values and the insular lifestyle that protects the values from external influence.

Many of the young lesbians and gay men in this study expressed pride in their culture, but they usually excluded themselves from cultural activities in order to avoid shaming their families. This alienation had painful consequences. The ethnic communities are not large enough in most cities to sustain a lesbian subculture of their own, and most ethnic lesbians find themselves in a largely White Protestant milieu. There are few role models from their own culture for these youth, and in an effort to integrate their sexual and ethnic identities, they are often left on their own to answer a question such as "What does it mean to be Japanese and lesbian?" Writer Audre Lorde expressed it this way:

> You see, I remember how being young and black and gay and lonely felt. A lot of it was fine, and knowing I had the truth and the light and the key, but a lot of it was purely hell and lonely. There were no mothers, no sisters, no role models as we call them these days. In other words, we had to do it alone, cold turkey, like our sisters and amazons, the riders on the loneliest outposts of the kingdom of Dahomey. (p. 223)

The researchers found further that many gay and lesbian youth are victimized by the stereotypes of their own culture and believe the misconceptions that being gay or lesbian means gender-role reversal, as is promulgated by many cultures. They may go through a phase of extreme cross-gender behavior that distresses and alienates their families and like-culture friends.

Among lesbians, ethnic and racial heritage is often celebrated in the visual and performing arts (and so is physical diversity—many lesbian events are signed for the hearing impaired, provide child care, and are wheelchair accessible), but racism, misunderstandings, and fears persist.

The authors conclude that all other things being equal, youngsters from many ethnic minorities face a greater challenge in being lesbian or gay than do their counterparts in mainstream North America. They suggest the following for service providers:

1. Ethnic background is not a predictable barrier between a lesbian and her parents, even when values, beliefs, and traditions strongly militate against acceptance of lesbianism. Consider each family individually, looking at its strengths and weaknesses, dynamics, functioning patterns in a crisis, communication, and the like in helping your client design her disclosure or her relationship with her parents after disclosure.
2. Help your client cope with family and cultural levels of acceptance

of her homosexuality. Many will achieve only tolerance, not a fully embraced acceptance. This can happen to all lesbians, but special attention should be given to the lesbian of color, whose lack of family acceptance means a possibly more difficult choice between her lesbian self and her ethnic self.

3. Examine with your client the effects of any loss of connection with her culture. Help her find a place where she can feel truly "at home."

4. Recognize that each ethnic group, and the subgroups within each group, must be treated as unique entities. Professionally, it is important to become conversant with the cultural perspective of each client in order to provide effective therapy.

There are still more factors to consider when evaluating the impact of culture and lesbianism. Touch, eye contact, personal space, and forms of greeting between you and your client can have particular meaning in particular cultures. Language can be a barrier, and bilingual therapists are greatly needed. Language usage also requires special attention if the therapist is of a different ethnic background than the client; the therapist may have to discuss with the client the meanings of particular phrases, both as used in English and in terms of the client's native culture. Economic level and its meaning to the individual, educational level, and other markers of achievement in the culture may also bear examination in relation to individual cultural norms. The therapy process itself must also be examined in cross-cultural situations:

> We are accustomed to using standard English in the therapy hour. We use verbal communication primarily. It's usually a 50-minute hour and we stick to that pretty stringently for a lot of practical reasons. It's usually—for most of us—individual-centered more than anything else. There's a lot of ambiguity and lack of structure for the most part. Because of the Western thinking on which psychotherapy is traditionally based, there's a very clear distinction between dealing with emotions, "mental" aspects, versus physical health aspects. And there's a logical cause-and-effect approach; in other words, understanding where I'm at now is a result of an interaction of variables in my history. All of the above generic characteristics of counseling can and do come into direct conflict with different people's various value systems which are not mainstream, and many times aren't even based on values of the Western world. (Bustamante, 1987, pp. 4–5)

In contrast to these Western approaches, in many cultures more focus is placed on the group than on the individual, and a person's life is viewed in relation to the generations that came before and those yet to come. These cultures are more attuned to nonverbal communication, are less rigid about time constraints, and are more accepting of emotional expression. All of these characteristics affect many aspects of the therapeutic environment.

These differences can apply to interracial couples as well, and you may be called upon to help clients understand how racism may manifest itself in the relationship, and how this might affect dynamics, communication, and esteem. As with individual therapy, you will have to know the cultures involved well enough to work with the interracial couple's understanding of why something of concern to one partner may be nonsense to the other, or why what is humorous teasing to one is insulting to the other. Or you may have to sort through differences in attitudes toward money, child raising, commitment, emotional expression, and degree of closetedness (Garcia et al, 1987).

It can be helpful to tell your client about the support groups that exist in larger cities. Some cities have joint support groups representing all lesbians of color, and other cities have groups for specific minority groups, such as Latina lesbian groups or Asian lesbian groups. Still others have groups for specified interracial couples, such as a group for couples where one partner is Black and the other White. Your client may want to contact such a group for support, even if it is located a long distance from her home. Also, although very little has been published on the psychology of color and lesbianism, several books of biography, poetry, and essays on lesbians and color are available; and most of the biographical collections of lesbians' coming-out experiences contain entries from women of color. Some of these are described in Appendix B. To find others, spend some time in a bookstore that carries gay and lesbian literature.

SEXUALITY AND SEXUAL DYSFUNCTION

The various stresses that lesbians experience as a hidden and stigmatized group produce effects in more than just psychological areas; sexual functioning and sexual satisfaction can be affected as well. Most lesbians report being fairly satisfied with their sex lives (Loulan, 1986a and 1987), and that their sexual experiences with women are more satisfying than sexual experiences with men (Moses, 1978). While the majority, then, appears to be satisfied with their sexual activities, a substantial minority has expressed some dissatisfaction with or dysfunction in their sex lives.

Lesbians are no more likely than other women to have suffered rape, sexual molestation, or other traumas that can affect sexual functioning (Loulan, 1986a, 1987). It therefore seems that most sexual dissatisfaction reported by lesbians is probably a result of myths and stigmatization, and the dynamics of being one of a couple composed of two partners who are socialized as females. Also, overidentification with religious or moral beliefs can occasionally play a part.

Although no data are currently available on the incidence and types of sexual dysfunction among lesbians, it is presumed that they are prone to some of the same dysfunctions that nonlesbian women are. These would include anorgasmia, vaginismus, and general dysfunctions related to aversion to specific sexual activities; lack of information; or lack of communication between the partners (Moses & Hawkins, 1982). Lesbians, however, may experience these difficulties in different relative percentages when compared with nonlesbian women. For example, anorgasmia appears to be much less prevalent among lesbians than among nonlesbians (Hite, 1976; Cavin, 1985), and vaginismus among lesbians seems to be quite rare (Moses & Hawkins, 1982; Nichols, 1983). An aversion to oral sex is likely to be more common among lesbians than among nonlesbians, simply because the opportunity to perform oral sex with a woman does not arise in a heterosexual relationship. Also, in our culture, a woman's body is considered less palatable than a man's—a myth with which many lesbians must struggle.

Among those lesbians who express some dissatisfaction with their sexual activity, the most common complaints are a lack of frequency and unequal desire (Blumstein & Schwartz, 1983; Nichols, 1982; Hall, 1987). Studies show consistently that by the second or third year of their relationships lesbian couples engage in genital sexual activity less frequently than do heterosexual or gay male couples.

For example, after two years of being in the relationship, 37% of lesbians in the Blumstein and Schwartz study reported making love at least once a week, compared with 73% of heterosexuals. Loulan's (1987) study showed that during the first year of the relationship, lesbian couples reported making love more than 10 times per month on the average; during years 1 to 3 of the relationship, they make love about five times a month; and from four years on, they make love a little less than once a week. These figures reflect less frequent genital sexual activity among lesbians as compared with nonlesbians, but it is important to remember that many lesbians are quite content with their level of frequency.

Hall (1984, 1987) suggests that sexual infrequency can be a response to distance-regulation problems in the relationship (see Chapter 6 on issues of merger and separation-individuation). Hall says,

There are a number of reasons cited for the plunge in sexual exchanges between lesbians in long-term relationships. Primary among them is a dissolution of the individual boundaries, submergence of self in the larger arena of the relationship. In the beginning, such a commingling of souls is intensely erotic. If each partner does not reclaim herself eventually, however, the relationship becomes stultifying, and the spark of difference that ignites eroticism disappears. (p. 138)

In Loulan's (1986a) survey of 1,361 lesbians, the most common reasons given for sexual dissatisfaction were unwanted celibacy, relationship problems, orgasmic problems, and sexual incompatibility. Loulan's results further indicate that no matter what sexual situation a lesbian is in (single, coupled, or casually involved), all report becoming less satisfied over time and having sex (through either masturbation or partner sex) less frequently the longer they were in their situation. Thus, a reduction in satisfaction with one's sexual situation over time may be a normal, not pathological, phenomenon.

Nichols (1982) also makes the point that since the literature has shown again and again that low sexual frequency is common in lesbian relationships, it is questionable to consider this a dysfunction rather than a normal situation. Nichols' report of 200 lesbians seen in clinical outpatient therapy indicates that low sexual frequency is often the case with couples where other, nonsexual physical affection is abundant; where sex, when it occurs, is good; and where the relationship itself seems loving and considerate. Low frequency also can be associated with a lack of fighting and a taboo on expressing anger in the relationship. Low frequency, it it is really a problem, thus may be less a primary problem than a circumstance that is secondary to other factors in the relationship.

Nichols (1982) further states that it is important for the clinician to make the diagnostic distinction between whether low frequency is being used to avoid intimacy or to escape fusion. Avoiding intimacy may be an unhealthy maneuver, while escaping fusion is a healthy, although misguided, attempt (see Chapter 6 on merger). In either case, however, low sexual frequency should be analyzed to help clients determine its function in the relationship, and whether it is a satisfying and normal state of affairs.

Lesbian couples are subject to the myth that lesbians are supposed to have great sex all the time, and thus may feel inadequate or may refrain from seeking help out of shame for not living up to the myth. Lesbians have average and below-average sexual experiences, just like everyone else, and may need permission to be like everyone else and to create their own sex life to their satisfaction (Moses & Hawkins, 1982; Loulan, 1986a: Califia, 1988). It is also common for lesbians to believe that since both partners are women, they will like the same approaches to love-making and so do not need to communicate their likes and dislikes to each other. When this occurs, it cannot help but lead to some level of dissatisfaction with sex.

Another area where stigmatization can make its mark is where one woman of a couple (or both) is reluctant either to touch her partner sexually or to be touched by her partner sexually. This is often a manifestation of internalized homophobia, and, as Moses and Hawkins (1982) state, is not so much a comment on how much love there is in the relationship, but on how well society is able to indoctrinate people; the reluctance to touch or to be touched stems from an internal belief that "If there's no actual sexual contact, then I don't have to see myself as a lesbian." A woman may believe that if she remains passive and does not actively make love to her partner, then she is not really a lesbian because she is not "doing anything." Or she may believe that if she were to allow herself to be made love to, to enjoy it, and to reach orgasm, she would "really" be a lesbian, which she may fear. Usually these processes are unconscious. In both of these instances, therapeutic intervention should be aimed at the underlying fear of being a lesbian, rather than at the sexual activity per se.

Many lesbians are distressed by sexual feelings, fantasies, and dreams about men, and fear that these experiences make their lesbianism dubious (Roth, 1989). In some areas, the lesbian community can look with disdain on any hint of heterosexual interests, and the lesbian in therapy may be relieved to be able to talk about these concerns in the treatment room. The therapist can guide the client to continue to develop an identity that is a best fit—remembering that a lesbian identity, behavior, erotic interests, and love are not always congruent with one another. Bisexuality or an inconsistent sexual preference can also be disfavored in the lesbian community, giving such a woman few places in which to feel accepted and at home, and again, a therapist may be a client's sole confidante.

Prairie had been in therapy with me for several months, working on recognizing and meeting her own needs while in a relationship. She had been identified as a lesbian for over 20 years. During the course of our work, she eventually left the relationship she had been in, and after being single a while, found that a few men were expressing interest in her. She was bewildered by her own reciprocal interest in them. She feared if she pursued these relationships with men, she wouldn't know what to call herself, lesbian or straight. Because the issue we had been working on all along was increasing her ability to know and meet her own self in a relationship, we stuck close to this topic as we examined her broadening knowledge of herself and her potentials. Prairie was able to some degree to shed her concerns about what others would think and to listen to her own values, and decided to take up the opportunities to become involved with men. She saw these male relationships as temporary, however, and indeed saw to it that they ended within several months. She found that she enjoyed their attention a great deal, but eventually her tension built again from her doubts regarding her lesbianism, as well as from having few friends who supported her new affairs. Prairie eventually decided to seek a next relationship with a woman. She was later able to feel resolved about this matter as she came to accept herself as a dynamic, changing being, whose needs are not static, but must be tended to on a regular basis as they change.

Additional factors that may affect sexual satisfaction stem from socialization as a female. Predictably, when two women are paired who share the common societal injunctions against sexual self-assertion, against sexual self-knowledge, and against recognition of the primacy of their own sexual desires, they will have some trouble defining and maintaining a sex life that is satisfying (Roth, 1985; Moses & Hawkins, 1982; Nichols, 1982). Neither partner may be willing to take on the role of sexual initiator. Also, many lesbians abhor any semblance of treating their partner "like a man would" and will refrain from any attempt to encourage or elicit a sexual response from their partner for fear that it would be too reminiscent of "objectifying"(seen as a male attitude) sexuality. Roth points out:

> Therapists who are called upon to assist lesbian couples in interrupting recurring sequences of sexual apprehension must take into account not only whatever models they have for addressing such sexual dysfunction; they must also be alert for the ways in which the social surrounding for the couple influences this private aspect of their lives and the ways in which the partners have learned their societally designated roles so well that they are inhibiting the expression of their womanliness. (p. 278)

In reference to the variety of sexual dissatisfactions that lesbians can experience, and the variety of reasons for those dissatisfactions, Moses and Hawkins (1982) state:

The uniqueness of problems involving communication difficulties, unwillingness to engage in or receive certain kinds of stimulation, and frequency of lovemaking all are based on learned fears of being lesbian, of one's own body, of being assertive, or of lack of skill. They are not indications of lesbian sexual pathology. (p. 109)

Lesbians who are physically disabled also face particular challenges. It is a common myth that disabled people are not whole people, that they need a great deal of help to function, and that they are unlikely to seek or find sexual partners. It is also a common myth that disabled women become lesbians because of an inability to succeed sexually in a predominantly heterosexual society (Wohlander & Petal, 1985). For some women, the experience of stigmatizing myth and oppression as a disabled person makes it easier to cope with the stigma of lesbianism, whereas for others, the experience of one stigma complicates the other. The therapist may be called upon to sort through these stigmas. Disabled women can be encouraged to express their sexuality to the fullest of their capacity.

Lesbians may also be prone to the negative effects of what Califia (1988) calls a "pro-lesbian myth"—for example, the assumption that two women know exactly how to please each other sexually since both are women. This assumes that sex is not a learned phenomenon—which, of course, to some degree it is. It also assumes that all women have the same pattern of sexual response and the same sexual preferences, which they do not. It further assumes that talking about sex with one's partner should be unnecessary.

These beliefs can lead to a very unsatisfactory sex life for many lesbians. It discourages women from paying attention to their own response patterns and touching preferences. And it discourages them from communicating this important and intimate information to each other, which can have a psychological effect on both self-esteem and the relationship dynamics.

In-depth sex therapy (such as treatment for vaginismus, anorgasmia, or aversions to specific sexual activities) for lesbians should be provided only by clinicians trained in that specialty. For therapists so trained, Nichols (1982) and Hall (1986, 1987) both recommend a model of sex therapy that is based soundly on the widely used therapies developed by Masters and Johnson (1971) and by Kaplan (1975 and 1979), with the addition of the special issues for lesbians mentioned above. Barbach's (1975) *For Yourself* is also a good resource on anorgasmia.

The typical clinician, who is not trained specifically as a sex therapist, nevertheless will encounter many of the sexual issues common to lesbians in the course of therapy. Loulan's (1984) book *Lesbian Sex* is unsurpassed as a resource, for both clients and therapists. Her homework exercises are very helpful for clients experiencing most types of sexual dissatisfaction, as well as for those who simply wish to enhance their sexuality. Califia's (1988) book, *Sapphistry: The Book of Lesbian Sexuality,* is another essential handbook; it presents extensive information in a very readable, non-judgmental manner.

To help your clients "normalize" their sexuality, or to help discover whether sexual dysfunction does truly exist, it can be valuable to furnish them with some of the statistics from Loulan's (1987) research on the sexual activity of 1,566 self-identified lesbians. Her figures show, among many other things, the following:

- Sixty-two percent were coupled, 26% were single, and 12% were casually involved with someone.
- Seventy-eight percent had been celibate at some time, mostly as a result being left by a lover, or experiencing stress, or because it felt good. Others reported celibacy owing to abuse memories, addiction recovery, illness, or motherhood.
- Ninety-two percent of single lesbians masturbate, 92% of those casually involved masturbate, and 88% of those in couples masturbate; 17% masturbate once a month or less, 38% masturbate two to five times per month, 22% masturbate six to ten times per month, and 23% masturbate ten or more times per month.
- During a typical month, 12% never have sex with their partner, 19% have sex once or less, 35% have sex two to five times, 20% have sex six to ten times, and 14% have sex 11 or more times.
- Eighty-six percent regularly have orgasms with masturbation, 81% regularly have orgasms with their partners; 13% occasionally have orgasms with their partners and 8% occasionally have orgasms with masturbation. Six percent never have orgasms with masturbation and 6% never have orgasms with their partner.
- Six percent state that they are not at all satisfied with their current sex life, 24% are somewhat satisfied, 8% are passably satisfied, 38% are fairly well satisfied, and 14% are completely satisfied.

Hall (1987) provides some guidelines for sex therapy with lesbian clients that goes well beyond the behavioral prescriptions on which most sex therapies are based. She recommends:

1. Part of the treatment must address a primary consequence of homophobia: the partners' sense of failure, the feeling that they are flawed, as evidenced by the fact that they do not have an ideal sexual relationship.
2. An equally critical treatment component is the delineation and modeling of a behavioral style that may seem alien and threatening to both partners—autonomous behavior within the context of the relationship that keeps a healthy separation of activities and, therefore, of psychological selves.
3. The final essential element of treatment is the exposure to and building of tolerance of differences in the partners.

As a final note, it is important to remember that lesbians as a group appear to prize nongenital physical contact, such as cuddling, hugging, and touching, more than other couples do. Further, they are likely to see this affection as an end in itself and not just as "foreplay" leading to genital sex (Blumstein & Schwartz, 1983). Therefore, unless the client herself defines sexual issues as a problem, they may not indeed be a problem. Also, even when the client does define her sexual issues as a problem, it is important for the therapist to ascertain whether a dysfunction actually exists or whether the client is simply judging herself as inadequate because of the mythical expectations about lesbian sexuality.

Sexual Molestation

Sexual molestation occurs at a horrifying rate in the United States, and the numbers of lesbians and nonlesbian women sexually molested as children are the same.

Loulan (1987) found a 38% rate of sexual molestation as a child among her lesbian sample, and a 16% incidence of rape as an adult; the *National Lesbian Health Care Survey* (NIMH, 1987) reported a 41% incidence of rape and sexual abuse across the life span and a 21% incidence in childhood. Sexual trauma, therefore, affects a great number of all lesbians personally. In addition, as you can conjecture from the figures, the likelihood of a lesbian's becoming partners with a woman who has been sexually traumatized is very high. As a result, most lesbian couples will encounter the effects of these traumas in one or both partners—especially if one of the partners is nonCaucasian. The *National Lesbian Health Care Survey* results showed that of those reporting molestation or rape, 16% were White, 29% were Latina, and 31% were Black.

Work with molestation and rape survivors in therapy is an area that calls for specialized training on the part of the therapist (and, of course, should not be undertaken without such training), but many therapists will see such clients in their offices regardless of expertise. Good referral resources are important in these instances. The information in the literature is quite sparse to date on lesbians and sexual molestation, but is presented here as a building block for further conceptualization.

Many of the symptoms and aftereffects of molestation are probably fairly similar among lesbian and nonlesbian women. According to Courtois (1988), the effects are:

- *Emotional reactions,* including fear, anxiety, depression, and self-destructive thoughts and behaviors.
- *Self-perceptions,* which are predominantly negative and indicative of low self-esteem, shame, and stigma.
- *Physical and somatic effects*—direct physical expressions of the abuse or physical manifestations of emotional reactions.
- *Sexual effects,* including the full range of disorders usually associated with anxiety and physical or psychological trauma.
- *Interpersonal relating,* characterized by mistrust and conflicted, non-nurturing, or superficial relationships.
- *Social effects,* ranging from underfunctioning to overfunctioning, from people-pleasing and extroverted behavior to extreme isolation and withdrawal, hostile schizoid behavior, and patterns of victimizing others or revictimization.

When a lesbian experiences these effects, the added dimension of internalized homophobia will often complicate assessment and treatment. Most lesbians who have been sexually abused must spend significant time sorting through the meaning of their lesbianism in light of the abuse. They may also have a distinctly difficult time with appropriate decisions about degree of openness about their lesbianism; any secrecy can be reminiscent of the secrecy of the molestation, which places great strain on her already vulnerable sense of stability and self-esteem. Further, there are instances where a woman's sexual identity becomes particularly difficult for her to integrate. As researchers and clinicians, both Courtois (1988) and Maltz and Holman (1987) have written on this topic.

These authors note that several permutations of sexual preference may occur concomitantly with molestation. About half of Maltz and Holman's sample of lesbians reported that they felt strongly that their sexual abuse had no bearing on their sexual orientation, while half felt that it was indeed related to their choice of same-sex partner. Maltz and Holman theorize that the first group consists of lesbians who also happen to be incest survivors and would have been lesbians with or without their molestation experience; the latter group may be basically heterosexual or bisexual and have been open to experimentation or love with female partners as part of their healing process. This second pattern may be seen as a healthy adaptation to a trauma, or it may be seen as a phase of healing, and the woman may choose heterosexual relationships in the future.

A third permutation can occur wherein a woman who is otherwise a lesbian is blocked from that awareness by one of two things: habitualized contact with males, which she then continues into adulthood, or anger at women—the result of anger at a mother who failed to protect her from abuse or a projected anger onto all women for her own perceived shame and weakness. Such a woman may experience a strong block to recognizing her attraction to women.

> Corky has come a long way in her therapy, working through significant effects of prolonged, tortuous molest by her twin brother. Her relationships, her career path, her self-esteem, her beliefs, and her view of the world had all been affected, some in strengthening ways, but many in detrimental ways. During her early adulthood, she engaged in very aggressive, physically damaging sex with male peers, this being the only type of sexuality she knew. She would become sexual with any male who showed the slightest interest. It wasn't until a gynecologist told Corky that sexual activity did not have to cause her physical damage that Corky began to realize that she had the capacity to define her own sexuality. She soon realized her deepest interests were in women, and she identified as a lesbian. She calls the era of her life when she was so active with men her "flight into heterosexuality." Corky is now beginning to realize that she can set her own standards of how she wants to be treated in many other areas of her life as well.

Finally, when the molestation has been perpetrated by a woman, the survivor may have a tough time sorting out her own sexual preference, being afraid that she is simply reenacting her own abuse or has somehow become "improperly" attached to the wrong sex by habituation.

The partners of sexual molestation survivors, whether or not they are abuse survivors themselves, often need guidance in how to be helpful to their partners, yet take good care of their own needs. Loulan notes that one of the major reasons that partners of incest survivors leave their relationships is that they find themselves caring for their partner at the expense of their own needs. A nonmolested partner may be in just as much need of a support group, understanding, and suggestions for balancing both partners' needs as is the molest survivor herself, especially since it cannot be assumed that the survivor will be completely understanding as she is busy with her own psychic struggle.

Loulan's *Lesbian Sex* (1984) is directed toward both survivors and their partners and contains healing exercises specifically relevant in the sexual arena. For the survivor, the exercises cover boundaries and limit-setting, self-protection, self-care and cleansing, talking about the abuse, and forgiving oneself; for the partner, exercises cover how to meet her own needs, feelings about having had a "less bad" childhood, and discovery about reasons for choosing a survivor as a partner. These exercises are highly effective. In addition, many larger cities have support groups or therapy groups specifically for lesbian survivors of molestation or rape run by trained therapists. I recommend against referring a lesbian survivor to an otherwise all nonlesbian women's survivor group unless the group leader herself is thoroughly trained in lesbian issues; such a referral creates too great a potential for the continuation of feelings of shame, misunderstanding, secrecy, internalized homophobia, and identity confusion.

ALCOHOL AND DRUG USE

The prevalance of alcohol overuse in the gay and lesbian community has been estimated to be considerably higher than in nongay populations. Studies show that from 25% to 35% of gays and lesbians appear to be alcoholic by various definitions (Zigrang, 1982). However, estimates of prevalence conflict, and the *National Lesbian Health Care Survey* (NIMH, 1987) indicated that drinking patterns are similar when comparing lesbians with matched heterosexual women, with the exception of a higher rate of alcoholism among older lesbians (55 and older). The survey also indicated that cocaine and other drug use among young lesbians was similar to usage patterns for other high stress groups, such as physicians and medical students. Loulan's (1986a) study of 1,361 lesbians showed that 30.2% of the respondents reported that they were previously addicted to chemical substances (alcohol or other drugs) and were currently clean and sober, and that 2% of the respondents considered themselves currently addicted. (Because drug and alcohol use is so often accompanied by denial of its impact, reports of current abuser rates are vastly underestimated.)

Unfortunately, studies of alcoholism among lesbians suffer methodological problems that make the results difficult to interpret or to generalize

(Nardi, 1982; Mosbacher, 1988). Most studies lack control groups, lack a representation of a cross section of gays and lesbians, and rely upon self-report. Nevertheless, the possibility of a high rate of alcoholism and drug use among gays and lesbians is a matter of some concern. Therapists must be alert to the need to do alcohol and drug screenings on some lesbian clients and they must be alert to the ways in which alcoholism or drug abuse can interact with lesbianism.

Historically, a shift has occurred from a psychoanalytic model to a more sociocultural perspective in describing the relationship between alcoholism and lesbianism (Nardi, 1982). The previous psychoanalytic views related homosexuality and alcoholism as two deviant conditions, both caused by oral fixations. More recent learning theory models offer some explanation of the prevalence of alcoholism by describing the common socialization of gays and lesbians into a positively reinforcing lifestyle that revolves around bars and various alcohol-oriented social functions. However, Nardi believes that sociocultural perspectives, rather than learning theory models, have the most to offer, by explaining labeling theories, conflict models, and interactionist perspectives. In these models emphasis is placed on the norms and values of the society toward drinking, the meaning people attach to drinking, and the definitions and laws imposed by those in power to enact and control norms. This viewpoint offers the most in-depth understanding of the problem by providing analyses of the meanings and definitions of alcohol use among gays and lesbians themselves.

Understanding how a given lesbian manages and controls her feelings in an oppressive social context illustrates this sociocultural perspective. As Nardi (1982) states, "A homophobic society instills in those coming to terms with their sexuality a variety of feelings about the immorality and deviant nature of homosexuality" (p. 21). Self-denial, self-hatred, and lowered self-esteem can lead to rigidity of ego defenses; hiding one's feelings becomes normative. This situation can lead some lesbians to increased alcohol consumption either to ease their coming-out process or to help maintain their concealed identity. Some lesbians who are fearful of their orientation only make love under the influence of alcohol or drugs, thereby creating the self-illusion that their sexuality is not within their conscious control, and therefore, they do not then have to face being lesbian.

Alcoholism has historically been treated as a crime, a sin, a moral issue, a legal matter, and, most recently, as a disease. This also has been true of homosexuality, and an alcoholic lesbian must thus contend with both stigmas. As Nicoloff and Stiglitz (1987) note, the medical disease model of alcoholism is the treatment approach most used today. Although this model has compelling explanatory advantages, it fails to explain the possibly higher incidence of alcoholism among lesbians than among nonlesbians. There is no indication that lesbians carry a genetic predisposition to alcoholism to any greater degree than do nonlesbians. These factors lend weight to treatment models that enlarge upon the medical model by also attending to social factors that contribute to the abuse of alcohol (and other drugs).

Diamond and Wilsnack's (1978) review of the literature names several factors contributing to alcohol abuse in gay and lesbian populations. First, the gay bar has served an important function as a safe meeting place and center of socialization. Second, it is the subcultural norm among lesbians and gays that social and romantic interaction frequently involves drinking. Third, alienation and isolation resulting from society's rejection and oppression can contribute to alcohol abuse. Finally, some lesbians, like heterosexual women, may abuse alcohol because they have experienced personal depression and loss.

Diamond and Wilsnack interviewed 10 lesbian alcohol abusers and found evidence of strong dependency needs, low self-esteem, and a high incidence of depression. Among their sample, drinking often occurred in response to disruption of dependency relationships. After drinking, many subjects engaged in power-enhancing behaviors such as increased assertiveness, aggressiveness, and sexual initiative, perhaps in response to their dependency needs. Depression and low self-esteem were reported to frequently precipitate drinking episodes. The subjects reported that drinking increased their self-esteem but also enhanced their feelings of sadness and depression. Comparisons were not made with nonlesbian drinkers.

Diamond and Wilsnack suggest several implications for therapy based on their study and review of the literature:

1. If lesbians drink in part to feel strong and powerful, therapists might help them explore ways to exercise real and effective social power, such as through political activity or membership in influential organizations.
2. If lesbians drink to improve self-confidence and self-esteem, therapists can help them develop new resources, both internally and through environmental support for their self-image (including their lesbianism).
3. The heightened assertiveness and creativity that many lesbians experience while drinking suggest treatment modalities such as assertiveness training and expressive therapies that will help them achieve these experiences without alcohol.
4. Many lesbian alcohol abusers have difficulty expressing their feelings directly when sober. This suggests therapeutic interventions that

enhance communication skills and help the client understand and overcome inhibitions about expressing feelings.

Therapists who are not specifically trained in the treatment of addictive disorders should refer a client to another therapist who is trained in both addictive disorders and in lesbianism, or to a similarly qualified treatment facility. In a survey of participants in gay alcoholism programs, Zigrang (1982) reports that 50% of these participants stated that they had previously participated in nongay alcohol treatment programs. This comparison stands in contrast with the reports from the staffs of these nongay agencies who believed that only 1% of their alcoholic clientele was gay! Clearly, many gays and lesbians who enter treatment programs do not reveal their sexual orientation. Zigrang notes the effects of this problem:

Nondisclosure results in the need to maintain considerable censorship and ultimately tends to result in radically decreased group participation; however, disclosure of their orientation is likely to result in considerable rejection and isolation from other group members. (p. 29)

Clients may not only fear the rejection of the group members in their treatment setting, but the rejection or misunderstanding of their counselors and treatment providers as well. They also may lose the benefit of the family treatment offered by many facilities. Surveys of facilities and agencies show that although gay people are seen as having unique service needs, few agencies offer special therapy groups for gay men and lesbians, conduct outreach to gay and lesbian clients, or provide staff training on gay and lesbian issues (Zigrang, 1982).

Ziebold (1978) recommends one solution to these problems. He urges the gay and lesbian community to take the responsibility for helping gay and lesbian alcoholics. His reasons are well-founded: (1) the gay community usually provides the supportive structure that heterosexuals receive from their families; (2) intervention can be facilitated by the gay and lesbian community without the threat of exposing sexual orientation to those whom the drinking person does not want this information revealed; (3) providing a drug-free reentry into social relationships is more effectively done within a gay- or lesbian-oriented setting; and (4) recovery must emphasize self-acceptance as a gay or lesbian person, and provide healthy role models, which a gay and lesbian agency is in a better position to offer than is a nongay agency.

Zigrang agrees with these arguments, but notes that only a few cities have visible gay and lesbian communities large enough to support such intervention efforts, and that the physical deterioration that can often accompany alcoholism and drug use requires medical backup that most gay and lesbian communities could not afford to provide. Further, Zigrang suggests that treatment facilities operated by the gay and lesbian community could maintain separation of gays and lesbians from the heterosexual community, and ultimately may perpetuate the homophobic attitudes that appear to have contributed significantly to gay alcoholism in the first place.

Zigrang describes the development of a special program for gays and lesbians at an alcohol treatment unit of a hospital that included an outpatient therapy group limited to gays and lesbians only, an inpatient program that mixed gays and lesbians with heterosexuals, and the presence on the staff of an openly lesbian therapist. This program has had limited success, the problems resulting mostly from the fact that gays and lesbians still have reason to fear that joining an all-gay group would be too stigmatizing. Lack of administrative support for this program was also an obstacle.

Other outpatient programs exist that have enjoyed long-term success. Some of these programs have individual and group treatment, structured groups, or ongoing recovery groups for gay men and lesbians. In some agencies, these services are advertised as part of the general program services, and in other agencies, such services are not directly advertised but are promoted by word of mouth throughout the local gay and lesbian community. Where these programs are successful, there is more likely to be outright administrative support for them and gay and lesbian staff are encouraged to be visible (V. Lawson, personal communication, June 12, 1987). Pride Institute in Minneapolis, Minnesota, is one example of an all-gay treatment facility that is showing success.

Most larger cities have all-gay or all-lesbian Alcoholics Anonymous or "12-Step" groups (as well as gay or lesbian Al-Anon, Narcotics Anonymous, and Adult Children of Alcoholics groups). These groups often provide the community support and the external structure needed to establish a new life that is drug-free. These groups are the mainstay of many recovering lesbian alcoholics, with many cities having one or more meetings per day. In addition, many lesbians want to be active in 12-step programs that are not just for lesbians; this can be a good adjunct to an all-lesbian group, assuming the client's lesbianism is accepted there. The therapist's referral to such groups can be a critical factor in successfully addressing the client's addictive process in a frame that is accepting of her lesbianism. The National Association of Lesbian and Gay Alcoholism Professionals provides a national list of nonhomophobic professionals and agencies; their address is listed in Appendix C.

YOUTH AND AGING

No matter what a woman's age, being a lesbian will have its joys and stresses. Because psychological development occurs across the life span, and is not complete by the time one reaches adulthood, all developmental issues throughout a woman's life will be interwoven with her lesbianism in some way. The special developmental issues of lesbian youth and elderly lesbians have been given some attention lately, however the literature still awaits discussion of developmental issues of special concern to the lesbian in her middle years.

Youth

The lesbian adolescent is in a unique situation. Maylon's (1981) discussion of the effects of social bias on the homosexual adolescent emphasizes the difficult double task that a lesbian adolescent is called upon to master. Both the developmental tasks of adolescence (transformation of parental dependence to an adult capacity for love and intimacy) and the developmental tasks of coming out (as described in Chapter 5) must be contended with in tandem. Completion of these tasks calls for extensive social interaction with peers, which are opportunities that an emerging lesbian will often be robbed of. Because of the antipathy associated with lesbianism, many critical social experiences will not be available to the young lesbian who usually finds herself in a hostile heterosexual milieu. The social disapproval she is likely to encounter interferes with social involvements that foster the evolution of maturity and self-respect.

The adolescent lesbian usually has three options open to her: (1) repression of same-sex desires, (2) suppression of lesbianism in favor of a heterosexual or asexual orientation, and (3) disclosure of lesbian identity and the decision to mobilize same-sex desires. According to Maylon, the adolescent who represses same-sex desires is making the most primitive and least satisfactory adaptation to the lesbian issue; the issues usually reemerge later and precipitate a crisis conflict and a disruption of coping strategies and life patterns.

For those who suppress their lesbianism, chronic psychological unrest and disequilibrium usually result; again, identity issues will reemerge in later life and a "second adolescence" often is required to complete developmental psychological growth.

The third option, disclosure, also has its drawbacks. Social attitudes militate against self-acceptance. Most young lesbians are not linked with any lesbian networks and so are alienated from their lesbian peers and have little access to the adult lesbian community. (The adult lesbian and gay male communities historically have been reluctant to accept minors into any agency or organizational activity for fear of being accused of fulfilling the myth that homosexuals "seduce" youth.) Those who remain in the heterosexual community face estrangement and confusion and must complete their developmental process in what could be a hostile and psychologically impoverished environment; those who attempt to enter the adult lesbian community often must prematurely assume adult responsibilities and may experience an abrupt separation from parents, either by their own choice or because the parents disown them. However, the self-respect and ego integrity that are possible only with disclosure are developmental advantages for the lesbian adolescent. For those young lesbians who are fortunate enough to learn about their resources, many cities do have social support systems, groups, and meeting places for youth.

Therapists are sometimes called upon to "decide" whether an adolescent is lesbian or not, usually by distraught parents, and occasionally by the confused adolescent herself. Maylon notes several things that are important to remember in these cases. Science has yet to be able to specify the process by which either heterosexuality or homosexuality is established, or the process by which a definition is made about one's "range" of sexual and affectional expression, but in many cases the process seems to tend toward immutability by the end of latency. Also, homoerotic fantasies or even overt behavior is not predictive of later homosexuality or heterosexuality. It is a therapeutic error to interpret adolescent homosexual impulses either as incidental or as evidence of homosexuality. Therefore disclosure of homoeroticism should be responded to with unbiased support and information about the meaning of homosexual desire; it should be described as a natural developmental outcome. The clinician should aim at facilitating safe and validating experimentation, understanding, and self-acceptance. The most appropriate stance for the therapist to take is to help the adolescent develop a positive self-concept and a genuine capacity for intimacy, irrespective of sexual orientation.

Woodman and Lenna (1980) provide additional suggestions for the therapist working with lesbian youth. Therapists can let the lesbian adolescent know that she has a right to define her identity in a way that is personally self-actualizing. She also can be helped to see that her lesbianism is somewhat separate from the pursuit of vocational satisfaction and avocational interests. When the lesbian youth is acting out the stereotypes of lesbianism, which occur with some frequency, the meaning and the effect of the stereotypes should be explored. The decision to come out to parents is often a difficult one for the lesbian adolescent; the decision is best based on factors such as the adolescent's comfort level with her identity, the flexibility and egalitarianism of her relationship with her parents, and the parents' ability to respect the adolescent's capacity to know that she is lesbian.

In a report of the Institute for the Protection of Lesbian and Gay Youth, Inc., a social service agency in New York City, Hetrick and Martin (1987) describe the most common presenting problems seen with their clientele. The primary problem among these youth is isolation. Three types of isolation were identified; first is social isolation, that is, clients who feel that they have no one to talk to; second is emotional isolation, clients who feel separated affectionally and emotionally both from social networks and from family; and third is cognitive isolation, a lack of access to accurate information about homosexuality, including a lack of good role models.

The secondary problem seen by these researchers is with family; lesbian and gay youth fear rejection by their parents, as well as fearing violence and expulsion from their homes. The tertiary problem identified is violence and suicide; one-third of the clientele suffer violence because of their sexual orientation, half of these incidents occur at the hands of their families. In addition, 20% report either attempted suicide or a strong suicidal ideation. Less frequently reported problems include emotional problems, shelter and job-related problems, drug use, and aftereffects of sexual abuse. A clinician should look for each of these problems in her or his assessment of a lesbian adolescent. The presenting problems will help guide toward appropriate interventions.

Anderson's (1987) description of a drop-in group for lesbian and gay youth provides further information useful to the therapist's assessment and treatment planning, especially where disclosure to parents is of concern. The majority of lesbian and gay youth studied did not disclose to their parents because they feared being rejected, punished, physically assaulted, or expelled from the family or the home. It appears that many youth defend against these fears by withdrawing emotional investment in the family as a means of diminishing the significance of possible rejection, or to limit the likelihood that the family will learn of her secret. Further, if the adolescent has found a peer group that includes other lesbians or gays, she may hide from her family her most commonplace social activities that heterosexual adolescents may easily share with their parents. The most innocent and healthy social activities thereby become tainted by the need to hide or lie. Such youth often feel guilty and sad, and they are in danger of displacing these feelings onto their sexual self-concept.

If a client does express a desire to tell her parents, it can be most helpful to describe and predict possible parental reactions. Although there is much variability, it is nevertheless fairly predictable that parents will proceed through a series of coping stages similar to that seen in the grief process. They may first be in shock and denial, and then have to work through their anger and tendency to feel guilty or to blame themselves, before they come to a stage of acknowledgment and an acceptance at whatever level they are capable of or willing to work toward.

Humans are socially influenced organisms—and this characteristic is especially apparent during adolescence. Because of this, accurate information and a diverse peer group that includes other gays and lesbians and solid role models are highly desirable ingredients for the healthy adjustment of a young lesbian. Many towns and cities have social groups for lesbian and gay male adolescents that can prove to be invaluable resources for the young lesbian who is in need of a peer group in which she can conduct the social developmental tasks of her age. Also, many young lesbians join their local Parents and Friends of Lesbians and Gays (see Appendix C, Resources), where they may find accepting parent surrogates and a group of supportive peers and adult gays and lesbians with whom they can feel a sense of belonging.

Elders

In contrast to the difficulties encountered by the lesbian youth, the aging lesbian appears to be in a surprisingly less difficult position. Moses and Hawkins's (1982) review of the literature on aging shows that the aging lesbian may have several advantages over her nonlesbian counterpart. The majority of lesbians look forward to their later years, whereas only a minority are apprehensive; they worry about the same things that nonlesbian women do—loss of physical attractiveness and loneliness—but perhaps less so than nonlesbians.

The reasons behind most lesbians not being apprehensive about growing older are many. Lesbians seem to emphasize personality, intellect, and hygiene in themselves and in others over physical appearance, which may make the aging process more acceptable. Also, lesbians can expect, statistically, that their partners will live as long as they do. Heterosexual women are statistically likely to outlive their male partners by several years. Lesbians are also significantly more involved in leisure time activities, artistic pursuits, and sports than are nonlesbian women, which can contribute to self-esteem and to the anticipation of having more time for those activities after retirement. Further, lesbians appear to have more close friends than do nongays, which can ease fears about loneliness in later years. Finally, Moses and Hawkins note, the years and years of stigmatization with which a lesbian has dealt appears to have a payoff in later years: having overcome the initial stigma of lesbianism, the additional stigma of age may be less likely to have a negative effect.

Friend (1987) confirms these perspectives in his discussion of homosexuality as a functional aspect in one's adaptation to older age. He describes the concept of "crisis competence" wherein the earlier coming-out process provided coping mechanisms that now generalize to a successful aging process. Friend further notes that the gender androgyny common to lesbians can protect them from the otherwise traumatizing effects of living alone, of losing the roles of parent, and of retirement; skills for independent living and role changes may often be already in the repertoire of most lesbians. Another facilitating aspect of lesbianism is that most lesbians are likely to have planned for their own futures, often being unable to rely on family members who may have decided to "keep a distance," and have developed some form of "chosen family" or community network.

A woman who comes to a lesbian awareness or lesbian identity in her later years is in a unique situation. On the one hand, her generational values may make the process of recognizing her lesbian interests particularly painful. On the other hand, she may have access to a lesbian community and social opportunities to which her age cohorts, who discovered their lesbianism earlier, were not privy. The older woman who is just coming out is also fairly likely to have previously married and to have grown children, all of whom she may need to contend with in her coming-out process. Finding available partners also may be a painstaking task, especially if she does not live in a large city or does not wish to associate closely with a younger or more "out" community.

My client Maya was 62 years old at the time I first saw her. She had separated from her husband, was preparing for divorce, and had realized she was a lesbian. She wanted help in adjusting to these changes, finding resources, and seeking a mate for what she hoped would be the rest of her life. When Maya told her grown children of her plans, they uniformly suggested that Maya not look for a life partner, and not change her life so drastically at this late stage. Maya was hurt by their lack of support, and this made her doubt whether it was really okay for a 62-year-old woman to be seeking sexuality, commitment, and companionship; her doubts melted away when we discussed the fact that if it were a male for whom she were looking, both her children and society would have not discouraged her from her dreams. With time and discussion, Maya's children eventually became her staunchest supporters. She is active in several lesbian social groups, some specifically for older lesbians, in search of a potential partner.

Perhaps one of the most difficult tasks of aging for a lesbian is the eventual need to be involved with health professionals, to whom she must decide whether or not to come out. Women who are currently in their elder years are likely to have lived most of their lives "pre-gay-liberation" and are perhaps more wary than today's middle-year or young lesbians about such disclosures. Issues of institutionalization and inheritance rights also may have an impact. Lastly, mourning the death of a lover can be a difficult process when the larger nongay community is unaccepting of the legitimacy of the relationship. A lesbian lover can experience being left out of the funeral plans and bereavement process by her partner's family, or may find that a will can be contested, or that no will at all was left, placing her in a position of great loss of personal possession on top of her grief.

Almvig (1982) surveyed 74 lesbians ranging in age from 50 to 70, and found that the respondents had generally positive feelings about their aging. More than half said they felt just as or more attractive than in their youths, and they were just as or more sexual than they always were. Like nongay women, they feared loss of physical capabilities above all else, and secondarily feared loss of financial capabilities and of mental capabilities. In planning for their declining years, most respondents said they would prefer a gay-oriented nursing home or retirement facility. Again, educating care givers was a major concern.

Perhaps Kehoe's (1988) descriptive study of 100 lesbians over 60 years of age sheds the most light to date on this population. Her respondents showed particular backgrounds and traits, as do all age cohort groups, that have a distinct effect on their aging processes. These respondents were frequently raised in rural or suburban areas or in small towns or they were born out of the country; their educational backgrounds were above average and they were heavily represented in professional careers. It was also common for them to have been in the military service during World War II.

These older lesbians grew up in a time when they were likely to face as severe discrimination in public life as females as they were to face as lesbians. Sexuality in general was not talked about openly in the early 1900s, let alone homosexuality. The most well-known piece of literature on lesbianism then available was Radclyff Hall's *The Well of Loneliness,* a novel that portrayed butch/femme roles and ended in tragedy—a model that all too many took to heart. Many came to believe that they must follow the heterosexual model of the time and play butch or femme roles, or believed that loving women must mean they really wanted to be men, and so tried to act and dress like men, resulting in much stigmatization and in difficulty obtaining jobs. This was especially the case for "working-class" women. The feminist movement had not yet liberated women from the conviction of their own inferiority or given them pride in their womanhood. Most were deeply closeted in small towns and seldom congregated in public places, which meant that they had little access to support and to normalization of their feelings. These women also lived through the Red-baiting and queer-baiting of McCarthyism, and they lived through a time when two million homosexuals were put to death in the Nazi death camps.

It wasn't until 1955 that the first lesbian liberation organization came into existence, which was begun by Del Martin and Phyllis Lyon and was called the Daughters of Bilitis (see their book *Lesbian/Woman*). Shortly thereafter, the first lesbian publication went into print; called *The Ladder,* and printed until 1972, it served as a rallying ground and support network across the nation. In 1969, the Stonewall riots occurred in New York City. Out of this protest against the continual police harassment of gay bars, Gay Pride was born.

Among those women who found small networks of other lesbians during this era, secrecy was the rule. Most women who came into contact with one another under such circumstances did not ask for and did not volunteer names or occupations, for fear of exposure. These are among the myriad events that have shaped the lives of many older lesbians, and that must be considered in any therapeutic setting.

Kehoe's respondents also described their present lives. Most restrict their social lives to a small group of other lesbians of similar age. Most do not use mainstream senior centers. The majority would prefer a retirement center designed for lesbians only. Many prefer to remain in a diverse neighborhood. Approximately half were in a coupled relationship, ranging in duration from new to over 50 years. Loneliness and isolation were reported as the biggest problems for older lesbians, especially for those not living in large cities. Three-quarters reported feeling very positive about their lesbianism and four-fifths reported being in good or excellent emotional health. In spite of describing past unhappy marriages to men, loss of lovers by death, unwanted celibacy, fears about aging and some debilitating illnesses, the majority of respondents fell above the mean score on a life-satisfaction scale.

Some cities have organizations for gay and lesbian elders, many of which are based on the prototypical organization SAGE (Senior Action in a Gay Environment) in New York City (see Appendix C). Because of the increased interest in gay- and lesbian-affirmative retirement centers and convalescent homes, several organizations across the country are undertaking projects to fill this demand. It is hoped that by the turn of the century, such facilities will be up and running.

LESBIANS AND AIDS

Lesbians as a group are in an extremely low-risk category for contracting Acquired Immune Deficiency Syndrome (AIDS). AIDS is spread primarily through contact with the blood or semen of another person whose body contains the AIDS virus. For most lesbians, contact with the blood or semen of another person is relatively rare. However, the human immunodeficiency virus (HIV), the virus thought to cause AIDS, is found to some degree in vaginal fluids and menstrual fluids, and can, theoretically at least, be transmitted to a partner through contact with these fluids.

As of this writing, only one documented case exists in the medical literature where AIDS was spread from one woman to another. In this case, one woman contracted the disease through intravenous drug use, and the disease apparently was passed on to her woman partner during vigorous sexual activity when some bleeding occurred. This one case out of the current approximate 50,000 reported cases of AIDS in the United States indicates the difficulty with which AIDS (and many other sexually transmitted diseases) is spread among lesbians. Despite the low-risk status of lesbians for contracting AIDS from each other, some lesbians are nevertheless at risk, and all lesbians may be feeling the effects of increased homophobia that has occurred toward homosexual people since the AIDS virus first arrived in this country in 1979.

Lesbians who are at risk for having AIDS are those who:

1. Share needles or any other paraphernalia if using intravenous drugs. This is the single most important risk category for lesbians.
2. Have had sexual contact with:
    (a) people who use intravenous drugs;
    (b) men who have had gay sex since 1979;
    (c) people of either gender whose sexual histories are unknown;
    (d) people who are hemophiliac, or who have received blood transfusions or blood products between 1979 and 1985.
3. Have used semen for donor insemination from a donor in a high-risk group who is known to be HIV antibody positive, or whose risk status is unknown.

4. Have received blood transfusions or blood products between 1979 and 1985.

For those lesbians who have reason to believe they may be infected with the AIDS virus, practicing safe sex is essential. These lesbians should not allow their menstrual blood, vaginal secretions, urine, feces, or breast milk to enter their partner's body through the mouth, rectum, vagina, or broken skin. Although the virus has been found in saliva, no evidence yet exists that it can be transmitted through this fluid.

Safe sex practices for lesbians at risk include:

- massage, hugging;
- social (dry) kissing;
- body-to-body rubbing;
- voyeurism, exhibitionism, fantasy;
- touching one's own genitals (masturbation);
- using one's own vibrators or other sex toys;
- other activities that do not involve bleeding or the exchange of body fluids.

Sex practices that are considered possibly safe for lesbians who are at risk include:

- oral-genital contact (cunnilingus) using a thin piece of latex (such as a dental rubber dam) placed between the vulva and tongue;
- hand- or finger-to-genital contact, vaginal or anal penetration with fingers using a disposable latex glove or finger cots;
- French (wet) kissing;
- external urine contact;
- anal-oral contact (rimming) with a latex barrier.

Sex practices that are considered unsafe for lesbians at risk include:

- unprotected cunnilingus (especially during menstruation);
- unprotected hand- or finger-to-vagina or anus contact, especially if there is a cut or sore on the hand;
- sharing IV needles or other skin-piercing needles;
- blood contact of any kind, including menstrual blood or shared IV needles;
- urine or feces in mouth or vagina;

- unprotected rimming (anal-oral contact);
- fisting (hand in rectum or vagina);
- sharing sex toys that have had contact with body fluids.

For lesbians who have sex with men who are in a high-risk category, it is essential to use condoms. All lesbians (as is true for all persons) are strongly urged to obtain a sexual, IV drug use, and blood transfusion history from any new sexual partner. Until a cure or a vaccine is developed, the only way to contain the spread of AIDS is through prevention based on knowledge of how the virus is spread. (Most of the above information is based on the brochure "Lesbians and AIDS: What's the Connection" available from the Women's AIDS Network. See Appendix C for address.)

Despite the fact that lesbians are generally at low risk for contracting AIDS (unless they are IV drug users who share needles with others), many lesbians are feeling the effects of the epidemic, especially the homophobia, fears, and hatred of gays that have been on the rise since the AIDS epidemic began. The National Gay and Lesbian Task Force reports that the incidence of violence against gays, both men and women, has been increasing over the past few years, and that perpetrators of assaults are referring to AIDS during the assault in 14% of the reported incidents of violence (Freiberg, 1987). The Task Force notes that "the AIDS virus has clearly fanned the flames of antigay bigotry, but it's unclear whether and to what extent 'AIDS backlash' is distinct from—or another manifestation of—this bigotry" (quoted in Freiberg, 1987, p. 17).

Many lesbians report increased fears of being out of the closet since the AIDS epidemic began. Many lesbians have also been personally affected by the AIDS-related illness or death of people close to them. It is not uncommon in therapy to find that a lesbian client is dealing with the effects of multiple deaths of dear ones or acquaintances. Also, many lesbians are actively involved in AIDS-related work, research, task forces, blood drives, and Shanti and Pal projects (providing home care, transportation, and other services to AIDS patients).

Therapists must become aware of what factors constitute a risk for AIDS, what are considered safe sex practices, what the AIDS testing procedure consists of and what the results mean, and the details of how AIDS can and cannot be spread, in order to inform their clients of the facts. The San Francisco AIDS Foundation (listed in Appendix C) or other local AIDS resources can provide the Surgeon General's Report on AIDS and other information essential to the therapist working with any clientele that is at risk.

8

TOWARD A PSYCHOLOGY OF LESBIANISM

This chapter provides a summary of the knowledge and experience that a psychotherapist is advised to have in order to consider herself or himself adequately prepared to provide clinical services to lesbian clients or to any clients who may at some point in their lives be working with matters that pertain to their sexuality or affectional preferences. Because there is evidence that from 10% to 50% of women are sexually or emotionally lesbian (Cavin, 1985; Hite, 1976; and Davis, 1929), it is important that all psychotherapists avail themselves of such information and experience.

This knowledge and experience falls into three categories: (1) knowledge of lesbian experiences, (2) knowledge of the application of lesbian experiences to therapeutic issues and the therapy work, and (2) the therapist's self-knowledge of her or his own level of homosexuality and heterosexist bias. Each of these categories is taken in turn. The final section of this chapter turns attention to future directions for research, to information still needed, and to further training of psychotherapists.

KNOWLEDGE OF LESBIAN EXPERIENCES

The lesbian experiences of which a therapist must be knowledgeable are elaborated upon in Chapters 1, 2, 6, and 7. Drawing upon these chapters, the following is a summary of the particular areas of lesbian experiences that the therapist must keep in mind.

1. Before all else, the psychotherapist must hold a positive view of lesbianism. Any beliefs, cultural stereotypes, religious biases, or psychological training that implies anything less than a positive outlook on lesbianism will negatively affect the therapist's ability to provide therapy. If the therapist finds herself or himself holding onto a negative view of lesbianism, she or he must be aware that such a view stems from emotional, cultural, or

value-laden sources and that this view will result in countertransferences that will have negative impact on the client (Collier, 1982). In practicing her or his profession responsibly, this therapist must refer clients to another therapist who is lesbian-affirmative.

In light of overwhelmingly negative socialization, it follows that a positive view of lesbianism does not just happen. Achieving a positive perspective may entail exposure to lesbian lifestyles and lesbian culture, examination of one's values, and an insight-oriented search into one's own fears and other feelings about homosexuality (Herek, 1984).

2. Exposure to the literature, both current and past, is also important to an understanding of the lesbian experience. The therapist should read materials on lesbians—and especially by lesbians—from the research literature, from the clinical literature, and from the lesbian community's literature. Materials from the past provide needed background and perspective, and current materials show us where we are and point toward possible future directions. (See Appendix B for some important current contributions.)

3. The therapist may want to maintain some regular involvement in the lesbian community. There is no better sensitization than through direct contact with lesbians from a variety of backgrounds and lifestyles.

4. Therapists may find it important to maintain knowledge of current local resources for lesbians, such as information lines, gathering places, and support groups in order to make appropriate referrals. (See Appendix C for national resources and ways to find local resources.)

5. Knowledge of demographics of lesbians is also indispensable. The therapist can keep abreast of the variety of lifestyle choices that lesbians make, of the fluidity of lesbian identity, of the continuum (rather than dichotomy) on which human sexuality falls, of styles of relationships sought, and of presenting issues in therapy. This information is important for the therapist's own perspective and it is often valuable for the client as well. (See Chapter 1.)

6. Knowledge of the special stresses of lesbians is another important ingredient. The therapist must remain sensitive to the very real fears of coming out (to self and to others); the costs of coming out and the costs of remaining hidden; the effects of discrimination, lack of visibility and social support; the costs and benefits of sex-role violations; and the effects of internalized homophobia. (See Chapters 2 and 4.)

7. Knowledge of relationship dynamics is essential whether or not the therapist works with couples. Therapists should be attuned to both the qualities of lesbian relationships that differ from those of heterosexual relationships and the qualities that are the same. Special characteristics of les-

bian relationships include issues of merger and separation-individuation, issues of power and equality, lack of support for the relationship, and similar matters (see Chapter 6).

8. Lesbianism interfaces with numerous other roles and aspects of the client's life. The therapist should be aware of the interplay between lesbianism and motherhood; sexuality; alcohol and drug abuse; matters of youth, middle age, and aging; and AIDS. Ethnicity and religion also are significant interrelating factors. (See Chapter 7.)

9. Research comparing the psychological health of lesbians with matched heterosexual women shows that lesbians have some special strengths: goal-directedness, self-acceptance, job satisfaction, interpersonal satisfaction, self-determination, and satisfaction with their bodies and with their abilities (Gartrell, 1981; Mannion, 1981; and LaTorre & Wendenburg, 1983). Not all lesbians have these qualities, but they are a reminder of the positive aspects of lesbianism and of the traits that therapists might seek to foster in clients. Therapists should keep current with this type of research.

KNOWLEDGE OF THE APPLICATION OF LESBIAN EXPERIENCES TO THERAPEUTIC ISSUES AND THE THERAPY WORK

Chapters 2, and 4, through 7 provide discussion of the application of lesbian experiences to the therapeutic setting and descriptions of the therapist's tasks in facilitating many aspects of healthy lesbian functioning. In order for the therapist to be adequately prepared to work in therapy with this clientele, the following skills and abilities are recommended:

1. The ability to ascertain to what degree lesbianism is a therapeutic issue is paramount. The client's lesbianism will always have some effect on her overall life and on her presenting problems in therapy. These effects must be assessed carefully with the client. (See Chapters 2 and 4).

2. Knowledge of identity formation theory is also critical. Chapter 5 describes several theorists' models of identity formation, some of which are described as sequential stages and others of which are seen as process models. Sexual orientations and identities are most likely fluid phenomena. Further, the development of a positive lesbian identity is a lengthy process. Perhaps most important, a differentiation must be made among lesbian identity, lesbian sexual activity, lesbian erotic interests, and lesbian emo-

tional attachments, and that these factors are not in strict correlation to one another. The management of lesbian identity and self-disclosure is another essential area of knowledge. (See Tables I, IV, and V, and the Self-Awareness Exercise in Appendix A.)

3. Therapists need to have the ability to work with and undo the effects of the client's negative conditioning to lesbianism. Therapists must be able to help the client reduce shame, be able to support the client's feelings and thoughts, be able to help the client expand the range and depth of her feelings, and assist in developing a system of values by which the client assesses herself rather than relying on society for validation (Collier, 1982). (See Chapters 2 and 5.)

4. The therapist must have an appreciation for a sociopolitical framework for understanding the stresses of being lesbian (Gartrell, 1984; Sophie, 1982). (See Chapters 2 and 5.)

5. The therapist also must have knowledge of the literature on the psychology of women. There is a critical relationship between female socialization and some of the problems and strengths inherent in lesbianism. (See Chapters 2 and 6 for discussion of the effects of female socialization on the stresses of lesbianism and on lesbian relationships.)

6. Therapists must have the skills to help clients explore the impact of homophobia on their lives, their beliefs, their feelings, and their relationships. Further, the impact of homophobia is often not conscious for the client, and the therapist must be able to evaluate such impact and present it to the client when appropriate, not necessarily waiting for the client to bring it up in session. It is vital to make interpretations of this material that are timely, done sensitively, and approached with clinical regard to defenses and traits. (See Chapters 4 through 7.)

7. Therapists must be skilled in exploring the risks and benefits of coming out with the client. There are pros and cons to every act of coming out. The client must decide for herself an appropriate level of being out that provides her with a balance between the safety of the closet, with its accompanying restrictions on her emotional life, and the freedom and integrity of being out, with its accompanying risk to job, home, and important relationships. It is important to remember that the literature shows that in the long run, more "out" lesbians are happier than those who are less "out" (Greene, 1977; Bell & Weinberg, 1978; and Gartrell, 1984).

8. In our own culture and in our own day, it is not possible for a woman to resolve the lesbian identity issue to the mutual satisfaction of both society and herself (Elliott, 1985). Therapists must help clients grapple with this reality, and perhaps grieve its unresolvability.

THE THERAPIST'S SELF-KNOWLEDGE

Therapists who wish to provide clinical services to the lesbian population are called upon to seriously examine themselves in two arenas: their own level of homosexual feelings, and their own manifestations of heterosexist bias or homophobia. The following is a summary of activities and skills, primarily taken from Chapter 3, that are suggested for a therapist to consider herself or himself qualified in a personal way to work with this clientele.

1. Therapists should attend workshops, join or start groups, and expose themselves to readings and events that are designed to help them get in touch with their feelings about lesbianism or homosexuality. This suggestion holds true even if the therapist is lesbian or gay. Fears, stereotypes, myths, assumptions, and misconceptions about lesbians can be very subtle, and facilitated activities may be required for the therapist to become aware of them. (See the Awareness Enhancing Exercise in Appendix A.)

2. Therapists should also attend workshops, attend groups, or read in order to examine their own degree of homosexual thoughts, feelings, behaviors, and fantasies. It is important for the therapist to find a level of comfort and an appreciation for her or his own degree of homosexuality. (See the Self-Awareness Exercise in Appendix A.)

3. Acknowledging one's own limits is often difficult, but it is essential for therapists to define their own limits to the best of their ability in order to practice their profession responsibly. If any substantial degree of heterosexist bias, confusion, or misunderstanding exists, the therapist must refer lesbian clients to another therapist, even if the client's lesbian leanings are not uncovered until well into therapy. Alternatively, if the therapist is willing to challenge her or his biases, consultation or supervision from a lesbian-affirmative therapist is an appropriate course of action, while keeping the client in one's practice. Further, if one believes a therapist colleague is not referring clients elsewhere when the therapist should do so due to her or his blind spots, that therapist should be approached and helped to see the danger to which her or his clients are being exposed.

4. Therapists are encouraged to work to change the society or environment that is the source of many of the difficulties that lesbians experience. Therapists can become active in political, social, and institutional policy making that influences lesbians' quality of life.

5. When therapists are learning to provide therapy to lesbian clients, supervision or consultation is imperative. Therapists can seek out a lesbian or lesbian-affirmative therapist to supervise their work, provide resources,

answer questions, help work with countertransference, and provide diagnostic and treatment-planning assistance.

6. Therapists can periodically obtain therapy for themselves. This is true for all therapists, but it is especially crucial for therapists working with lesbians to have a therapist with whom they can explore their own feelings about lesbianism and heterosexism. A lesbian-affirmative therapist is imperative for this.

FUTURE DIRECTIONS

The fields of psychology, psychiatry, counseling, and social work have come a long way in the last 10 years in advancing our knowledge about lesbianism. But we still have a great distance to go. The illness model of homosexuality, which sees homosexuality as a failure or fixation in development and in which a cure or change to heterosexuality is sought, has by now been more than satisfactorily refuted. However, this former stance is still clung to by some therapists, and has yet to be replaced by a solid system of approaches and treatment guidelines for lesbian clients. Such a system would provide an approach to lesbian issues that is affirming and would set the goal of psychotherapeutic treatment as one in which the client is assisted in understanding herself, understanding the effects of her feelings and choices on her life, maximizing the quality of her relationships, and living a satisfying life while embracing her lesbianism. This volume provides much-needed material toward this end—however, more research, more therapy guides, and more elaboration are still required.

As a base for such clinical literature, a robust, explanatory, clinically based psychology of lesbianism is greatly needed. A psychology of lesbianism would view lesbianism as positive, would not seek to cure a "pathology," would acknowledge special stresses and their effects on emotional health, would acknowledge the different experience of lesbians from that of gay men, and would be based on an understanding of the lesbian experience as described by lesbians themselves. A psychology of lesbianism would also incorporate a psychology of women. It would likewise be clinically explanatory, diagnostically useful for treatment planning, and developmentally applicable over the life span.

A discussion of countertransference issues for therapists working with lesbian clients is also missing from the present body of knowledge. Only a few therapists have as yet put in writing their feelings and experiences in treating lesbian clients. Providing this information for other therapists would be an important addition to the state of current information. A

description of experiences could be translated into a list of common countertransference issues to which a clinician could refer for personal awareness, to enhance the therapy she or he provides, and to help determine
when consultation with another professional is needed.

Considerably more information on diagnostic matters also is necessary.
Lesbianism may interface with specific personality disorders or with specific clinical syndromes in certain ways of which we are not yet aware.
These interactions may change as societies change. This would be
extremely useful information for clinicians, statistically and diagnostically;
however, the individual client will always present a unique picture.

Further studies also must be undertaken on psychotherapy outcome for
lesbian clients. Such studies could attempt to correlate therapy outcome
with the gender of the therapist, the sexual identity of the therapist, the
amount or type of training in treatment of lesbians that the therapist has
undertaken, and the style of therapy utilized. It seems possible that therapy
outcome studies for lesbian clients may have different results than studies
for nonlesbian clients.

More research and theory development on the process of lesbian identity
formation (and any other sexual identity) would also be a welcome addition. There is a special need to understand the fluidity of identity over the
life span and the lack of strict correlations among lesbian behaviors, lesbian
erotic interests, emotional attachments to women, and a lesbian identity.

The mental health professions would be enhanced by a set of guidelines
for training all therapists to work with gay and lesbian clients as part of
their training programs. Therapists who prefer not to work with this clientele, or who are aware that their personal feelings would prevent them
from responsibly working with this group, could be taught referral skills
that would not make the client feel rejected for her lesbianism; because
such a large percentage of the population is gay or lesbian, a therapist cannot help but see clients from this group at some time in her or his career.
(Many therapists have seen lesbian clients without knowing it because the
client detected an atmosphere in which it was not safe to bring it up and
because the therapist was not trained to be sensitive to the client's cues.)
Most therapists hold a somewhat positive view of lesbianism, according to
the research, yet remain unaware of much essential information, such as
demographic data; the effects of internalized homophobia, of the
homophobia of others, and of oppression and invisibility; and the specific
issues that are of concern when doing psychotherapy with lesbians.

Finally, the mental health professions are in need of ethical guidelines
that pertain specifically to psychotherapy with lesbians (and gay men).
Guidelines are needed in two arenas. One arena is for therapists who are

themselves lesbians. Issues of dual relationships, transference and counter-transference difficulties, confidentiality difficulties, and loss of privacy for the therapist are special circumstances for lesbian therapists who need to be somewhat active in their own lesbian community for their own emotional health, yet derive some of their clientele pool from that very community. A lesbian therapist must further make choices about her own degree of being "out" based on the possibly conflicting need to model healthy levels of "outness" to clients and the need to preserve discretion for referral sources and client populations that would not take a positive view of her lesbianism.

The second arena for ethical guidelines would apply to all therapists, lesbian or nonlesbian, and apply to a number of issues and circumstances. Guidelines are needed for therapists who find a degree of homosexuality in either the adult or the child in a custody assessment or adoption assessment. Guidelines also are needed for determining the applicability of present testing norms to lesbian clients when providing psychological testing. Guidelines also would be useful in determining whether to inform a hospital staff of a client's lesbianism and whether and how to record lesbianism in a client's file, which in some cases could be damaging to the client, yet is a requirement for the therapist who is practicing his or her profession responsibly.

It is probable that that the specific concerns that lesbians have in a therapy setting may change over time, as society's attitude evolves and as psychotherapists' training improves. Lesbians have life experiences and emotional issues that are different from gay men, from nongay men, and from nongay women, and it is likely that these differences will remain in the foreseeable future. Therefore, therapists are called upon to keep abreast of the realities of being lesbian, to take an active part in reducing fear and misinformation about lesbians, and to promote a positive value of lesbianism—among peers, political leaders, and the population at large.

APPENDIX A: EXERCISES

The following exercises are designed with a twofold purpose: to facilitate understanding of the experience of being homosexual and to increase understanding of one's own feelings about homosexuality. Although these exercises can be done effectively individually, their effects are enhanced if done with a group of colleagues where a discussion can follow.

The "Self-Awareness Exercise" asks one to examine feelings and rate oneself on a continuum of heterosexual-homosexual aspects.

The "First Impressions Exercise" helps one explore the earlier—and therefore potentially deeply held—impressions of gays and lesbians.

The "Awareness Enhancing Exercise" offers suggested activities to allow a nongay therapist to spend some time in the shoes of a gay or lesbian person, to experience the stigma of being out of the closet, and to understand the effort required when one is staying in the closet. It also provides an opportunity for gay or lesbian therapists to experience a different level of being in or out of the closet from the one they may have chosen in their lives.

SELF-AWARENESS EXERCISE

The Kinsey research of the 1940s and '50s determined that human sexuality was not classifiable as a dichotomy between heterosexual and homosexual, but as a continuum. The research team developed a scale of the degree of heterosexuality/homosexuality that could be used to rate individuals on the continuum. However, Kinsey's team studied only the sexuality components of arousal and experience, which is now often regarded as an incomplete picture of the components of sexuality.

This exercise asks you to rate yourself on Kinsey's scale in many additional areas that are thought to be components of sexuality—thoughts, feelings, fantasies, and behaviors: *Thoughts* are defined as ideas, opinions, or cognitive perceptions. *Feelings* are defined as emotions or sense perceptions. *Fantasies* are imaginative fancies, daydreams, or images. *Behaviors* are actions that are carried out.

For each of the numbered items, rate yourself by placing an "x" at the place on the continuum line that best describes you overall. In some cases you might find it interesting to place more than one "x" on a continuum if there have been notable changes over your life span; in this case, use different colors or otherwise label the "x's" to show that they apply to certain times in your life.

COMPONENT

CONTINUUM OF EXPERIENCE

COMPONENT	Exclusively Other Sex	Predominantly Other Sex	Generally Other Sex	Equally Both Sexes	Generally Same Sex	Predominantly Same Sex	Exclusively Same Sex
1. Erotic or Sexual Thoughts	0	1	2	3	4	5	6
2. Erotic or Sexual Feelings	0	1	2	3	4	5	6
3. Erotic or Sexual Fantasies	0	1	2	3	4	5	6
4. Erotic or Sexual Behaviors	0	1	2	3	4	5	6
5. Affectionate or Loving Thoughts	0	1	2	3	4	5	6
6. Affectionate or Loving Feelings	0	1	2	3	4	5	6
7. Affectionate or Loving Fantasies	0	1	2	3	4	5	6
8. Affectionate or Loving Behaviors	0	1	2	3	4	5	6

Note your responses to making these ratings

FIRST IMPRESSIONS EXERCISE

Directions: Consider your responses to the following questions, noting how your impressions of gays and lesbians may be affected. Discussing these with colleages can enhance the experience.

What was the first reference to gays or lesbians you ever remember hearing?

What do you remember about the first person you ever saw or met who you identified as gay or lesbian?

What do you remember first being taught about homosexuality in your therapy or counseling courses?

How were gay and lesbian clients treated in your practicum, internship, or residency?

How were gay or lesbian student therapists treated in your training program? Gay or lesbian supervisors or instructors?

Do you presently have friends or acquaintances whom you know to be gay or lesbian? Who you think might be gay or lesbian?
  If not, why do you think this is so?
  If so, what are they like? Do you think they are typical of gays or lesbians?

What is the most memorable same-sex experience of your life?
  The most traumatic?
  The most meaningful?
  The most educative or eye-opening?

AWARENESS ENHANCING EXERCISES

Directions: Choose several of the exercises below. It is suggested that you keep a record or journal of your experience in doing the exercises. Note your willingness or resistance to doing them. Note your own feelings and actions as well as the reactions you receive from others.

From a nearby women's bookstore or a bookstore that carries pro-gay materials, purchase a button that says "Don't Assume I'm Heterosexual" or "Gay and Proud." Wear it for two months.

Purchase a copy of *Lesbian Sex* by JoAnn Loulan or *Homosexualities* by Bell and Weinberg. (These books have very large title print on their covers.) Carry the book with you wherever you go for one week; make sure it is always in prominent view.

For one month, say nothing to anyone about your spouse/partner that would reveal his or her gender. Do not use his or her first name; do not use the pronoun "he" or "she"; do not use "wife" or "husband," or "girlfriend" or "boyfriend"; take his or her picture off your desk if you have one there.

Spend two weeks solely in the company of members of your own gender for all social and recreational events. Whether you are going to the movies or are dining out, whether you going shopping or attending a sports event, always take at least one adult of your gender along with you.

Purchase a local periodical for gays and lesbians and attend a few events of your choice listed in it.

Attend a Gay Pride March in your nearest town. They're held in late June.

From a bookstore that carries pro-gay materials, purchase a button that has a pink triangle on it. Wear it from now on, placed perhaps on the lapel of your favorite jacket. Inform all who'll listen that you are wearing it in solidarity for the many thousands of homosexuals who were exterminated in Nazi death camps. (Homosexuals were made to wear a pink triangle on their sleeve or chest while interred in the camps.)

Volunteer some counseling services to a nearby gay and lesbian hotline or counseling center. (Be sure you are being properly supervised if you are not already experienced in counseling gays and lesbians.)

Purchase a few record albums, tapes, or CDs of lesbian music. Make sure they are among the selections you play when you are entertaining family or friends. These are available in women's bookstores; many mainstream record shops also have "Women's Music" sections that are primarily comprised of lesbian music. Some of the more well-known "out" lesbian albums are "The Changer and the Changed" by Cris Williamson, "Face the Music" by Meg Christian, "Imagine My Surprise" by Holly Near, "Living with Lesbians" by Alex Dobkin, "Michigan Live 85" from the 10th Michigan Womyn's Music Festival, "Phranc Folksinger" by Phranc, "Closer to Home" by Jamie Anderson, "Freedom to Love" by Faith Nolan, and "More than Friends" by Robin Flower. Other woman-identified music artists include Kay Gardner, Sweet Honey In the Rock, Ferron, Mary Watkins, Teresa Trull, Lucie Blue Tremblay, Willie Tyson, and Tret Fure.

APPENDIX B: ANNOTATED BIBLIOGRAPHY

There are two current texts that contain high-quality, extensive bibliographies: *Counseling Gay Men and Women* by Woodman and Lenna (1980), which includes an annotated bibliography that covers some of the best and most "classic" literature both for the lesbian client and for the therapists who counsel them; and *Counseling Lesbian Women and Gay Men* (1982) by Moses and Hawkins, which offers a lengthy, nonannotated bibliography that covers most of the available books and articles on lesbianism, both from the general literature and from the therapy literature. These two sources list works referring to both gay men and lesbians.

Although I highly recommend both of these bibliographies as sources for the therapist's bookshelf, neither bibliography offers material after 1980. The following bibliography updates these sources, listing primarily materials published since that date. Only works that refer solely or largely to lesbians are listed. I have attempted to include a broad range of good materials. For more complete references, visit your nearest women's or feminist bookstore and peruse the titles to keep abreast of periodicals. Subscribing to journals that regularly discuss lesbian-affirmative therapy issues is also useful.

COUNSELING AND THERAPY

Counseling Lesbian Women and Gay Men, A. Elfin Moses and Robert O. Hawkins, Jr. St. Louis: C.V. Mosby. 1982. Coverage of background information important to understanding the gay or lesbian client. Material on development of sexual identity, coming out, the gay lifestyle, sexual activity, and relationships. Chapters on special issues, such as Third World and rural clients, college students, gay parents, and aging. Good beginning text for therapists.

Counseling with Gay Men and Women, Natalie Jane Woodman and Harry R. Lenna. San Francisco: Jossey-Bass. 1980. Sound, basic information useful to the clinician. Covers the basics of counseling procedures with gays and lesbians. Chapters on sexual identity, promoting a positive self-image, relationships, special problems of adolescents, and building community-based support systems.

Contemporary Perspectives on Psychotherapy with Lesbians and Gay Men, Terry S. Stein and Carol J. Cohen (Eds.). New York: Plenum. 1986. A very fine collection of articles written by clinicians. Full of case material, addressing both theory and practice. Covers historical trends, developmental factors, lesbian couples, and lesbian mothers, as well as material on gay men. Primarily psychodynamic in orientation.

The Lavender Couch, Marny Hall. Boston: Alyson. 1985. A consumer's guide for gays and lesbians seeking psychotherapy services. Helps clients determine what they can realistically expect therapy to accomplish and discusses types of therapy, how to choose a therapist, and how to leave therapy if the therapist is not gay-affirmative. Highly recommended reading for both therapists and clients.

Lesbian Psychologies, Boston Lesbian Psychologies Collective (Eds.). Urbana: University of Illinois. 1987. A collection of diverse articles, covering identity, relationships, family, therapies, and community. A valuable reference.

"Beyond Homophobia: Learning to Work with Lesbian Clients," Rachel Josefowitz Siegel, in *Handbook of Feminist Therapy,* L.B. Rosewater and L.E.A. Walker (Eds.). New York: Springer. 1985. Suggests avenues for improving one's ability to work with lesbian clients, including learning from one's own therapy, from the literature, from lesbian colleagues, and from lesbian clients. Written by a nongay therapist and therefore especially helpful to that group.

"Some Issues in the Treatment of Gay and Lesbian Patients," April Martin. *Psychotherapy: Theory, Research and Practice, 19*(3), 341–348. 1982. Describes some of the more subtle heterosexual biases that can occur unwittingly in therapy. Alternatives are suggested for therapeutic exploration of heterosexist bias.

Bridges of Respect: Creating Support for Lesbian and Gay Youth, American Friends Service Committee, 1988. Designed for parents, educators, and human service providers. Analyzes the effects of homophobia on youth and presents creative ideas and resources for constructive change and new program models.

"Combating Homophobia in the Psychotherapy of Lesbians," Nanette Gartrell. *Women & Therapy,* 3(1), 13–29. 1984. Discussion of psychotherapy with lesbians in a sociopolitical context. The author is an "out" lesbian therapist, and discusses the effects of that status on her clients.

Journal of Homosexuality. Published quarterly by Haworth Press. Subscriptions: 10 Alice Street, Binghamton, NY, 13904–1580. This journal has been in publication since 1974 and always carries scholarly and useful articles, both for the theorist and the practicing clinician.

Journal of Gay and Lesbian Psychotherapy. Published quarterly by Haworth Press. Subscriptions: 10 Alice Street, Binghamton, NY, 13904–1580. Began publishing in 1989. Especially for psychotherapists who treat gay and lesbians clients, emphasizing broad practical applications.

SEXUALITY

Sapphistry: The Book of Lesbian Sexuality, Pat Califia, Third Edition, Tallahassee, FL: Naiad. 1988. A down-to-earth, sex-positive approach to sex between women that the author describes as "an alternative to conformity." Covers common sexual concerns for lesbians, communication, eroticism, age and disability changes, variations, and sexually transmitted diseases. An excellent resource.

Lesbian Sex, JoAnn Loulan. San Francisco: Spinsters Ink. 1984. A guide to enhancing sexuality for lesbians, written by a therapist. An open, easy, and freeing approach to sex. Covers myths, expectations, physiology, and numerous special issues, such as being partners with (or being oneself) a survivor of incest. Helpful exercises.

Lesbian Passion, JoAnn Loulan. San Francisco: Spinsters/Aunt Lute. 1987. Based on Loulan's research on lesbian sexuality and love. Covers lesbian self-esteem, intimacy in drug and alcohol recovery, survival after incest and advice for partners of incest survivors, sexuality patterns, and keeping passion in relationships.

"Sex Therapy with Lesbian Couples: A Four Stage Approach," Marny Hall. *Journal of Homosexuality,* 14(1/2), 137–156. 1987. Suggestions for tailoring traditional sex therapy to lesbian clients, taking into account the cultural, social, and psychological factors that shape lesbian sexuality.

LESBIAN EXPERIENCE

Another Mother Tongue, Judy Grahn. Boston: Beacon. 1984. An artistic unraveling of the history and culture of gays and lesbians. The poet-author describes history, myth, tribal traditions, personal experience, and interview material in a manner that traces the traditions of gay life as it has existed from ancient times to the present.

Lesbian/Woman, Del Martin and Phyllis Lyon. New York, Bantam. 1972, updated 1983. One of the classics has been recently updated. A good source for understanding the lesbian as a whole person, written by the founders of the oldest lesbian organization in the United States, the Daughters of Bilitis. Discusses self-image, sexuality, lifestyles, lesbian mothers, youth, and a social and political framework for the lesbian experience.

The Gay/Lesbian Almanac—A New Documentary, Jonathan N. Katz. New York: Thomas Y. Crowell, 1983. Katz is a great archivist, who brought us *Gay American History* in the 1970s. This new book is a collection of documents of personal testimony, news reports, diaries, medical records, letters, laws, songs, cartoons, and reviews of books, movies, and plays over two formative periods. The subtitle of the book reads "In which is contained, in Chronological Order, Evidence of the True and Fantastic History of those Persons now called Lesbians and Gay Men, and of the Changing Social Forms of and Responses to Those Acts, Feelings, and Relationships now called Homosexual, in the Early American Colonies, 1607–1740, and in the Modern United States, 1880–1950."

Looking at Gay and Lesbian Life, Warren J. Blumenfeld and Diane Raymond. Boston: Beacon Press. 1988. A comprehensive source of information on subjects including socialization, religion, theories of "causes" of homosexuality, discrimination, history of the gay and lesbian political movements, AIDS, lifestyle and culture, and literature.

The Alyson Almanac: A Treasury of Information for the Gay and Lesbian Community, Alyson Publications, 1989. A collection of historical and recent events that are relevant to the lives of gays and lesbians.

"Compulsory Heterosexuality and Lesbian Experience," Adrienne Rich. *Signs: Journal of Women in Culture and Society,* 5(4), 631–660, 1980. An in-depth analysis of the invalidation of women's choice of women as passionate comrades, lovers, and life partners, with a special eye to the virtual neglect of lesbian experience not only in the mainstream literature, but in the feminist literature as well. Rich says, "Feminist theory can no longer afford merely to voice a toleration of 'lesbianism' as an 'alternative lifestyle,' or make token allusions to lesbians. A feminist critique of compulsory heterosexual orientation for women is long overdue."

The Lesbian Path, Margaret Cruikshank. San Francisco: Grey Fox Press. 1980, revised 1985. An anthology of stories from lesbians' lives. Thirty-six autobiographical stories provide affirmation of lesbians' strength, resilience, and diversity. The stories are personal and powerful.

Long Time Passing: Lives of Older Lesbians, Marcy Adelman. Boston: Alyson. 1986. This volume came out of the author's research on lesbian aging. Rather than compiling academic opinions, the author records the voices of the women she interviewed for her study. The stories shatter the stereotype of the depressed and lonely older lesbian, showing instead that the most important factor in determining the psychological well-being of lesbians in later life is the level of homophobia in society and in ourselves. The stories are compelling.

We Are Everywhere: Writings By and About Lesbian Parents, Harriet Alpert (Ed.). Freedom, CA: Crossing. 1988. An anthology describing the experiences of lesbian parents from many different cultures and walks of life. A supportive and useful resource for therapists and clients alike.

Women-Identified Women, Trudy Darty and Sandee Potter (Eds.). Palo Alto, CA: Mayfield. 1984. A lively collection of articles on the lesbian experience. Articles include lesbian identity, relationships, older lesbians, lesbians of color, motherhood, oppression, jobs, health care, and lesbian culture in literature, poetry, and music.

COMING OUT

"Theory and Research on Lesbian Identity Formation," Phyllis E. Elliot. *International Journal of Women's Studies,* 8(1), 64–71. 1985. A review of the literature on lesbian identity formation. Covers the differences from the coming-out process for gay men. Discusses definitions and models of lesbian identity formation, and makes a case for seeing it as a developmental process.

"Counseling Lesbians," Joan Sophie. *Personnel and Guidance Journal,* 60(6), 341–345. 1982. Recommendations for counselors and therapists working with clients who present issues concerning any kind of thoughts, feelings, or behaviors related to lesbianism. Describes the process of developing a lesbian identity and the facilitative factors that therapists can provide.

Lesbian Crossroads, Ruth Baetz, Tallahassee, FL: Naiad. 1988. Personal stories of the struggles and triumphs of the coming-out process. The author records the diverse experiences—good and bad—of the women she has interviewed, as they describe the process of discovering their sexual identity.

The Original Coming Out Stories, Julia Penelope & Susan J. Wolfe (Eds.). Freedom, CA: Crossing. Revised 1989. Personal narratives and poetry about the intensely emotional and personal experience of coming out, as described by a wide range of women.

There's Something I've Been Meaning to Tell You, Loralee MacPike (Ed.). Tallahassee, FL: Naiad. 1989. A collection of stories by women who have told their children of their love for women. Particularly meaningful for lesbian mothers.

Now That You Know, Betty Fairchild and Nancy Hayward. San Diego: Harcourt Brace Jovanovich, 1989. An award-winning book about coming out to parents. Covers what every parent should know about homosexuality, couples, religion, parenting, and how to be supportive.

RELATIONSHIPS/COUPLES

"Psychotherapy with Lesbian Couples: Individual Issues, Female Socialization, and the Social Context," Sallyann Roth. In *Women in Families: A Framework for Family Therapy,* M. McGoldrick, C. Anderson, and F. Walsh (Eds.). New York: Norton. 1989. Describes relationship patterns among lesbian couples that are different from patterns among heterosexual couples, especially because the couple is composed of two females, has a stigmatizable identity, and lacks social recognition. The therapeutic aspects of these issues are discussed from the perspectives of boundary maintenance in the relationship, sexual expression, financial arrangements, breaking up, and differences in acceptance of lesbian identity.

"The Problem of Fusion in the Lesbian Relationship," Jo-Ann Krestan and Claudia S. Bepko. *Family Process, 19,* 277–289. 1980. Outlines hypotheses about issues that intensify the problems of fusion in committed lesbian partnerships. Also discusses why fusion is common in lesbian relationships. Issues are addressed from a systems perspective. Includes applications for treatment.

"Lesbian Couples: The Implications of Sex Differences in Separation—Individuation," Dianne Elise. *Psychotherapy, 23*(2), 305–310. 1986. The dynamics of merging in lesbian couples are addressed from an object relations perspective. Different patterns seen in gay male couples and lesbian couples illustrate crucial gender differences that affect the overall pattern of lesbians' relationship style. Excellent compilation of the literature on merging in lesbian relationships.

Lesbian Couples, D. Merilee Clunis & G. Dorsey Green. Seattle: Seal. 1988. A manual on lesbian relationships. Covers topics of practical concern for lesbians who are building couplehood, including resolving conflict, living arrangements, monogamy, children, community, abuse recovery, race and class differences, disability, and growing old together.

Unbroken Ties: Lesbian Ex-Lovers, Carol S. Becker. Boston: Alyson. 1988. Addresses the common lesbian phenomenon of maintaining friendships with ex-lovers. The author observes the diverse anatomy of breakups and the transitions that are possible, from the couple's initial pain and loss to "the opportunity to increase their self-awareness, to clarify their interpersonal needs and desires, and to build more durable relationships in the future."

Permanent Partners, Betty Berzon. New York: E.P. Dutton. 1988. Written by a psychotherapist who has worked extensively with gay and lesbian couples. Chapters on building compatibility, communication, sex, power and control, weathering changes in the partnership, and how to fight constructively.

Gay Relationships, Tina Tessina. Los Angeles: Jeremy P. Tarcher. 1989. A guide to lesbian and gay relationships. Addresses dating and commitment, living arrangements, coming out, support networks, and making relationships last.

APPENDIX C: RESOURCES

RESOURCE GUIDES

Gaia's Guide International by Sandy Horn.
147 West 42nd St., Suite 603
New York, NY 10036
United States and worldwide guide to local lesbian meeting places, resources, bookstores, religious groups, mental health services, Alcoholics Anonymous groups, guest houses, restaurants, campus student unions, publications, and organizations. A good way to learn what is available in your own town. Published yearly. $10.00.

Places of Interest to Women
Ferrari Publications
P.O. Box 35575
Phoenix, AZ 85069
Another worldwide guide to local information, geared especially for the traveller. Lists accommodations, events, bars, merchants, publications, services, and information lines. Published yearly. $9.95.

Inn Places
Ferrari Publications
P.O. Box 37887
Phoenix, AZ 85069
Gay and lesbian accommodation guide for the U.S. and worldwide. Includes detailed descriptions of accommodations and their clientele, plus nightlife, dining, and shopping.

ORGANIZATIONS

National Gay and Lesbian Task Force
1517 U Street, N.W.
Washington, DC 20004
(202) 332-6483
The largest gay and lesbian civil rights organization in the United States. Also serves as a clearinghouse for the national gay movement and a political force promoting gay rights legislation and a positive image of gay men and lesbians in the media.

Federation of Parents and Friends of Lesbians and Gays
P.O. Box 24565
Los Angeles, CA 90024
A large national organization with local chapters in most towns across the U.S. Provides resources and support groups for the parents, family, and friends of lesbians or gay men, who themselves seek assistance with accepting and understanding their lesbian/gay loved one. Also a good resource for lesbians and gay men who are just coming out.

National Gay Youth Network
P.O. Box 846
San Francisco, CA 94114

Senior Action in a Gay Environment (SAGE)
208 W. 13th St.
New York, NY 10011

Society for Senior Gay and Lesbian Citizens, Project Rainbow
255 S. Hill St. Rm. 410
Los Angeles, CA 90012

Lesbian Archives
P.O. Box 1258
New York, NY 10001

PUBLICATIONS

Off Our Backs
2423 18th St. N.W.
Washington, D.C. 20009

A monthly women's news journal.

Lesbian Connection
P.O. Box 811
East Lansing, MI 48823

A monthly vehicle for personal communications; from Ambitious Amazons.

Sinister Wisdom
P.O. Box 3252
Berkeley, CA 94703

A quarterly of fiction, poetry, essays, and graphics.

Common Lives, Lesbian Lives
P.O. Box 1553
Iowa City, IA 52244

A quarterly of literature documenting the experiences of lesbians.

The Advocate
Liberation Publications, Inc.
6922 Hollywood Blvd., Tenth Floor
Los Angeles, CA 90281

A national bi-weekly newsmagazine for lesbians and gay men.

Visibilites
P.O. Box 1258
Peter Stuyvesant Station
New York, NY 10009-1258

A lesbian magazine published bi-monthly.

National Lesbian Health Care Survey—Mental Health Implications
National Institute of Mental Health, 1987
Dept. of Health and Human Services
Washington, DC

Lesbian and Gay Issues: A Resource Manual for Social Workers
H. Hidalgo, T.L. Peterson, and N.J. Woodman (Eds.), 1985
Published by the National Association of Social Workers
Silver Springs, MD 20910

Publications from the American Psychological Association Committee on Lesbian and Gay Concerns
1200 Seventeenth St. N.W.
Washington, DC 20035

1. Lesbian and Gay Issues in Psychology Series booklets:
   The Development of Sexual Orientation by Michael C. Storms
   Homophobia by Kristin A. Hancock
   Some Information for Parents and Families of Lesbians and Gays by Helena M. Carlson
   American Psychological Association Policy Statements on Lesbian and Gay Issues

2. Graduate Faculty Interested in Gay and Lesbian Issues

3. *Division 44 Newsletter* (Division 44 is the Society for the Psychological Study of Lesbian and Gay Issues)

Publications published jointly by the APA's Committee on Lesbian and Gay Concerns (address above) and the Association of Lesbian and Gay Psychologists, 210 Fifth Ave., New York, NY 10010:

Research Roster A listing of persons conducting or interested in research on lesbian, gay, and bisexual topics.

Therapist Roster A listing of psychotherapists and mental health professionals who define themselves as interested in and able to work with lesbians and gay males.

ORGANIZATIONS FOR PSYCHOTHERAPISTS

American Psychological Association
Committee on Lesbian and Gay Concerns
1200 Seventeenth St. N.W.
Washington, DC 20036

Association of Lesbian and Gay Psychologists
210 Fifth Ave.
New York, NY 10010

American Psychiatric Association
Committee on Gay, Lesbian and Bisexual Issues
1400 K St. N.W.
Washington, DC 20005

American Psychiatric Association
Caucus of Gay, Lesbian and Bisexual Members
c/o Stuart Nichols, Jr.
245 E. 17th St.
New York, NY 10003

National Association of Social Workers
Committee on Lesbian and Gay Issues
7981 Eastern Ave.
Silver Springs, MD 20910

American Association for Marriage and Family Therapy
Caucus for Gay, Lesbian, and Bisexual Concerns
c/o Keith Schrag
304 Lynn
Ames, Iowa 50010

American Association of Physicians for Human Rights
P.O. Box 14366
San Francisco, CA 94103

National Association of Lesbian and Gay Alcoholism Professionals
204 West 20th Street
New York, NY 10011

MISCELLANEOUS RESOURCES

Alcoholism and Drug Treatment Programs, Inpatient:
Pride Institute
14400 Martin Drive
Eden Prairie, MN 55344
1-800-54-PRIDE

Alcoholism and Drug Treatment Programs, Outpatient:
Many towns have groups for Alcoholics Anonymous (12 Step), Al-Anon, Adult Children of Alcoholics, and Narcotics Anonymous. Check *Gaia's Guide* for your local area resources.

Legal Issues:
A Legal Guide for Lesbian and Gay Couples by H. Curry and D. Clifford, 1980, Addison-Wesley Publishing Co., Reading, MA.

Lesbian Mothers' National Defense Fund
P.O. Box 21567
Seattle, WA 98111

Local chapters of the American Civil Liberties Union, or
ACLU Lesbian and Gay Rights Project
132 W. 43rd Street
New York, NY 10036
(212) 944-9800

Lamda Legal Defense and Education Fund
666 Broadway, 12th Floor
New York, NY 10012
(212) 995-8585

Religious Issues:

Dignity
1500 Massachusetts Ave.
Washington, DC 20005
(202) 861-0017

An organization for gay and lesbian Roman Catholics, with chapters throughout the country.

Lutherans Concerned/North America
P.O. Box 10461
Chicago, IL 60610

Integrity
P.O. Box 5202
New York, NY 10185
(718) 448-2006

An organization for gay and lesbian Episcopalians.

Metropolitan Community Church
A network of Christian churches that openly accept gays and lesbians, with congregations in most major cities. Check *Gaia's Guide* for local information.

Jewish lesbian organizations can be found in many major cities. Check *Gaia's Guide*.

Lesbians of Color:
National Coalition of Black Lesbians and Gays
930 F Street, N.W., Suite 514
Washington, DC 20004
(202) : . /-5276

Many cities have groups or organizations for lesbians of color as a group or for lesbians of specific races. Check *Gaia's Guide*.

Lesbians and AIDS:
Women's AIDS Network
San Francisco AIDS Foundation
333 Valencia Street, 4th Floor
San Francisco, CA 94103
(414) 864-4376

Women's AIDS Project
8235 Santa Monica Blvd., Suite 201
West Hollywood, CA 90046
(213) 650-1508

The Gay Men's Health Crisis—Women's Program
132 West 24th Street, Box 274
New York, NY 10011
(212) 807-6655

REFERENCES

Allen, P.G. (1984). Beloved women: The lesbian in American Indian culture. In T. Darty & S. Potter (Eds.), *Women-identified women* (pp. 83–96). Palo Alto: Mayfield.

Almvig, C. (1982). *The invisible minority.* Published thesis.

American Psychiatric Association. (1987). *Diagnostic and statistical manual of mental disorders.* (Third Edition, Revised). Washington, DC: American Psychiatric Association.

American Psychological Association, Committee on Professional Standards. (1980). *Specialty guidelines for the delivery of services by clinical psychologists.* Washington, DC: Author.

American Psychological Association. (1981). *Ethical principles of psychologists.* Washington, DC: Author.

Anderson, D. (1987). Family and peer relations of gay adolescents. *Adolescent Psychiatry, 14,* 162–178.

Anthony, B.D. (1982). Lesbian client-lesbian therapist: Opportunities and challenges in working together. In J.C. Gonsiorek (Ed.), *Homosexuality and psychotherapy* (pp. 45–57). New York: Haworth.

Armon, V. (1960). Some personality variables in overt female homosexuality. *Journal of Projective Techniques, 24,* 292–309.

Atkinson, D.R., Morten, G., & Sue, D.W. (1979). *Counseling American minorities: A cross-cultural perspective.* Dubuque, IA: William C. Brown.

Barbach, L. (1975). *For Yourself.* New York: Doubleday.

Becker, C.S. (1988). *Unbroken ties: Lesbian ex-lovers.* Boston: Alyson.

Bell, A.P., & Weinberg, M.S. (1978). *Homosexualities: A study of diversity among men and women.* New York: Touchstone.

Berman, J.R.S. (1985). Ethical feminist perspectives on dual relationships with clients. In L.B. Rosewater & L.E.A. Walker (Eds.), *Handbook of feminist therapy* (pp. 287–296). New York: Springer.

Berzon, B. (1978). Sharing your lesbian identity with your children: A case for openness. In G. Vida (Ed.), *Our right to love* (pp. 69–77). Englewood Cliffs, NJ: Prentice-Hall.

191

Berzon, B. (1988). *Permanent partners.* New York: E.P. Dutton.

Blumstein, P., & Schwartz, P. (1983). *American couples.* New York: William Morrow.

Bolen, J.S. (1984). *Goddesses in Everywoman.* New York: Harper & Row.

Boston Lesbian Psychologies Collective. (1987). *Lesbian psychologies: Explorations and challenges.* Urbana: University of Illinois.

Boston Women's Health Book Collective. (1973). *Our bodies, ourselves.* New York: Simon & Schuster.

Brannock, J.C., & Chapman, B.E. (1990). Negative sexual experiences with men among heterosexual women and lesbians. *Journal of Homosexuality, 19*(1), 105–110.

Brooks, V.R. (1981). Sex and sexual orientation as variables in therapists' biases and therapy outcomes. *Clinical Social Work Journal, 9*(3), 198–210.

Broverman, I.K., Broverman, D.M., Clarkson, F.E., Rosenkrantz, P., & Vogel, S.R. (1970). Sex role stereotypes and clinical judgements of mental health. *Journal of Consulting and Clinical Psychology, 34,* 1–7.

Brown, L. (1984). The lesbian feminist therapist in private practice and her community. *Psychotherapy in Private Practice, 2*(4), 9–16.

Brown, L. (1985). Ethics in business practice in feminist therapy. In L.B. Rosewater & L.E.A. Walker (Eds.), *Handbook of feminist therapy* (pp. 297–304). New York: Springer.

Brown, L. (1989). Lesbians, gay men and their families: Common clinical issues. *Journal of Gay and Lesbian Psychotherapy, 1*(1), 65–77.

Burch, B. (1985). Another perspective on merger in lesbian relationships. In L.B. Rosewater & L.E.A. Walker (Eds.), *Handbook of feminist therapy* (pp. 100–109). New York: Springer.

Burch, B. (1986). Psychotherapy and the dynamics of merger in lesbian couples. In T.S. Stein & C.J. Cohen (Eds.), *Contemporary perspectives on psychotherapy with lesbians and gay men* (pp. 57–71). New York: Plenum.

Burch, B. (Work in progress). *Being different: Individuation and lesbian identity.* Unpublished manuscript.

Bustamante, A.L. (1987, January). *Cultural and class differences in defining boundaries.* Paper presented at "Boundary dilemmas in the client-therapist relationship: A working conference for lesbian therapists," Los Angeles, CA.

Cabaj, R.P. (1988). Homosexuality and neurosis: Considerations for psychotherapy. *Journal of Homosexuality, 15*(1/2), 13–23.

Califia, P. (1988). *Sapphistry: The book of lesbian sexuality.* Tallahassee, FL: Naiad.

Caprio, F. (1954). *Female homosexuality: A modern study of lesbianism.* New York: Grove.

Cass, V.C. (1979). Homosexual identity formation: A theoretical model. *Journal of Homosexuality, 4*(3), 219–235.

Cass, V.C. (1984a). Homosexual identity: A concept in need of definition. *Journal of Homosexuality, 10,* 105–126.

Cass, V.C. (1984b). Homosexual identity formation: Testing a theoretical model. *Journal of Sex Research, 20*(2), 143–167.

Cavin, S. (1985). *Lesbian origins.* San Francisco: Ism.

Chan, C.S. (1989). Issues of identity development among Asian-American lesbians and gay men. *Journal of Counseling & Development, 68,* 16–20.

Chesler, P. (1972). *Women and madness.* New York: Doubleday.

Chodorow, N. (1978). *The reproduction of mothering.* Berkeley: University of California Press.

Clark, D. (1977). *Loving someone gay.* Millbrae, CA: Celestial Arts.

Clark, D. (1987). *The new loving someone gay.* Berkeley: Celestial Arts.

Clunis, D.M., & Green, G.D. (1988). *Lesbian couples.* Seattle: Seal Press.

Cohen, C.J., & Stein, T.S. (1986). Reconceptualizing individual psychotherapy with gay men and lesbians. In T.S. Stein & C.J. Cohen (Eds.), *Contemporary perspectives in psychotherapy with gay men and lesbians* (pp. 27–54). New York: Plenum.

Coleman, E. (1982). Developmental stages of the coming out process. In J.C. Gonsiorek (Ed.), *Homosexuality and Psychotherapy* (pp. 31–43). New York: Haworth.

Collier, H.V. (1982). *Counseling women: A guide for therapists.* New York: Free Press.

Courtois, C.A. (1988). *Healing the incest wound: Adult survivors in therapy.* New York: W. W. Norton.

Cruikshank, M. (Ed.). (1985). *The lesbian path.* San Francisco: Grey Fox Press.

Davis, K.B. (1929). *Factors in the sex life of twenty-two hundred women.* New York: Harper & Bros.

Decker, B. (1983–1984). Counseling gay and lesbian couples. *Journal of Social Work and Human Sexuality, 2*(2/3), 39–52.

DeCrescenzo, T.A. (1983/84). Homophobia: A study of the attitudes of mental health professionals toward homosexuality. *Journal of Social Work and Human Sexuality, 2*(2/3), 115–135.

de Monteflores, C. (1986). Notes on the management of difference. In T.S. Stein & C.J. Cohen (Eds.), *Contemporary perspectives on psychotherapy with lesbians and gay men* (pp. 73–101). New York: Plenum.

de Monteflores, C., & Schultz, S.J. (1978). Coming out: Similarities and differences for lesbians and gay men. *Journal of Social Issues, 34*(3), 59–72.

Diamond, D.L., & Wilsnack, S.C. (1978). Alcohol abuse among lesbians. *Journal of Homosexuality, 4*(2), 123–142.

Doell, R.G., & Longino, H.E. (1988). Sex hormones and human behavior: A critique of the linear model. *Journal of Homosexuality, 15*(3/4), 55–78.

Eichenbaum, L., & Orbach, S. (1983). *Understanding women.* New York: Basic Books.

Elliott, P.E. (1985). Theory and research on lesbian identity formation. *International Journal of Women's Studies, 8*(1) 64–71.

Elsie, D. (1986). Lesbian couples: The implications of sex differences in separation-individuation. *Psychotherapy, 23*(2), 305–310.

Epsín, O.M. (1987). Issues of identity in the psychology of Latina lesbians. In Boston Lesbian Psychologies Collective (Eds.), *Lesbian psychologies* (pp. 35–55). Urbana: University of Illinois.

Erhardt, A.A., Meyer-Bahlburg, H.F.L., Rosen, L.R., Feldman, J.F., Veridiano, N.P., Zimmerman, I., & McEwen, B.S. (1985). Sexual orientation after prenatal exposure to exogenous estrogen. *Archives of Sexual Behavior, 14,* 57–77.

Falk, P.J. (1989). Lesbian mothers: Psychosocial assumptions in family law. *American Psychologist, 44*(6), 941–947.

Freiberg, P. (1987, June 23). NGLTF report shows increase in antigay violence. *Advocate,* p. 17.

Friend, R.A. (1987). The individual and social psychology of aging: Clinical implications for lesbians and gay men. *Journal of Homosexuality, 14*(1/2), 307–331.

Garcia, N., Kennedy, C., Pearlman, S.F., & Perez, J. (1987). The impact of race and cultural differences: Challenges to intimacy in lesbian relationships. In Boston Lesbian Psychologies Collective (Eds.), *Lesbian Psychologies* (142–160).

Garrison, D.C. (1988, December). *Social support correlates of life stress and well-being in self-disclosed and nonself-disclosed lesbian women.* Paper presented at Association for Women in Psychology Conference, Baltimore, Maryland.

Gartrell, N. (1981). The lesbian as "single" woman. *American Journal of Psychotherapy, 35*(4), 502–509.

Gartrell, N. (1984). Combating homophobia in the psychotherapy of lesbians. *Women & Therapy, 3*(1), 13–29.

Gilligan, C. (1982). *In a different voice.* Cambridge, MA: Harvard University Press.

Gochros, H.L. (1984). Teaching social workers to meet the needs of the homosexually oriented. *Journal of Social Work and Human Sexuality, 2*(2/3), 137–156.

Golden, C. (1987). Diversity and variability in women's sexual identities. In Boston Lesbian Psychologies Collective (Ed.), *Lesbian psychologies.* Urbana: University of Illinois.

Gonsiorek, J.C. (Ed.). (1982a). *Homosexuality and psychotherapy: A practitioner's handbook of affirmative models.* New York: Haworth.

Gonsiorek, J.C. (1982b). Introduction: Present and future directions in gay/lesbian mental health. In Gonsiorek, J.C. (Ed.), *Homosexuality and psychotherapy: A practitioner's handbook of affirmative models* (pp. 5–7). New York: Haworth.

Gonsiorek, J.C. (1982c). The use of diagnostic concepts in working with gay and lesbian populations. In Gonsiorek, J.C. (Ed.), *Homosexuality and psychotherapy: A practitioner's handbook of affirmative models* (pp. 9–20). New York: Haworth.

Graham, D.L.R., Rawlings, E., Halpern, H.S., & Hermes, J. (1984). Therapists' needs for training in counseling lesbians and gay men. *Professional Psychology: Research and Practice, 15*(4), 482–496.

Grahn, J. (1984). *Another mother tongue.* Boston: Beacon.

Gramick, J. (1983). Homophobia: A new challenge. *Social Work, 28,* 137–141.

Gramick, J. (1984). Developing a lesbian identity. In T. Darty & S. Potter (Eds.), *Women-identified women* (pp. 31–44). Palo Alto: Mayfield.

Greene, D.M. (1977) Women loving women: An exploration into feelings and life experiences. *Dissertation Abstracts International, 37,* 3608.

Hall, M. (1984). Lesbians, limerence and longterm relationships. In Loulan, *Lesbian Sex* (pp. 141–150). San Francisco: Spinsters Ink.

Hall, M. (1987). Sex therapy with lesbian couples: A four stage approach. *Journal of Homosexuality, 14*(1/2), 137–156.

Hancock, K.A. (1986). *Homophobia.* American Psychological Association.

Hanley-Hackenbruck, P. (1988). 'Coming out' and psychotherapy. *Psychiatric Annals, 18*(1), 29–32.

Hart, M., Roback, H., Tittler, B., Weitz, L., Walston, B., & McKee, E. (1978). Psychological adjustment of nonpatient homosexuals: Critical review of the research literature. *Journal of Clinical Psychiatry, 39,* 604–608.

Herek, G.M. (1984). Beyond "homophobia": A social psychological perspective on attitudes toward lesbians and gay men. *Journal of Homosexuality, 10,* 1–21.

Hess, E.P. (1983). Feminist and lesbian development: Parallels and divergencies. *Journal of Humanistic Psychology, 23*(1), 67–78.

Hetrick, E.S., & Martin, A.D. (1987). Developmental issues and their resolution for gay and lesbian adolescents. *Journal of Homosexuality, 14*(1/2), 25–43.

Hite, S. (1976). *The Hite report: A nationwide study of female sexuality.* New York: Dell.

Hooker, E. (1957). The adjustment of the male overt homosexual. *Journal of Projective Techniques, 21*(1), 18–31.

Jensen, J.P., & Bergin, A.E. (1988). Mental health values of professional therapists: A national interdisciplinary survey. *Professional Psychology: Research and Practice, 19*(13), 290–297.

Kahn, M. (1988, December). *Factors affecting the coming out process.* Paper presented at the Association for Women in Psychology Conference, Baltimore, MD.

Kaplan, H.S. (1975). *The illustrated manual of sex therapy.* New York: Times.

Kaplan, H.S. (1979). *Disorders of sexual desire.* New York: Brunner/Mazel.

Katz, J. (1976). *Gay American history.* New York: Thomas Y. Crowell.

Kaufman, P.A., Harrison, E., & Hyde, M.L. (1984). Distancing for intimacy in lesbian relationships. *American Journal of Psychiatry, 141*(4), 530–533.

Kehoe, M. (1988). Lesbians over 60 speak for themselves. [Entire issue]. *Journal of Homosexuality, 16*(3/4).

Kingdon, M.A. (1979). Lesbians. *The Counseling Psychologist, 8*(1), 44–45.

Kinsey, A.C., Pomeroy, W.B., Martin, C.E., & Gebbhard, P.H. (1953). *Sexual behavior in the human female.* Philadelphia: W.B. Saunders.

Kirkpatrick, M., Smith, C., & Roy, R. (1981). Lesbian mothers and their children: A comparative survey. *American Journal of Orthopsychiatry, 51*, 536–544.

Kirkpatrick, M. (1987). Clinical implications of lesbian mother studies. *Journal of Homosexuality, 14*(1/2), 201–211.

Krajeski, J.P. (1986). Psychotherapy with gay man and lesbians. In T.S. Stein & C.J. Cohen (Eds.), *Contemporary perspectives on psychotherapy with lesbians and gay men* (pp. 9–25). New York: Plenum.

Krestan, J., & Bepko, C.S. (1980). The problem of fusion in the lesbian relationship. *Family Process, 19*, 277–289.

Kurdek, L.A., & Schmitt, P. (1986). Relationship quality of partners in heterosexual married, heterosexual cohabiting, and gay and lesbian relationships. *Journal of Personality and Social Psychology, 51*(4), 711–720.

LaTorre, R.A., & Wendenburg, K. (1983). Psychological characteristics of bisexual, heterosexual and homosexual women. *Journal of Homosexuality, 9*, 87–97.

Lewis, K. (1980). Children of lesbians: Their point of view. *Social Work, 25*(3), 203.

Lewis, L.A. (1984). The coming out process for lesbians: Integrating a stable identity. *Social Work,* Sept-Oct, 464–469.

Lindenbaum, J.P. (1985). The shattering of an illusion: The problem of competition in lesbian relationships. *Feminist Studies, 11*(1), 85–103.

Lorde, A. (1978). I've been standing on this street corner a hell of a long time! In G. Vida (Ed.), *Our right to love,* (pp. 222–225). Englewood Cliffs, NJ: Prentice-Hall.

Loulan, J. (1984). *Lesbian Sex.* San Francisco: Spinsters Ink.

Loulan, J. (1986a). *Preliminary report on survey of lesbian sex practices.* Unpublished manuscript.

Loulan, J. (1986b). Psychotherapy with lesbian mothers. In T.S. Stein & C.J. Cohen (Eds.), *Contemporary perspectives on psychotherapy with lesbians and gay men* (pp. 181–208). New York: Plenum.

Loulan, J. (1987). *Lesbian passion: Loving ourselves and each other.* San Francisco: Spinsters/Aunt Lute.

Mach, H.J. (1987, October). Shrink, shrank, shrunk. *Advocate,* pp. 43–49.

Mahler, M. (1975). *The psychological birth of the human infant.* New York: Basic Books.

Maltz, W., & Holman, B. (1987). *Incest and sexuality.* Lexington, MA: Lexingon Books.

Mannion, K. (1981). Psychology and the lesbian: A critical review of the research. In S. Cox, (Ed.), *Female Psychology* (pp. 256–274). New York: St. Martin's.

Margolies, L., Becker, M., & Jackson-Brewer, K. (1987). Internalized homophobia: Identifying and treating the oppressor within. In Boston Lesbian Psychologies Collective (Eds.), *Lesbian psychologies* (pp. 229–241). Urbana: University of Illinois.

Marmor, J. (1980). Overview: The multiple roots of homosexual behavior. In J. Marmor (Ed.), *Homosexual behavior: A modern reappraisal.* New York: Basic Books.

Martin, A. (1982). Some issues in the treatment of gay and lesbian patients. *Psychotherapy: Theory, Research and Practice, 19*(3), 341–348.

Martin, D., & Lyon, P. (1983). *Lesbian/woman.* New York: Bantam.

Masters, W. & Johnson, V. (1971). *Human sexual inadequacy.* Boston: Little Brown.

Masters, W.H., Johnson, V.E., & Kolodny, R.C. (1986). *Masters and Johnson on sex and human loving.* Boston: Little, Brown.

Maylon, A. (1980, September). *Toward a definition of gay-affirmative psychotherapy.* Paper presented at the annual convention of the American Psychological Association, Montreal.

Maylon, A.K. (1981). The homosexual adolescent: Developmental issues and social bias. *Child Welfare, 60*(5), 321–330.

McCandlish, B.M. (1982). Therapeutic issues with lesbian couples. In J.C. Gonsiorek (Ed.), *Homosexuality and psychotherapy* (pp. 71–78). New York: Haworth.

McConaghy, N., Armstrong, M.S., Birrell, P.C., & Buhrich, N. (1979). The incidence of bisexual feelings and opposite sex behavior in medical students. *Journal of Nervous and Mental Disease, 167,* 685–688.

Mogul, K.M. (1982). Overview: The sex of the therapist. *American Journal of Psychiatry, 139*(1), 1–11.

Money, J. (1988). *Gay, straight and in between.* Oxford.

Morin, S.F. (1977). Heterosexual bias in psychological research on lesbianism and male homosexuality. *American Psychologist,* 629–637.

Morin, S.F. & Charles, K.A. (1983). Heterosexual bias in psychotherapy. In J. Murray & P. Abramson (Eds.). *Bias in psychotherapy.* (pp. 309–338).

Mosbacher, D. (1988). Lesbian alcohol and substance abuse. *Psychiatric Annals, 18* (1), 47–50.

Moses, A.E. (1978). *Identity management in lesbian women.* New York: Praeger.

Moses, A.E., & Hawkins, R.O. (1982). *Counseling lesbian women and gay men.* St. Louis: C.V. Mosby.

Murphy, B.C. (1989). Lesbian couples and their parents: The effects of perceived parental attitudes on the couple. *Journal of Counseling & Development, 68,* 46–51.

Nardi, P.M. (1982). Alcoholism and homosexuality: A theoretical perspective. In T.O. Ziebold & J.E. Mongeon (Eds.), *Alcoholism & homosexuality* (pp. 9–25). New York: Haworth.

National Institute of Mental Health (NIMH). (1987). *National lesbian health care survey* (Contract No. 86MO19832201D). Washington, DC: DHHS Publication.

Nichols, M. (1982). The treatment of inhibited sexual desire (ISD) in lesbian couples. *Women & Therapy, 1*(4), 49–66.

Nicoloff, L.K., & Stiglitz, E.A. (1987). Lesbian alcoholism: Etiology, treatment, and recovery. In Boston Lesbian Psychologies Collective (Eds.), *Lesbian psychologies* (pp. 283–293). Urbana: University of Illinois.

Ort, J.D. (1987). *Enablers and inhibitors of lesbian self-disclosure.* Unpublished manuscript.

Parloff, M.B., London, P., & Wolfe, B. (1986). Individual psychotherapy and behavior change. *Annual Review of Psychology, 37,* 321–349.

Peplau, L.A., Cochran, S., Rook, K., & Pedesky, C. (1978). Loving women: Attachment and autonomy in lesbian relationships. *Journal of Social Issues, 34*(3).

Peplau, L.A., Pedesky, C., & Hamilton, M. (1982). Satisfaction in lesbian relationships. *Journal of Homosexuality, 8*(2), 23–35.

Petry, R.A., & Thomas, J.R. (1986). The effect of androgyny on the quality of psychotherapeutic relationships. *Psychotherapy, 23*(2), 249–251.

Ponse, B. (1978). *Identities in the lesbian world.* Westport, CT: Greenwood.

Pope, K.S., Tabachnick, B.G., & Keith-Spiegel, P. (1987). Ethics of practice: The beliefs and behaviors of psychologists as therapists. *American Psychologist, 42*(11), 993–1006.

Rand, C., Graham, D., & Rawlings, E. (1982). Psychological health and factors the court seeks to control in lesbian mother custody trials. *Journal of Homosexuality, 8*(Fall), 27–39.

Rich, A. (1980). Compulsory heterosexuality and lesbian experience. *Signs: Journal of Women in Culture and Society, 5*(4), 631–660.

Riddle, D.I. (1978). Finding supportive therapy. In G. Vida (Ed.), *Our right to love* (pp. 87–91). Englewood Cliffs, NJ: Prentice-Hall.

Riddle, D.I., & Sang, B. (1978). Psychotherapy with lesbians. *Journal of Social Issues, 34*(3), 84–100.

Rochlin, M. (1982). Sexual orientation of the therapist and therapeutic effectiveness with gay clients. In J.C. Gonsiorek (Ed.), *Homosexuality and psychotherapy* (pp. 21–29). New York: Haworth.

Ross, M.W., Paulsen, J.A., & Stalstrom, O.W. (1988). Homosexuality and mental health: A cross-cultural review. *Journal of Homosexuality, 15*(1/2), 131–152.

Roth, S. (1985). Psychotherapy with lesbian couples: Individual issues, female socialization, and the social context. *Journal of Marital and Family Therapy, 11*(3), 273–286.

Roth, S. (1989). Psychotherapy with lesbian couples: Individual issues, female socialization, and the social context. In M. McGoldrick, C. Anderson & F. Walsh (Eds.). *Women in families: A framework for family therapy.* New York: Norton.

Rothberg, B., & Ubell, V. (1985). The co-existence of system theory and feminism in working with heterosexual and lesbian couples. *Women & Therapy, 4*(1), 19–36.

Rothblum, E.D. (1989, August). *Depression among lesbians: An invisible and unresearched phenomenon.* Paper presented at the annual convention of the American Psychological Association, New Orleans.

Saghir, M.T., & Robins, E. (1973). *Male and female homosexuality: A comprehensive investigation.* Baltimore: Williams and Wilkins.

Saghir, M.T., & Robins, E. (1980). Clinical aspects of female homosexuality. In J. Marmor (Ed.). *Homosexual behavior* (pp. 280–295). New York: Basic.

Sang, B.E. (1977). Psychotherapy with lesbians: Some observations and tentative generalizations. In E.I. Rawlings & D.K. Carter (Eds.), *Psychotherapy for women* (pp. 266–275). Springfield, IL: Charles C Thomas.

Sang, B.E. (1978). Lesbian research: A critical evaluation. In G. Vida (Ed.), *Our right to love* (pp. 80–87). Englewood Cliffs, NJ: Prentice-Hall.

Sang, B.E. (1984). Lesbian relationships: A struggle toward partner equality. In T. Darty & S. Potter (Eds.). *Women-identified women*. Palo Alto: Mayfield.

Schlossberg, N.K., & Pietrofesa, J.J. (1978). Perspectives on counseling bias: Implications for counselor education. In L.W. Harmon, J.M. Birk, L.E. Fitzgerald & M.F. Tanney (Eds.), *Counseling women* (pp. 59–73). Monterey, CA: Brooks/Cole.

Schneider, M.S. (1986). The relationships of cohabiting lesbian and heterosexual couples: A comparison. *Psychology of Women Quarterly, 10,* 234–239.

Sharratt, S., & Bern, L. (1985). Lesbian couples and families: A co-therapeutic approach to counseling. In L.B. Rosewater & L.E.A. Walker (Eds.), *Handbook of feminist therapy* (pp. 91–99). New York: Springer.

Siegel, R.J. (1985). Beyond homophobia: Learning to work with lesbian clients. In L. B. Rosewater & L. E. A. Walker (Eds.), *Handbook of feminist therapy* (pp. 183–190). New York: Springer.

Smith, J. (1988). Psychopathology, homosexuality, and homophobia. *Journal of Homosexuality, 15*(1/2), 59–73.

Sophie, J. (1982). Counseling lesbians. *Personnel and Guidance Journal, 60*(6), 341–345.

Sophie, J. (1987). Internalized homophobia and lesbian identity. *Journal of Homosexuality, 14*(1/2), 53–65.

Statistical Abstract of the United States. (1986). U.S. Bureau of the Census. Washington, D.C.

Stein, T.S. & Cohen, C.J. (Eds.). (1986). *Contemporary perspectives in psychotherapy with gay men and lesbians.* New York: Plenum.

Tanney, M.F., & Birk, J.M. (1978). Women counselors for women clients? A review of the research. In L.W. Harmon, J.M. Birk, L.E. Fitzgerald & M.F. Tanney (Eds.), *Counseling women* (pp. 208–217). Monterey, CA: Brooks/Cole.

Task Force on the Status of Lesbian and Gay Male Psychologists. 1977. Removing the stigma. *APA Monitor.*

Tessina, T. (1989). *Gay relationships.* Los Angeles: Jeremy P. Tarcher.

Tremble, B., Schneider, M., & Appathurai, C. (1989). Growing up gay or lesbian in a multicultural context. *Journal of Homosexuality, 17*(3/4), 253–267.

Troiden, R.R. (1988). *Gay and lesbian identity: A sociological analysis.* Dix Hills, N.Y.: General Hall.

Vance, B.K., & Green, V. (1984). Lesbian identities: An examination of sexual behavior and sex role attribution as related to age of initial same-sex sexual encounter. *Psychology of Women Quarterly, 8*(3), 293–307.

Vargo, S. (1987). The effects of women's socialization on lesbian couples. In Boston Lesbian Psychologies Collective (Eds.), *Lesbian psychologies* (pp. 161–173). Urbana: University of Illinois.

Vetere, V.A. (1982). The role of friendship in the development and maintenance of lesbian love relationships. *Journal of Homosexuality, 8*(2), 51–65.

Wohlander, K. & Petal, M.A. (1985). People who are gay or lesbian and disabled. In H. Hidalgo, T.L. Peterson & N.J. Woodman (Eds.). *Lesbian and gay issues: A resource manual for social workers* (pp. 38–42). Silver Springs, MD: NASW.

Woodman, N.J. (1989). Mental health issues of relevance to lesbian women and gay men. *Journal of Gay and Lesbian Psychotherapy, 1*(1), 53–64.

Woodman, N.J., & Lenna, H.R. (1980). *Counseling with gay men and women.* San Francisco: Jossey-Bass.

World Health Organization (WHO). (1977). Manual of the international statistical classification of diseases, injuries, and causes of death (9th rev.). Geneva: Author.

Wyers, N.L. (1987). Homosexuality and the family: Lesbian and gay spouses. *Social Work,* March-April, 143–148.

Zevy, L., & Cavallaro, S.A. (1987). Invisibility, fantasy, and intimacy: Princess charming is not a prince. In Boston Lesbian Psychologies Collective (Eds.), *Lesbian Psychologies* (pp. 83–94). Urbana: University of Illinois.

Ziebold, T.O. (1978). *Alcoholism and the gay community.* Washington DC: Blade.

Zigrang, T. (1982). Who should be doing what about the gay alcoholic? In T. O. Ziebold & J.E. Mongeon (Eds.), *Alcoholism & homosexuality* (pp. 27–35). New York: Haworth.

NAME INDEX

SUBJECT INDEX